MUSIC FROM FAR AND WIDE

MUSIC FROM

WITH A FOREWORD BY
JIM CUDDY OF BLUE RODEO

FAR AND WIDE

CELEBRATING

40
YEARS OF THE
JUNO
AWARDS

KAREN BLISS

NICK KREWEN

LARRY LEBLANC

JASON SCHNEIDER

KEY PORTER BOOKS

Library and Archives Canada Cataloguing in Publication

Music from far and wide : celebrating 40 years of Canadian music / CARAS.

ISBN 978-1-55470-339-5

1. Juno Awards. 2. Music--Canada--20th century--History and criticism.
3. Music--Canada--21st century--History and criticism. 4. Canadian Academy of Recording Arts and Sciences.
I. Canadian Academy of Recording Arts and Sciences

ML37.C212M98 2010   780.79'71   C2010-902033-2

Every reasonable effort has been made to trace ownership of copyrighted materials.

The publisher gratefully acknowledges the support of the Canada Council for the Arts and the Ontario Arts Council for its publishing program. We acknowledge the support of the Government of Ontario through the Ontario Media Development Corporation's Ontario Book Initiative.

We acknowledge the financial support of the Government of Canada through the Canada Book Fund (CBF) for our publishing activities.

Key Porter Books Limited
Six Adelaide Street East, Tenth Floor
Toronto, Ontario
Canada M5C 1H6

www.keyporter.com

Text design: Sonya V. Thursby, opushouse.ca
Electronic formatting: Sonya V. Thursby, opushouse.ca

Mixed Sources
Cert no. SW-COC-001271
© 1996 FSC
FSC

carbonzero CERTIFIED

Printed and bound in Canada

10 11 12 13 14 5 4 3 2 1

This book is dedicated to
Stan Klees (left) and Walt Grealis (right)
without whom we would not have a history to tell.

CONTEN

FOREWORD

BY JIM CUDDY

Blue Rodeo

LET'S think back to the early seventies and the Juno gathering in Toronto. There's the cool-looking Lothario Gordon Lightfoot, the straggle-haired prairie boys from The Guess Who, the sexy-like-your-math teacher Anne Murray, and then, maybe scattered around the room, the likes of Ginette Reno, Murray McLauchlan, Terry Jacks, or Stompin' Tom Connors in his big black cowboy hat blocking everyone's view of the stage. And that's it: a few quality stars, no television, no adoring fans, and did Lightfoot really say upon winning a Juno, "I need another one of these like a hole in the head"? Probably not, but you get the picture.

Fast forward to the arena extravaganzas of the 2000s: big audiences, screaming fans, a city on fire with Juno celebration, scores of bands, and artists walking the red carpet and cruising the town until all hours of the morning. Lots of success stories every year with lots of stars, and most of it homegrown talent. We've come a long way these past four decades.

The road from humble beginnings to the spectacle of today is measured in song after glorious song. Each one made its way to the ears of the Canadian music lover and took up residence. Even in the early days we all knew "Hot Child in the City" or "Seasons in the Sun" or "These Eyes"; we just didn't know whether they held Canadian passports or not. Gradually that changed as we got to know ourselves through these songs and artists. The songs were our stories. The lyrics described things just as we would if we had the gift. We knew the artists or had at least gone to school with someone just like Gord Downie or Burton Cummings. We loved our musicians, admired their talent and their humble ways. They were us. When Leonard Cohen recited "Tower of Song" upon being inducted into the Canadian Music Hall of Fame, we were flushed with pride. He spoke for us and spoke so beautifully. Each new chapter that was written in song by Lightfoot, The Tragically Hip, Ron Sexsmith, Sarah McLachlan, and all our musical brothers and sisters brought us closer together, filling in the colours of our beautiful nation's portrait. The songs stand as testament to our collective lives, our character, and our culture. They mark the important moments in our lives and they accompany us like beloved friends as we move around the world.

Frances Juriansz

PREFACE

FORTY years ago, a group of Canadian music pioneers decided that the music of this country, which had resonated and united its people for a little over a century, deserved greater recognition and respect.

Walt Grealis and Stan Klees of *RPM*, Canada's only music-industry trade magazine at the time, organized a small, one-night celebration in 1970 called the Gold Leaf Awards. The following year the name changed to the Juno Awards, in honour of Pierre Juneau, then chairman of what's known today as the Canadian Radio-television and Telecommunications Commission (CRTC), and a champion of Canadian music. If not for Mr. Juneau, who radically changed radio programming by establishing strict Canadian content broadcast requirements, the music and musicians of this country would not be where they are today.

Paul Alexander

BY MELANIE BERRY

President and CEO
The Canadian Academy of Recording Arts
and Sciences and MusiCounts

Once Canadians were exposed to more of their own music, we discovered our passion for it and how much we excelled in it. As a result, our national music industry grew exponentially. More artists broke through, more original compositions received airplay, and more Canadian music began to be heard both within and beyond our borders.

There was ever more to celebrate at the Juno Awards. Just as the awards themselves gained distinction through greater scope and depth of musical artistry, the country too was entering a golden age. If the twentieth century was to belong to Canada, as Prime Minister Wilfrid Laurier said, certainly from a musical point of view the last thirty years of the century heartily demonstrated that Canadian music was equal to any in the world.

It is an inescapable fact that the Juno Awards have been both a chronicle and a bellwether of some of the most marvellous music on the planet over the last forty years. As the country progressed, as our industry evolved, and as technologies advanced, it's no stretch to say that the Juno Awards have reflected Canada's socio-cultural development from a musical perspective.

From its early one-night Toronto beginnings that honoured a tightly knit community of artists, the now week-long public event celebrates not only a resoundingly successful industry and its artistic achievements, but also the fascinating mosaic that is Canada.

Music from Far and Wide is evidence of our success. It records and revels in the dynamism of a nation's art. And it represents the Juno Awards' sustained reflection of our highly diverse artistic excellence.

We are very proud of the journey you are about to embark on through the musical history of this country. What you will also find here is testament to the effort that's gone into organizing and supporting Canada's musical artists by The Canadian Academy of Recording Arts and Sciences (CARAS), which I'm extremely honoured to lead.

I am so very privileged to be a part of all the work done on behalf of the artists and professionals in the music industry by our valuable CARAS staff, as well as their accomplishments in conjunction with the Juno Awards' host cities and charitable partners.

A special note of personal gratitude also must go to the many passionate and dedicated board members and chairmen, past and present, presidents, plus the jurors and industry personnel who have been so invaluable to CARAS and in making Canadian music second to none.

We have seen our ups and downs in this ever-changing industry for over forty years of the Juno Awards. We have had the privilege of welcoming new artists and celebrating musical icons. We have evolved the Juno Awards by taking the show on the road over the last nine years and, in this fortieth year, we happily return home to Toronto, where our roots were planted. Enjoy this book and join us in celebrating forty incredible years of Canadian musical history. We at CARAS and the Juno Awards look forward to the brilliant future our rich musical culture has to offer in Canada and we hope you do too.

The proceeds from *Music from Far and Wide* will go to benefit MusiCounts, Canada's music education charity associated with CARAS. Since 1997, MusiCounts has donated more than $4 million through its Band Aid musical instrument grants and scholarships, impacting more than 265,000 students, their schools, and communities across the country. Thank you for helping to keep music alive in schools.

1970s

1980s

1990s

2000s

I didn't take the Junos seriously at the beginning. I was very busy. I was doing a lot of writing, and making an album every year and a half at that point. I took it more seriously as time went by. I realized the significance of it. The award points out the people who are doing meaningful things here. It also brings interest from the big market south of the border. From there, it can go right out around the world, as we very well know.

—GORDON LIGHTFOOT

I was all in favour of the Junos in those early days. You know me: if it was for the industry I was always in there like a dirty shirt. But I only remember half of what happened back then. I was so busy. It's all hazy. No wonder it's hazy. I was going from pillar to post, being pushed here and there. I didn't know which end was up I was so busy.

—ANNE MURRAY

AN INDUSTRY IS

MUSIC is one of Canada's best-known exports.

This wasn't always the case.

In the 1950s, as rock and roll blew apart the U.S.-dominated global music industry, Canada's best-known musical exports were limited to orchestrator Percy Faith; classical pianist Glenn Gould; singers Paul Anka, Félix Leclerc, and Hank Snow; and the polished vocal acts The Diamonds and The Four Lads.

In the early 1960s, there weren't equivalents of The Beatles or Bob Dylan coming from Canada. Still, there were artists who were stars within the emerging music industry here.

Singers Bobby Curtola, The Guess Who, Catherine McKinnon, Pat Hervey, Debbie Lori Kaye, Shirley Matthews, and Terry Black made their voices heard in pop; Oscar Peterson and Moe Koffman in jazz; Ian & Sylvia, Buffy Sainte-Marie, Gordon Lightfoot, and Gilles Vigneault in folk; and The Mercey Brothers, Myrna Lorrie, Dianne Leigh, Gary Buck, Jerry Palmer, Hank Smith, and Bob King in country.

"There wasn't much of an industry," recalls Larry Mercey. "We'd go to Prince Edward Island to play and people would think we were American because we had gone to Nashville to record, and we had the 'Nashville Sound.'"

"Bobby Curtola inspired me," remembers legendary guitarist Randy Bachman. "Being in Winnipeg and hearing a guy from Thunder Bay on the radio with 'Fortune Teller' and all these great songs was a great inspiration. Then he hired The Guess Who in 1964 to be his backup band. Our first road trip. We did 'Shakin' All Over' and we were big."

The first announcement of the new Canadian music awards came in the May 18, 1964, issue of the Toronto music trade *RPM Weekly*. The awards were the idea of *RPM* publisher Walt Grealis and his close friend, record producer Stan Klees, also *RPM*'s special projects director.

BORN

"The reason we started the year-end poll was to attempt to give some credibility to the industry we were creating with our publication," recalled Grealis later.

"We thought it'd create interest in Canadian artists," adds Klees. "At that time there wasn't a great deal of interest in Canadian artists. There were very few artists. You really couldn't call them recording stars. There were a handful."

A four-by-nine-inch ballot appeared in the December 7, 1964, issue of *RPM* asking subscribers "to help *RPM* pick our year-end notable Canadian artists and industry figures" for the RPM Gold Leaf Awards.

The votes would be tabulated by a "neutral body" and announced December 31.

"We polled the industry, and made the announcement the same month," recalled Grealis in *RPM* in 1976.

Topping the poll were Terry Black as top male singer, Shirley Matthews as top female singer, and Ottawa's Esquires as the top group. Also picked were Gary Buck as top country male singer and Vancouver's Pat Hervey as top female country singer. The year's top album was *That Girl* by jazz singer Phyllis Marshall, one of Canadian TV's first stars and a pioneer among black Canadian performers.

About thirty people turned out for the wine-and-cheese party Grealis threw in an east-end ballet rehearsal hall that he rented for fifty dollars. "The only thing that the winners received was a scroll in the mail," says Klees.

The RPM Gold Leaf Awards became an annual feature in the magazine.

"The awards gave some credibility to Canadian artists and helped at radio, which was slow on coming aboard on records then," says Ed Preston of RCA Records of Canada. "The fact that Walt and Stan kept talking about the awards meant something to people."

Bruce Cockburn's manager, Bernie Finkelstein, argues the awards contributed greatly to the growth of the Canadian music industry. "The Junos have been a miraculous story," he says. "It started out of the imagination of Walt and Stan, and it has grown into quite an industry event."

"We all owe a lot to Walt and Stan," agrees singer Andy Kim. "There was no Canadian industry. Walt Grealis and Stan Klees and others were pounding the drums here, but you had to go somewhere else."

For many, securing an American recording deal was the gateway to a career. "All that was on our minds was trying to stay alive long enough to make a record [in order] to get an American record deal, and get south of the border into the real game," explains Rich Dodson of The Stampeders.

Many top Canadian musical figures, in fact, left Canada to achieve stardom in the U.S., including Paul Anka, Hank Snow, The Diamonds, The Four Lads, David Clayton-Thomas, Neil Young, Joni Mitchell, and Denny Doherty.

"Those great Canadian artists may have had to move to the United States, but they weren't really apologizing for who they were," says Lighthouse co-founder Paul Hoffert. "Also the songs they were writing had a lot of Canadian influences."

The Guess Who, Gordon Lightfoot, and Anne Murray stayed—the first to prove that you could be a major international star and remain in Canada.

"People have no idea what we went through," says Guess Who singer Burton Cummings. "In the summer of '66 and '67 we'd be playing places for one hundred people every night, a different place every night in northern Saskatchewan. It meant nothing careerwise. It toughened us up. It gave us road chops to continue on."

"You met other bands at service centres going back and forth to Ottawa or to Montreal or out west," remembers Dodson.

Meanwhile, Yorkville Village's bustling coffeehouse scene developed in the mid-sixties. Walk down the street any summer evening, and you'd hear Lightfoot, Clayton-Thomas, Joni Mitchell, Bonnie Dobson, Jon & Lee & The Checkmates, Jack London and The Sparrows (later renamed Steppenwolf), The Ugly Ducklings, The Mynah Birds (with Rick James and Neil Young), and The Dirty Shames.

Vancouver also developed a bold musical style in the sixties. Groups like The Collectors, the Tom Northcott Trio, Mother Tucker's Yellow Duck, Papa Bear's Medicine Show, Spring, and Seeds of Time populated the numerous ballrooms and theatres in "The Hippie Capital of Canada."

Top: *RPM Magazine* publisher Walt Grealis at the 1973 RPM Gold Leaf Awards.

Centre: *RPM Magazine*'s special projects director Stan Klees.

Bottom: Andy Kim performing at the 1975 Junos. He won Best Male Vocalist in 1970.

Characterized by an exceptionally high level of foreign ownership, Canada's music industry was primarily based in Toronto. Canadian head offices of Capitol Records (later renamed Capitol-EMI), MCA Records, RCA, Kinney Music (later to be WEA), and Columbia were in the city. PolyGram and London Records were in Montreal. Quality Records was in Scarborough, a suburb of Toronto.

Despite some notable successes, the Canadian music industry represented an inevitable circle with limited potential. The majority of Canadian records remained stranded in lower chart positions. Other than Capitol, the majors weren't interested in Canadian artists.

"The majors just didn't care about Canadian talent," Toronto record retailer Sam Sniderman told *Billboard* in 1971.

However, the Canadian Radio-television Commission (CRTC) and its chairman, Pierre Juneau, had proposed Canadian content regulations for AM radio in 1970. After a public hearing in April of that year, the regulations were finalized, and set to come into effect January 1, 1971. Canadian AM radio stations would now have to play at least 30 per cent Canadian music during the broadcast day. Similar regulations for commercial Canadian FM stations followed in 1975.

When these AM content regulations were introduced, Canada's music industry was largely regional. It was hoped that the regulations would lead to a stronger

recording industry—that their passage would spur on the activities of the small independent labels here.

The immediate impact was greater radio exposure and increased popularity of homegrown talent: Crowbar, April Wine, Max Webster, Triumph, Saga, Prism, Chilliwack, Lighthouse, Fludd, Mashmakhan, and A Foot in Coldwater soon racked up impressive domestic sales.

Country acts such as Carroll Baker, Stompin' Tom Connors, The Mercey Brothers, Family Brown, The Carlton Showband, and Dallas Harms came to the forefront nationally.

A handful of Canadian-owned labels, including Attic, Aquarius, Axe, True North, Daffodil, Nimbus 9, Music World Creation, and Boot also emerged in less than a year.

Another key domestic player would be GRT Records, which opened in Canada in late 1970. The tiny American-owned label signed Ronnie Hawkins, Everyday People, Dr. Music, and Beverly Glenn-Copeland in the space of a month. Signings of Lighthouse, Moe Koffman, James Leroy, Cathy Young, Ian Thomas, and Downchild Blues Band soon followed.

Right: CRTC chairman Pierre Juneau in 1972, for whom the Juno Award was renamed. He was responsible for the CanCon guidelines that regulate how much Canadian music is played on the radio.

"The environment seemed good for picking up Canadian artists," GRT president Ross Reynolds told *Billboard* in 1971.

There was certainly considerable industry excitement when *RPM* announced in early 1970 that there would be a formal ceremony for the Gold Leaf Awards, honouring the fourteen winners of the December 1969 poll.

The event held on February 23, 1970—the first to be held in public—was, in effect, the first Juno Awards. For six years, the magazine had honoured musicians using its reader surveys until this formal ceremony at the historic St. Lawrence Hall in Toronto.

Plum Communications Inc.

"We hired a catering firm and invited about 125 people," recalled Grealis later. "We didn't realize that we needed good security at the door. By seven o'clock, 250 people arrived [twice the number who were invited]. The food lasted about twenty minutes, and the bartenders started to worry about the liquor. We closed the bar before the liquor ran out."

"I remember the first one so well," says Finkelstein. "It felt like a family affair to me. It felt like that for years. The first four or five years, it just felt like a big family dinner to me."

"The fact that the award shows at the St. Lawrence happened was a positive step for the growth of the industry," says Attic Records co-founder Al Mair. "What I liked about the early Junos was that it was such a small crowd. You could mingle. It was the artists, and the record company people."

For the occasion, Klees designed an eighteen-inch metronome-shaped walnut trophy. "That was no spot of genius," he says. "I thought, 'What is it about music? Well, there's a treble clef, and a staff.' I went through all of the symbols in my mind. I suddenly said, 'metronome.'"

Broadcaster George Wilson, newly arrived at CFRB in Toronto as host of "Starlight Serenade," emceed the event, and would do so for the next four years.

The evening's first presenter was Apex Records VP George Offer, who named Dianne Leigh as Best Country Female Artist. Leigh had to struggle through the

Plum Communications Inc.

Plum Communications Inc.

crowded room to get onstage while the small hired trio played her current hit, "I'm a One-Man Woman."

Among the other winners were Andy Kim (Best Male Vocalist), Quebec's Ginette Reno (Best Female Vocalist), Tommy Hunter (Best Country Male Artist), and The Mercey Brothers (Best Country Group).

"I don't remember any of that," laughs Anne Murray, who had only just released her album *This Way Is My Way*, featuring "Snowbird." "What I do remember was being sick for the first awards. I got out from what felt like a death bed to go to that thing. I wasn't going to go. Brian [Ahern] said, 'You have to come.' I had the flu. I remember being miserable. Brian

physically carried me up onto the stage and held my arm. That's how sick I was. I wasn't there long."

"In those days you really didn't see a lot of those people like Anne Murray," recalls Larry Mercey of The Mercey Brothers. "You were working someplace, and they were working. You just never got to see them. It was really something."

"Most everybody knew about everybody else," recalls folksinger Murray McLauchlan. "There was an Ottawa scene, and there was a Toronto scene with an overlap. Occasionally, you would hear about this weird place on the other side of the planet called Vancouver because the odd group came out of there. Everybody

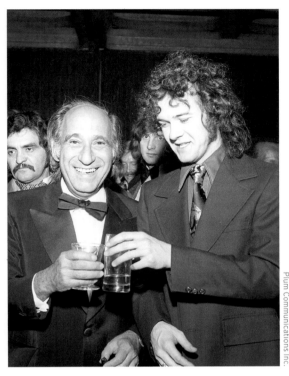

Opposite left: Quebec chanteuse Ginette Reno in 1972. She won Best Female Vocalist honours in 1970, 1972, and 1973.

Opposite right: Lighthouse drummer Skip Prokop. The band won Best Group in 1972, 1973, and 1974.

Left: Best Female Vocalist Anne Murray at the 1972 awards ceremony.

Right: Music retailer Sam "The Record Man" Sniderman and Murray McLauchlan toasting the folksinger's 1974 Juno win.

Canada's foremost singer of the past four decades, Anne Murray still holds the record for the most Juno Awards won by an artist—twenty-four trophies in all.

In 1993, she was inducted into the Canadian Music Hall of Fame.

knew about Winnipeg, but artists got out of there as quickly as they could and came to Toronto."

Paul Hoffert of Lighthouse believes that these ceremonies provided the Canadian music industry with a sense of community and fellowship.

"The concept of having awards and celebrating success instilled a lot of pride," he says. "Also getting a critical mass of successful Canadian artists seeing and meeting each other did a lot to create a sense of community among Canadian artists and the other people in the industry. That doesn't happen unless you have some kind of physical event where people can get together, do a face-to-

face and hang in a way. When you are on the road performing with one another, it doesn't usually happen. You are in your dressing room, and they are in their dressing room."

After their first successful event, Grealis and Klees sought a nickname for the awards. So they ran a contest in the May 16, 1970, edition of *RPM*. On July 25, the magazine picked Hal Philips' winning entry "Juno." Philips had, in fact, suggested "Juneau" (to honour the CRTC chairman). Grealis asked him to resubmit the shorter name.

"The name Juno was like magic," recalled Grealis. "It caught on immediately."

The nickname was apt, folksinger Bruce Cockburn explains. "In a sense the Junos were the manifestation of that groundswell of opinion that led to the CanCon regulations. I don't know if one caused the other, but I think that the same body of popular feeling led to both. That you could have a Juno Awards ceremony because people were starting to care."

In 1970, Canadian artists experienced significant breakthroughs. Lightfoot had a North American pop hit with "If You Could Read My Mind," Murray became an international star overnight with "Snowbird," and The Guess Who topped charts on both sides of the border with "American Woman."

Meanwhile, Toronto had become a formidable recording centre.

Toronto Sound, an upscale twenty-four-track studio facility, had opened in 1969. The next year Eastern Sound upgraded to twenty-four-track; and Moses Znaimer, Ed Cowan, and Will Webster opened Thunder Sound. This was followed in 1971 by Andy Hermant's fortress-like Manta Sound.

Roughly six hundred people crowded into the ballroom of Toronto's St. Lawrence Hall on February 22, 1971, to witness the newly nicknamed Juno Awards presentation.

The audience stood because Grealis and Klees couldn't afford to rent tables. As well, the hall again didn't provide catering. Recalls Klees, "My mother said, 'I can make finger sandwiches and for dessert I can make chrusciki [a Polish bow-tie pastry also known as angel wings].' They went crazy for the chrusciki."

"I liked [the awards] better in their earliest days when it was down-home and personal," says Cockburn. "My feeling was, 'okay, if the music industry wants to get together and congratulate itself on what it's up to, that's great. And, if I'm part of that, that's great too. It is nicer to be thought of than to be ignored.'"

Gordon Lightfoot received his first Gold Leaf Award in 1966. "There are fifteen Junos altogether," he says. "I'm quite proud of them. They mean a lot."
In 1980, he was inducted into the Canadian Music Hall of Fame by Bob Dylan.

The highlight of the night was Pierre Juneau receiving a lengthy ovation upon receiving the Music Industry Man of the Year Award. He held his award and, clutching a copy of *RPM*, declared, "I shouldn't be here receiving an award, I should be here to give an award to *RPM*."

Two new award categories were added this year: Special Award, Canadian Composer (won by Gene MacLellan for "Snowbird") and Journalist of the Year (won by Dave Bist of the *Montreal Gazette*). The journalist category was dropped in 1973.

Murray won her first Juno ever, for Best Female Vocalist. Her producer, Brian Ahern, won for Best Produced Single for "Snowbird" and Best Produced Middle of the Road (MOR) Album for Murray's *Honey, Wheat & Laughter*.

Established stars were the big winners overall. Lightfoot won again as Best Male Vocalist, The Guess Who won Best Group honours again, and The Mercey Brothers were named Best Country Act for the second consecutive year. As well, two veteran country artists, Stompin' Tom Connors and Myrna Lorrie, won their first Junos that night.

Cockburn was named Top Folksinger. "When I won, I looked at the award, and I looked at the people," he says. "I had no idea of what to say to them. So I said, 'Thanks,' and I walked off. Everybody laughed. They thought it was great."

With Maritimers like herself, Ahern, MacLellan, and Connors winning, Murray declared, "The Maritime Mafia has just scratched the surface," as she accepted her Best Female Vocalist award.

Two decades later in *RPM*, Grealis addressed the importance of Murray's attendance at those first awards as her career was soaring. "The fact that Anne Murray had come to the awards was something of a milestone. Her very presence gave the awards a new stature."

Interest in the Junos had grown so much that a thousand people attended the ceremonies on February 22, 1972, at the Inn on the Park, in Toronto.

The following day, *Toronto Star* writer Marci McDonald claimed that the Junos had "graduated from a sophomoric affair into a posh and polished night."

For Rich Dodson, Ronnie King, and Kim Berly of The Stampeders, the night began unglamorously low-key. Suited in leather, frilly shirts, and large bow ties, the Calgarians met up in front of the hotel. They then hopped into a black limousine for a thirty-second ride around the building so they could arrive with style at the hotel's Centennial Ballroom side entrance.

That night, however, the band and their manager, Mel Shaw, celebrated in high style with three wins—Best Group, Best Produced Single (Shaw for "Sweet City Woman"), and Composer honours for Dodson.

"I brought a film crew to the awards," recalls Shaw. "The footage is on the Stampeders' DVD [*Hit the Road*, released in 2006]. It shows the group getting an award, me getting an award, and the group with Anne Murray. [With the film] I wanted to take advantage of the night, and let people know [about the wins]. I also took a full-page ad out in *Billboard* saying that 'This is the top group in Canada.'"

The U.S. popularity of The Guess Who, Gordon Lightfoot, and Anne Murray had been a watershed for the Canadian music industry in the late sixties. Following the introduction of the CRTC's Canadian Content (CanCon) regulations for radio in 1971, The Stampeders, Bachman-Turner Overdrive, Rush, Five Man Electrical Band, Motherlode, The Bells, Bruce Cockburn, and others broke onto American pop music charts as well.

The awards, however, again presented few surprises.

Murray accepted her Best Female Vocalist award from Juneau. Ahern won as Best Producer for Murray's album *Talk It Over in the Morning*. Stompin' Tom and Myrna Lorrie again won their respective country categories. Cockburn's

folksinger award was picked up by Murray McLauchlan, who quipped, "Bruce is out boogyin' around the country."

Leading up to the 1973 Junos, there was discontent about the balloting system as well as sharp criticism that the awards were slanted toward MOR and country acts. There was also grumbling that many of the same acts were winning every year.

Despite such rock bands as Bachman-Turner Overdrive, April Wine, and Rush becoming huge concert draws in the country, there was no category for rock albums. Indeed, the only album category was for Best Produced MOR Album, which had been won by Murray's producer, Brian Ahern, for three consecutive years. Her *Annie* album, in fact, was a virtual shoo-in in the category in 1974 (and did win).

Grealis responded to the criticism by promising to restructure the awards for 1974.

Meanwhile, the show went on.

The 1973 Juno Awards were held March 12, with 1,200 people filling the Inn on the Park's Centennial Ballroom in Toronto. Twenty awards were handed out.

For the first time, all award winners were on hand to receive their trophies, including the elusive Gordon Lightfoot, there for the first time. That night, he won for Best Male Vocalist and Best Songwriter.

"I've been accepted in my native country on a scale I never dreamed possible," he said in his heartfelt speech.

"I'm going to sing the praise of Canada far and wide for as long as I can."

There were other repeat winners. Anne Murray was selected Best Female Vocalist for the third straight year; Stompin' Tom won again as Best Country Male Artist, while The Mercey Brothers again won for Best Country Group. Shirley Eikhard took home her first Juno for Best Country Female Artist.

Edward Bear—whose single "Last Song" had recently reached number 1 on *RPM*'s chart—won for Outstanding Group Performance. Their producer, Gene Martynec, won Best Produced Single for "Last Song." Accepting the awards were the band's singer/songwriter Larry Evoy, keyboardist, Bob Kendall, and guitarist Roger Ellis.

Bob McBride, who had left Lighthouse for a solo career, won for Best Male Vocalist, while Lighthouse was named Best Group. A new award, for Outstanding Performance by a Folksinger, was won by Valdy.

David Clayton-Thomas flew in from Los Angeles to receive a Juno for his contributions to the growth of Canadian music. The award was presented by Walt Grealis.

"In 1973, they realized that a Canadian had already won five Grammy Awards and had never been nominated for a Juno," says the former Blood, Sweat & Tears singer. "So they came up with a new category, Outstanding Contribution to the

Plum Communications Inc.

Canadian Music Industry, and gave it to me. I don't think they have ever done it again."

For the first time the Junos aired nationally. CBC Radio's "The Entertainers" recorded the presentation for a two-hour special that featured interviews with many of the winners.

In a *RPM* editorial following the awards, Grealis pondered the Junos' future. "Could it be that the event has become too big to be of any importance, and might it be impossible for the trust fund, which is heavily subsidized by *RPM*, to continue with the awards?"

This was to be the last Junos by invitation. "The food and liquor bill was incredible," recalled Grealis in *RPM* in 1976.

A lobby sign at the entrance of the Centennial Ballroom at the Inn on the Park on the evening of March 25 told the story of the 1974 ceremonies.

Plum Communications Inc.

Top: Quality Records' Brenden Lyttle, Bob Morten, and Gene Lew at the 1973 Juno Awards. The Hellzapoppin' poster lists events featuring "Chelsea Wind," 'Quality' Magic with Ron Leonard, "Miss Quality Q-Tips Miss Toronto Pat Mazurick," "The Cycle," "Stampeders Movie," "Stampeders phone call direct from London, Eng," "Charlee Symons," "Special Guest—Michael Quatro."

Bottom: Three pillars of Canadian music: Anne Murray, Gordon Lightfoot, and Stompin' Tom Connors at the 1973 Juno Awards.

"THE JUNO AWARDS SOLD OUT."

For the first time *RPM* charged for the event: $12.50 a ticket.

Local press took notice of a new industry glitz.

"Murray McLauchlan, folk-singer, was wearing a tie at last night's Juno Awards, and Bernie Finkelstein, his manager, had a jacket on," noted Jack Batten in the *Globe and Mail*. "It was a first for both in the sartorial department and all by itself, that shows just how classy the Junos, those annual prizes for the best in Canadian pop music, have suddenly grown."

This year's Junos was a fitting close to *RPM*'s Communication 8 conference, which had attracted 1,500 music-industry figures. Speakers had included Kal

Rudman, the founder/publisher of the influential U.S. radio trade, *The Friday Morning Quarterback*, who declared, "If I was getting started in the record industry today, I think I'd head for Canada. This is really where it's at. This is the Old West in music."

There were twenty-four Juno Awards presented in 1974, the highest number to date. Boosting the number were Single and Album of the Year awards in the contemporary, pop, country, and folk categories.

The night kicked off with an ugly confrontation between Grealis and the twenty-three-piece orchestra hired for the night. The American Federation of Musicians had learned that he planned to

tape the show for radio, and refused to let the orchestra go on. In time, the matter was resolved, and Grealis was able to record the show.

The delay, however, resulted in the bar staying open and many presenters not receiving their tickets, leading to several presentation mishaps during the night.

"The [musicians] held up the show for almost forty-seven minutes," Klees remembers. "During that time, people were out there drinking. The bartenders were told not to close the bar until the music started. The bar bill was enormous."

Bottom left: The lobby sign at the entrance of the Centennial Ballroom at the Inn on the Park.

Bottom right: Valdy (left), seen here in 1976 taking time out with Charley Pride (right), won Outstanding Performance by a Folksinger in 1973.

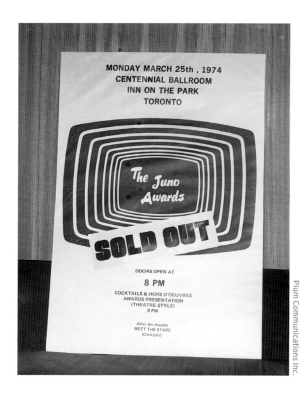

16

Unlike past years, *RPM* had published the nominations in advance. For the first time, winners' names were withheld. While most of the winners were predictable, there were still surprises.

Top folksinger was neither Lightfoot, McLauchlan, nor Cockburn but Valdy, then living in Victoria. He received thunderous applause from the audience. In another upset, Terry Jacks won Best Male Vocalist honours, which usually went to Lightfoot. The night, in fact, resembled a victory party for the West Coast singer/producer. His hit "Seasons in the Sun" was honoured as both Best Contemporary Single and Best Pop Single.

McLauchlan also walked to the podium on three occasions. He won as Best Songwriter for "Farmer Song," which was also named both Best Country and Folk Single.

"There's a real weird picture that someone sent me of me wearing bell bottom jeans and looking really pissed off," says McLauchlan. "With a lot of curly hair and a cigarette dangling from my mouth. I looked like I would rather kill Walt Grealis than take whatever was in his hand."

He also accepted the Canadian Independent Label Award on behalf of True North Records owner Bernie Finkelstein, then managing him and Bruce Cockburn.

Top: Murray McLauchlan at the 1974 Junos accepting an award.

Bottom: Terry Jacks, performing his award-winning single "Seasons in the Sun" in 1975, when he took home three trophies.

"We always won," boasts Finkelstein. "I don't mind admitting that I like things where we win. I always thought the Junos were so valuable."

Anne Murray was named Best Female Vocalist for the fourth time, while her album *Danny's Song* was named Best Pop Album. Stompin' Tom won for Best Country Male Artist and his recording *To It and At It* was named Best Country Album. Bachman-Turner Overdrive won Best Contemporary Album for *Bachman-Turner Overdrive,* as well as Best New Group.

Toronto's Cathy Young was named Most Promising Female Vocalist, while Ian Thomas took home the award for Most Promising Male Vocalist.

"It was the kiss of death to my career," jokes Thomas tongue-in-cheek. "God knows the music business should ever make any promises. [The show] wasn't even televised. That would have done [my career] some good."

Criticisms of the awards continued unabated. Concerns included the unclear categories, the show's disorganization, and the lack of nominations of French-language artists. The latter would lead to the Association québécoise des producteurs de disques setting up its own awards, the Grand prix du disques Québécois, in 1977.

For the first time the evening ended with a round of label parties—which became a Juno tradition—upstairs in the Inn on the Park suites. Burton Cummings remembers, "I went around singing with MacLean & MacLean. Everybody was crazy. God, people used to drink a lot then."

On March 24, 1975, the Junos moved to the Queen Elizabeth Theatre on the grounds of the Canadian National Exhibition in Toronto. An hour-long pre-taped show, before an audience of 1,400, was broadcast by CBC-TV amidst controversy over whether the Junos were ready for TV.

"In 1975, we had to go to television," said Grealis in *RPM* in 1976. "We had no choice."

Many were skeptical. "Does anybody really care about the Juno awards?" asked Robert Martin in the *Globe and Mail* on March 8, 1975.

Plum Communications Inc.

Left: Stompin' Tom Connors, in his signature hat, accepting his Best Country Male Artist honours in 1973. He would win six Junos in the seventies.

The night's performers included Andy Kim, Stompin' Tom Connors, Susan Jacks, Terry Jacks, and Anne Murray.

Viewers, however, nearly missed out on seeing Anne Murray.

A week before the awards, Murray's management representative Leonard Rambeau threatened to withhold her from the broadcast after hearing that CBC was selling commercial time to record companies. But the CBC didn't air any label spots, and Murray performed Lennon and McCartney's "You Won't See Me" dressed in palazzo pants and a print blouse.

With the move to television, Klees designed a new award fashioned from acrylic and stretched to twenty-three inches in height. It would continue to read "RPM Annual Gold Leaf Award" until 1978, when The Canadian Academy of Recording Arts and Sciences (CARAS) officially took over the awards. Since then, each trophy has been labelled as a Juno Award.

With the move to television, and control over the Junos shifting initially to the hastily formed Canadian Music Awards Association (CMAA, which later became CARAS), the awards moved away from being industry awards. Sales came to be entered into tabulating some categories. As well, ballots were to be audited by Thorne Riddell, which had the job for several years.

The selection of the year's top recordings caused an industry stir. The

Plum Communications Inc.

choices were made from recordings released over the preceding fourteen months.

This meant that with sales of nine million worldwide, Terry Jacks' "Seasons in the Sun" won as Best Selling Single for the second consecutive time. "You see," he explained afterwards, "its sales lapped over from '73 to '74. It just kept selling and selling."

Meanwhile, leading up to show time, things were not running smoothly.

Top: Lead singer David Clayton-Thomas with Blood Sweat & Tears in 1976. Bobby Colomby is on drums and Bill Tilman on backup vocals performing "Mean Old World.

With only twenty minutes before the curtain came up, Juno organizers asked Toronto Sound recording engineer Terry Brown to handle the engineering for the $120,000 production. "It was all very much a last-minute thing," says Brown.

While it was a coup to get Canadian Paul Anka to host the show, the former fifties teen idol would come only if he could have a private jet. The CMAA was cash strapped, so United Artist Records Canada's president, Stan Kulin, agreed to pay the $5,000 jet rental for his label's artist.

"We looked for the biggest name that we could get at the time, and Stan Kulin put us in touch with Paul," recalls the

show's co-producer Brian Robertson. "He was appearing at Caesar's Palace. I went down there with the CBC director [John Thompson] and we met Paul with all his entourage in this plush room at Caesar's Palace that was about 5,000 square feet. He agreed to do it. We sent scripts to him. Never heard anything back."

Through Anka's lawyer, Robertson finally received the showman's travel plans. Anka was to come in on the Wednesday before the show on Saturday. That was changed to Thursday, and then Friday. Then he was coming on the private jet on Saturday morning, the day of the show.

Plum Communications Inc.

laughs Ian Thomas about the crooner's pre-recorded show intro.

Thomas caused a stir when he glibly satirized the glitzy stage setting, saying "I think the CBC would like to thank Alcan for this set." Thomas says, "I don't think the CBC was very happy with that. Okay, I brought the show down to a new level. But it was like they had raided all of the kitchen cupboards in Toronto for tin foil."

When Randy Bachman announced Rush as best new group, the band's co-managers Ray Danniels and Vic Wilson came onstage to pick up the award. "We were not there," recalls Rush bassist Geddy Lee. "I think we were in [the American] Midwest opening for Aerosmith. I remember getting the call from Vic that we had won. Of course, we proceeded to celebrate and drink too much. It was a huge thrill."

Keeping with tradition, Anne Murray again won as Top Female Artist, and as Top Female Country Artist; and Gordon Lightfoot won Top Male Artist and Top Folksinger honours.

"This is really difficult," Lightfoot quipped as he peered over his rimless glasses, accepting his Top Male award. "I've been doing it so long."

"I remember it as being a stellar evening," he says. "I went in and took my awards, and I was very grateful, and gracious."

Left: Jet-setting Paul Anka hosted the first televised Juno Awards in 1975 on CBC.

Recalls Robertson, "I go out to the airport figuring Paul had read the script. He gets off the plane with a guy he introduces as his ski instructor. In the car, I asked if he was comfortable with the script, keeping in mind that we had a dress rehearsal at 2 p.m. It's now eleven. He looks at me blankly. It's obvious that he's never read anything. So, I said 'We will give you some ideas for the opening, and we will give you cards to introduce the segments.'

"We did the dress [rehearsal] and it was okay. Paul said not to worry about the intros. In the evening—and it's all live—we were giving him these [cue] cards as he went out onstage. Anyway, he was terrific. We finish at eleven. Paul goes out to the car, goes out to the airport and left with his ski instructor. That was it. That was Paul."

"Paul Anka turned the Junos into a Vegas show as he walked through the crowd singing 'You're Having My Baby,'"

Myrna Lorrie presented Stompin' Tom with his Country Male Vocalist award with Anka, then joked, "That's a nice hat there, son. Glad you dressed for the occasion there, Tom." She also handed The Carlton Showband their award for Country Group of the Year.

Cathy Young and Edward Bear's Larry Evoy presented Anka with his Composer award, which he accepted, joking that he had lost two other awards during the evening.

"It's really nice to know people like what I do," Suzanne Stevens said in accepting her Top New Female Artist award from The Mercey Brothers.

Rosalie Trombley, music director of the powerhouse Top-40 radio station CKLW in Windsor, presented the Producer award to Randy Bachman. Bachman-Turner Overdrive also took Group of the Year

honours as well as Best Selling Album for *Not Fragile*.

"It was a very lump-in-the-throat, gut-wrenching tears moment," declares Bachman, who had left The Guess Who four years earlier on bitter terms. "It was really something to go up there, get that [award], and be cheered on."

Bachman-Turner Overdrive had opted not to perform. Instead, a short promotional film was shown. "We made some stupid stance that we didn't want to play on television," recalls the band's manager, Bruce Allen.

Canada's music industry, as Grealis had feared, was not ready for its prime-time moment. Gaffes and stiff performances dotted the evening. Few artists dressed up, and there were few sparks between co-presenters.

"We were under the misapprehension that most music people knew each other, but there was an obvious lack of familiarity and casual warmth between many participants before the camera," admitted producer/director John Thompson to *RPM* the following year.

"Paul Anka mispronounced my name and the audience corrected him," recalls Bruce Cockburn. "People yelled at him. I think I saw it on TV. It can happen to

anybody, but it's one of those things that stand out. Both of us being Ottawa boys and all."

"Performing on the first televised Juno Awards was thrilling," says Andy Kim, who sang "Rock Me Gently." "Here is a record that I wrote and produced. That I put out first in Canada. I had two hundred records pressed and London Records sent it out to Canadian radio stations. Then it became a number 1 record in the U.S. and John Lennon gives me my gold record. I now had the ability to stand in front of my peers and perform. That was exciting."

"It was pretty much a blur," reveals Gino Vannelli about accepting his Juno for Most Promising Male Vocalist. "Things were just happening around me. I was sort of caught in a storm. In those days events like the Junos or the Grammys were interjected into a life of writing and touring and planning. It was all happening to me as I was trying to create."

Top: Tommy Hunter presenting at the 1975 Junos. In 1970, he won Best Country Male Artist.

Right: A pensive Gino Vannelli awaiting the announcement of 1977 Best Male Vocalist award.

Plum Communications Inc.

superstars like Gordon Lightfoot and Anne Murray didn't need that extra encouragement. But would-be pop singers and composers and record-makers have told me at rock concerts how much it has boosted their confidence."

"Before we had nothing," explained Sam Sniderman of the thirty-store Sam the Record Man national chain in the same *Star* article. "Now we have a little bit of a Canadian industry. . . . My wife and I could run a record store profitably, if we wanted to, just by selling Canadian products."

This was reflected in the continued growth of the recording studio sector in Canada. In 1974, Guess Who producer Jack Richardson opened Soundstage (later renamed Nimbus 9), Jeff Smith opened Sounds Interchange, also in Toronto, and Doug Hill and Paul Gross opened Phase One in the city's Scarborough suburb. Also opened were Little Mountain Sound in Vancouver and Andre Perry's rural retreat, Le Studio, in Morin Heights, Quebec.

At this time The Stampeders and April Wine became the first two Canadian bands to do full-scale tours across Canada. "We did the first national tour," recalls The Stampeders' Rich Dodson. "We played all of the condemned arenas. Take the sign down, play, and then put it back up now. There weren't many promoters booking Canadian acts."

At the show's conclusion, the audience gave Anka a standing ovation as he walked among them singing his upcoming single, "I Don't Like to Sleep Alone." "I'm happy with the way things turned out," he declared backstage. "It's good to see this thing get off the ground."

By the mid 1970s, it was clear that the Canadian music industry had passed out of its cottage-industry period.

Prime Minister Pierre Trudeau had coined the phrase "a yowling infant of a musical recording industry" in 1974 to describe the impact of the CRTC's CanCon regulations on radio.

"The squalling infant has developed beyond my fondest hopes, and I am happy to have been its grandfather," proudly said former CRTC head Pierre Juneau in the *Toronto Star* in 1974. "Established

Left: The stage show at the 1976 awards.

The biggest crisis in Juno history began when the Canadian Recording Industry Association (CRIA) was founded in 1974, replacing the Record Manufacturers Association.

Brian Robertson, president of the new organization, had recently left his job as account supervisor at MacLaren Advertising in Toronto to launch his own company, Marketplace Communications.

"The record companies wanted a more dynamic trade association that would lobby and represent their interests with one effective voice," he recalls. "At the first board meeting, I said that we needed a national awards structure that could be sold to a television network. The obvious one was the Juno Awards."

Juno co-founders Walt Grealis and Stan Klees, however, sought to keep the awards an industry show.

After a flurry of meetings, it was obvious the two parties could not work together. "We were being squeezed out," says Klees. "The labels weren't willing to pay a cent for the Juno Awards. They wanted them for nothing."

Then CRIA dropped a bombshell. It would establish a rival awards, The Maple Music Awards, which would be televised.

"Walt and Stan were in a position of losing everything," recalls their friend, Stampeders' manager Mel Shaw, who became the first president of the Canadian Academy of Recording Arts and Sciences (CARAS).

On February 4, Grealis and CRIA president Arnold Gosewich issued a joint statement indicating the two parties would work toward developing a new broad-based awards system.

In late 1975, CARAS was founded to oversee the planning and the presentation of the awards. In 1984, CARAS negotiated the name and the rights to the awards show.

The 1976 Junos confirmed Bachman-Turner Overdrive's stature as Canada's top group, boosted Hagood Hardy's standing, and launched country singer Carroll Baker's career.

CBC-TV extended the 1976 Juno show to ninety minutes. Jack McAndrew, who had recently become head of CBC-TV programming, declared that the 1975 broadcast was "a satisfactory first effort" but demanded changes from CBC-TV and music-industry people.

McAndrew told RPM that the broadcaster was beginning to pay more attention to the Canadian music industry. "The Junos itself is a big boost for CBC-TV because it helps to establish as TV fare the same artists we want to expose throughout the year. The Junos on TV are not preaching to the converted as were the Junos of the past. If we all produce a good show, all our interests are served."

As proof of this, CBC-TV was about to begin production of a one-hour Hagood Hardy special, Murray McLauchlan had taped a special in Vancouver, and specials were scheduled for Anne Murray, Gordon Lightfoot, Sylvia Tyson, The Irish Rovers, and Gino Vannelli.

"That period was the flowering of Canadian music," remembers McAndrew.

In an ironic twist, Juno emcee and Cape Breton singer John Allan Cameron hosted a successful show on the rival CTV network.

The Juno ceremonies were held at the Ryerson Polytechnic Institute and about 8,800 people attended.

It took a week to set up the show. The production crew doubled the area of the existing 2,000-square-foot stage and brought 7 cameras and a 100-input audio control board. More than 55 CBC personnel were on hand on Juno night.

"Ryerson Theatre is just four walls," explained producer/director John Thompson in RPM. "We have to rebuild the entire theatre to be a television studio for just one night."

Meanwhile, there was growing media criticism that the Junos had been overhauled by the music industry in order to sell more records."Sales is its own reward," groused CHUM-FM news director Larry Wilson on air. "Why can't these [awards] be strictly artistic awards? After all, Juno recipients all jealously consider their awards to be recognition of artistic prowess, not bloody sales bonuses. The record industry's greed is only underlined and spotlighted by this type of format."

"Of course, it was to sell more records," laughs one of CARAS' founding directors, Ross Reynolds, who was CARAS chairman from 2001 to 2006.

While the music industry body would control the awards ceremony in coming years, CBC-TV would rigidly control the in-house television production of the Junos until the mid-eighties.

"There was a modest budget from CBC, but the show was modest," recalls Reynolds. "The record companies agreed that they would provide the talent while CBC would produce the show. That formula is still in existence [at the Junos]."

"Those early Juno shows were by the seat of the pants," admits the show's co-producer Brian Robertson, then head of the Canadian Recording Industry Association (CRIA), and president of CARAS from 1977 to 1984. "We were trying to get the show done as inexpensively as we could. We had to try to find locations where we didn't have the IATSE [union] costs."

"The CBC put money in, but they didn't put much money in," adds Peter Steinmetz, then counsel to CARAS, and its

president from 1984 to 1993. "That was reflected in the quality of the shows."

Certainly, the 1976 presentation reflected more CBC-TV's approach to light entertainment than what was going on within Canada's music community.

The twenty-seven-piece show orchestra, under the direction of David Woods, was upfront that year as opposed to being buried off-camera as it was in 1975. Artist backup and medley performances were also arranged to better highlight eight singer/dancers who,

among things, crooned the songs under the Composer of the Year category.

Michel Pagliaro, one of Quebec's leading stars, opened the show with his raucous hit "What the Hell I Got." He was followed by Montreal-based Suzanne Stevens, who sang "Make Me Your Baby," and the down-home Valdy, who performed his new single "Yes I Can." For the finale, Blood, Sweat & Tears, fronted by singer David Clayton-Thomas, raised the roof with "Mean Old World."

Among those performing with the orchestra was twenty-one-year-old Dan Hill, singing "You Make Me Want to Be." Hill won that night as Most Promising Male Vocalist; Patricia Dahlquist won for Most Promising Female Vocalist; and Myles and Lenny won for Most Promising Group.

"I remember bombing out," says Hill. "I had to sing and play guitar live but the drums didn't come in until halfway through the song. I just freaked out and panicked. I lost my rhythm, my breathing, and totally blew it on nationwide TV. I was so embarrassed that I couldn't leave my house the next day."

A disappointment was that there were no-shows by many of the marquee acts: Anne Murray, Gordon Lightfoot, Gino Vannelli, Joni Mitchell, and Murray McLauchlan. Lightfoot was playing in Reno, Nevada, so his sister Bev picked up his Folksinger of the Year award; WEA Music Canada president Ken Middleton accepted for Mitchell; and Top Country

Opposite: Ross Reynolds with Murray McLauchlan at the 1974 Junos.

Top: Twenty-one-year-old Dan Hill performing "You Make Me Want to Be" in 1976 when he won Most Promising Male Vocalist.

Centre: Carroll Baker won the 1977 Country Female Vocalist of the Year after a stellar performance the previous year.

Bottom: Valdy accepting his award at the 1978 Junos.

Male Vocalist McLauchlan was working in Vancouver.

Anne Murray's Country Female Vocalist award was accepted by her brother Bruce. Murray had recently married TV producer Bill Langstroth, and she was expecting in August.

Though Vannelli was touring in Europe, he appeared on the show in a film clip performing his current hit "Keep On Walking." A&M Records of Canada executives Doug Chappell and Jean-Pierre Guilbert accepted his Male Vocalist of the Year award.

"If the industry is going to grow, we can't depend on those big Canadian stars showing up each year," newly named CARAS president Mel Shaw told *Billboard* afterwards. "The new acts are there with enthusiasm and high hopes because for most of them it is their first opportunity to be seen on national television. That also gives the show excitement."

Country singer Carroll Baker's performance of "I've Never Been This Far Before" received one of the most boisterous audience reactions in Juno history.

Reynolds remembers, "Nobody knew who Carroll Baker was. She sang her heart out. And everybody went 'whoa.'"

"Carroll Baker stole the show," confirms Hill.

Plum Communications Inc.

Plum Communications Inc.

Baker's performance led to her being signed by RCA Records, as well as to a deal with CBC-TV for shows. "I was knocked out by her," McAndrew says. "I went up and talked to her. That led to me doing a number of specials with her."

"That performance was an introduction to country music for many Canadians," states Baker. "I was only one of two people to sing live [on the show]. Just before I went onstage, they lost the mic I had rehearsed with. So they just threw me a mic. I remember looking up, and saying, 'Please Lord, just let this turn out good for country music. This is our one and only shot.' When I finished I could hear people murmuring, 'Who is she?'"

Also drawing attention that night was Hagood Hardy. His evocative instrumental "The Homecoming," originally a commercial jingle for Salada tea, won him awards for Composer and Instrumental Artist of the Year. Its producer, Peter Anastasoff, won the Producer award.

"Hagood was not the kind of person who got excited; he was Mr. Mellow," says his widow, Martha. "He would never have considered doing a cartwheel down the aisle like I would have done. But he was very excited."

One emotional moment came when Randy Bachman, his brother Robbie, and Blair Thornton were accepting Bachman-Turner Overdrive's award for Group of the Year. Randy pulled a maple leaf-styled plaque from a brown paper bag. He called

Juno co-founder Walt Grealis to the stage, and then read the plaque's inscription: "To Walt Grealis, You Were Always There When We Needed You. Signed: The Musicians of Canada 1976." The crowd gave Grealis a standing ovation.

This Juno show ran into twenty minutes of national news time, but ratings of more than 3 million viewers proved that Canadian music had identifiable stars. "The very high rating shows that the public is interested in the Junos as a prestige event," said CBC-TV's McAndrew at the time.

Yet, despite the impressive reaction, prior to the 1977 Juno show Canada's music industry was stunned to read comments attributed to Grealis describing the Junos as "first rate awards that we give to a bunch of nobodies."

"We just haven't got it right," Grealis was quoted as saying. "It's not working at all. We have bush-league artists receiving awards they don't deserve." He continued, "We haven't got any real stars in Canada. Who have we got? Anne Murray, Gordon Lightfoot, and Bachman-Turner Overdrive? And they're not exactly setting the world on fire."

Top: Randy Bachman in the audience at the 1976 Junos.

Bottom left: Burton Cummings won both New Male Vocalist and Best Male Vocalist in 1977.

Opposite: Trooper with MCA's Randy Sharrard promoting their debut album *Two for the Show* at the 1977 Junos.

Plum Communications Inc.

World's Goin' Crazy, Gordon Lightfoot's *Summertime Dream* (featuring the "The Wreck of the Edmund Fitzgerald"), Harmonium's *L'Heptade*, Bruce Cockburn's *In the Falling Dark*, and Max Webster's masterful self-named debut.

There would also be riches throughout 1977, including April Wine's *Forever for Now*, Dan Hill's *Longer Fuse*, Kate & Anna McGarrigle's *Dancer with Bruised Knees*, Murray McLauchlan and the Silver Tractors' *Hard Rock Town*, and Stan Rogers' debut, *Fogarty's Cove*. As well, Toronto-based Klaatu, rumoured to be all or parts of The Beatles, enjoyed brisk sales of its album *3:47 EST*.

Grealis' alleged outburst led to comedian David Steinberg starting off the 1977 Juno broadcast with, "Hello, fellow nobodies."

In his opener, the host also took a shot at CanCon regulations while mentioning the Male Vocalist category. He said, "I have bad news for the five nominees. We have just learned that Stevie Wonder was born in Saskatchewan."

The March 16 event was held before a capacity crowd of 1,000 people in the Canadian Room of the Royal York Hotel in Toronto. The ceremonies followed dinner and were broadcast on a two-hour CBC-TV special that drew an impressive 2,075,000 viewers. Directed by Ron Meraska, the show was produced by Paddy Sampson in association with CARAS president Mel Shaw and Brian Robertson of CRIA.

Though Grealis would claim that the article by Ian Haysom of the *Ottawa Journal*, syndicated by Canadian Press, was "a hatchet job," both media outlets stood by the story.

"Can you imagine me referring to artists as nobodies?" Grealis fumed in the March 19, 1977, issue of *RPM*. "I've been trying to help Canadian artists become somebodies for 13 years."

He may, however, have been resigned to the changes in the awards. Paul McGrath had recently written in the *Globe and Mail* that "Grealis, as more than an interested bystander, isn't all that pleased with the way the Junos are handled. . . . He admits that he's 'fighting like hell to remain positive' about it all, and hopes that 'out of this mediocre cornball thing, something of value will surface.'"

The past year had actually been good for Canadian music. In 1976, Rush released their pivotal *2112* album, and there was such killer fare as April Wine's *The Whole*

27

Two new categories for jazz and classical music, both based on voting only, were presented prior to the broadcast. Phil Nimmons won the Best Jazz Album award for *Atlantic Suites*, and pianist Anton Kuerti won Best Classical Album for *Beethoven, The Complete Piano Sonatas, Vol. 1-3*.

During the night Ian Tyson sang "Summer Wages," Keath Barrie read a moving dissertation entitled "On Being Canadian," Quebec pianist André Gagnon performed his instrumental hit "Wow" backed by the band led by musical director Jimmy Dale, and Patsy Gallant slinked through a choreographed dance routine with the Eddy Toussaint Dancers while lip-syncing her disco-styled national pop hit "From New York to L.A."

Gagnon, one of the few French-Canadian acts to be nominated due to the split from the Junos in 1976 by the French-language segment of the music industry in Quebec, triumphantly beat out Bachman-Turner Overdrive, Heart, and Gordon Lightfoot for Best Selling Album with *Neiges*.

While Joni Mitchell, Anne Murray, Carroll Baker, and Charity Brown were nominated for Female Vocalist, it was feisty New Brunswick underdog Patsy Gallant who won. Gallant was in tears as she came to the podium to accept the award.

"Anne Murray kept winning; it was a big deal beating her," says Gallant. "I

didn't expect to win at all. I had decided to go to the dressing room, and hang out. All of a sudden, they were calling me because they couldn't find me at my seat. The director was going berserk. They found me in the dressing room. I freaked out. I was saying, 'It's not me.' I couldn't believe it."

Gallant, a major star in Quebec singing in French, had become a star nationally a

year earlier with her hit single "From New York to L.A.," a translated version of Gilles Vigneault's signature song "Mon Pays." Her engineer, Paul Page, won his category for his work on Gallant's LP *Are You Ready for Love?*

It also proved a memorable night for former Guess Who singer Burton Cummings. Gallant presented him with the Male Vocalist award, his second Juno

up the Best Selling Single trophy for Sweeney Todd's hit "Roxy Roller" (actually sung by Nick Gilder, who had left the Vancouver band), which had topped *RPM*'s chart.

In the country category, Carroll Baker predictably won as Top Country Female Vocalist. She announced that Murray McLauchlan had won Country Male Vocalist for the second consecutive year. However, he was not present. The Juno for Country Group of the Year went to The Good Brothers. Bruce Good's wife, Margaret, accepted for the siblings who were playing in Vancouver that night.

For the second consecutive year, Hagood Hardy won the Juno for Instrumental Artist. He accepted his award from Rush drummer Neil Peart and CBC Radio host Jim Millican.

Lightfoot picked up two Junos that year. Music retailer Sam Sniderman presented him with the Composer award, and Bruce Murray and John Allan Cameron handed him his Folksinger of the Year trophy.

of the night. The first, for Most Promising Male Vocalist, had been presented earlier to the Winnipegger by Gordon Lightfoot and Liona Boyd.

"Don't let people say that things don't happen fast in Canada," Cummings quipped at the podium. "In forty-five minutes, I went from Best New Male Vocalist to Best Male Vocalist."

"That was a special night, and I won't forget it in a hurry," says Cummings.

The Juno for Most Promising Female Vocalist was presented to Colleen Peterson. She had, in fact, won a Gold Leaf Award as Most Promising Vocalist in 1967. Grinning widely, Peterson assured the crowd she was "still promising."

Many Canadians got their first glimpse of Bryan Adams when he and his producer/manager, Martin Shaer, picked

Opposite: Lavender Hill Mob performing at the 1977 Junos. Note the cue cards at the front used before teleprompters became the norm.

Top: Grant Smith and Barbara Law getting "disco fever" at the 1978 Juno stage show.

Heart won Group of the Year honours but, enmeshed in legal tangles with Vancouver's Mushroom Records after deciding to sign with Columbia's Portrait label in the U.S., only the band's bassist, Steve Fossen, was on hand to accept the award.

A nonchalant Gino Vannelli accepted his Top Male Singer award by saying, "Hey, thanks a lot," which drew criticism.

Watching the televised show at home, Anne Murray was aghast. "It was embarrassing when they decided to televise it," she says. "It was just a big party. [The award show] was for the people at home. We were televising it, and all of these people there were drunk. They were talking and yelling. I was just disgusted with the whole thing. I said, 'I'm not going to perform in front of an audience like this.' It was awful."

Murray steered clear of the Junos until 1986. If she had any reservations, the Junos of 1978 would have resolved her decision.

Hosted for the second consecutive year by David Steinberg, they took place March 29, 1978, at Toronto's Harbour Castle Hilton convention centre.

The show's opener was pure cornball.

On a grid of coloured squares, Toronto soul singer Grant Smith, dressed in a *Saturday Night Fever*-inspired white suit, alongside Irish singer/actress Barbara Law, vamped and kicked his way through "Step Out," a song co-written by Paul

Hoffert and his wife, Brenda, for the 1977 Craig Russell cult film *Outrageous!*

Dan Hill was the night's big winner. He was named Composer of the Year for his massive North American hit "Sometimes When We Touch" (co-written with American songwriting legend Barry Mann) and Male Vocalist of the Year, beating out frontrunner Burton Cummings as well as Gordon Lightfoot, Gino Vannelli, and Valdy.

Hill also won for Best Selling Album with *Longer Fuse*, over such popular works as Cummings' *My Own Way to Rock* and Rush's *A Farewell to Kings*. Although he had not been scheduled to perform, Hill sang "Sometimes When We Touch." "Burton was having a huge year," the Toronto singer/songwriter recalls. "During rehearsals, he said to me, 'You may win some of these, but you aren't going to win them all.'"

Top: Accepting the award for Ronnie Prophet as Country Male Vocalist, Nashville's Charley Pride said he was "just comin' through and dropped by" in 1978.

Centre: Nineteen-year-old Lisa Dal Bello performing in 1978. Upon presenting her with the Most Promising Female Vocalist award, Burton Cummings observed, "Boy, she's beautiful."

Bottom: Nick Gilder performing his 1979 award-winning single "Hot Child in the City." He also won Most Promising Male Vocalist that year.

Opposite: Singer Geddy Lee and guitarist Alex Lifeson of Rush accept 1978 Group of the Year honours.

Despite its international success, Rush had been unable to win Group of the Year honours at the Junos. This year, they did. Alex Lifeson, accepting with Geddy Lee, told the audience, "We'd like to thank Dan Hill for not being a group." A video clip of Rush performing the title track to *Farewell to Kings* was shown.

Backstage, Lee had run into future film star Rick Moranis, then a writer on the show, who asked, "So, you need any jokes when you go on?" Says Lee, "I knew Rick from public school. I hadn't seen him in years."

On accepting his Folksinger of the Year award, Gordon Lightfoot joked, "This I don't need, but nevertheless there it is." He clarified the comment later in the broadcast saying he'd already won fifteen awards.

"I didn't take the Junos seriously at the beginning," Lightfoot admits. "I was

very busy. I was doing a lot of writing, and making an album every year and a half at that point. I took it more seriously as time went by. I realized the significance of it. The award points out the people who are doing meaningful things here. It also brings interest from the big market south of the border. From there, it can go right out around the world as we very well know."

That night Patsy Gallant got so overexcited in presenting the Most Promising awards with Burton Cummings that she practically sidetracked the show. Cummings, after giving the award for Most Promising Female Vocalist to sultry nineteen-year-old Toronto singer Lisa Dal Bello, observed, "Boy, she's beautiful." Gallant brashly shot back, "Well, she's gone, and I'm here."

When she arrived again at the podium, Gallant promised not to cry (as she did in 1977), but she did everything else when

she won the Juno for top-selling single for her disco hit "Sugar Daddy."

"When Patsy Gallant crawled up onstage, and didn't go up the steps, she [accidentally] mooned the crowd," recalls Ross Reynolds.

Laughs Gallant, "It was okay. I was wearing the same colour [red] as my dress. I was colour coordinated. Luckily, I was wearing panties."

As one of Canada's top stars, Cummings was allowed a fat chunk of airtime to perform a medley of his hits as well as "Break It to Them Gently," performed in public for the first time. "What more could I ask for?" Cummings crowed after the show. "It was eight minutes of uninterrupted playing, more time than even David Steinberg got in one shot."

Heart's win as top Canadian group in 1977 was controversial.

Their debut album *Dream Boat Annie*, released in Canada in 1975 on Vancouver's Mushroom Records, sold 2.5 million albums. By mid-1976, its singles "Magic Man," "Crazy on You" and the title track had become big hits throughout North America.

As most of the members of Heart were from Seattle, many felt that the band should have been ineligible for a Juno. However, the American members of the band were landed Canadian immigrants, which made them eligible at the time.

"They collected their award and went back to the States," says Daisy Falle, then national coordinator of CARAS. "We then changed the rules to say that a [landed Canadian] act had to be in the country for six months during the past year."

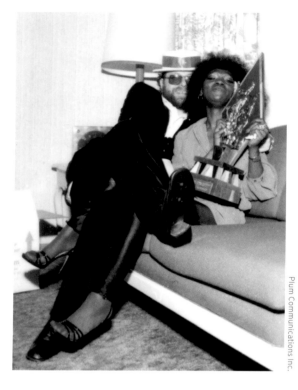

At a news conference following the 1978 Junos, Stompin' Tom Connors announced he would return his six trophies to CARAS as a protest against rewarding "Juno jumpers," or artists who do not maintain a residence or presence in Canada.

True to his word, Stompin' Tom sent them back accompanied by a letter to the CARAS board of directors.

Says Daisy Falle, then national coordinator of CARAS, "He got those Junos when Stan (Klees) and Walt (Grealis) were running the Junos. It had nothing to do with us. And do you know what? I threw them out. I did. I didn't have room in storage."

Accepting the award for Ronnie Prophet as Country Male Vocalist, Nashville's Charley Pride allowed he was "just comin' through and dropped by." Carroll Baker was again named Country Female Vocalist, while The Good Brothers barely made it to the stage to jointly accept their Country Group or Duo of the Year trophy.

For the Junos' first Canadian Music Hall of Fame inductions, CARAS' executive board had selected two legendary Canadian figures: jazz pianist Oscar Peterson and band leader Guy Lombardo, who had passed away the year before. Lombardo's award was accepted by Saul Richman, who had handled Lombardo's affairs for more than three decades.

Having Peterson on hand to accept his award and receive a standing ovation was one of the evening's highlights. Peterson said, "I would like to accept this award not just for myself but on behalf of some of the great players we have not only in this orchestra but in Canada that will be in line I'm sure for many awards, certainly many of these."

The 1979 Junos took place as the music industry, already facing a declining number of adolescent buyers, was being battered by home taping and competition from video games. As well, a gas crunch and a recession had hit North America.

Layoffs, roster reductions, and management reorganizations were happening throughout the industry.

It was in this environment that the awards were presented on March 21 at the Harbour Castle Hilton convention centre with Burton Cummings hosting for the first time.

CARAS and CBC-TV were over the moon with having Cummings as host. "Finding a host was our annual Juno headache," recalls Daisy Falle, CARAS' national coordinator from 1978 to 1984, executive director from 1984 to 1999, and president from 1999 to 2002. "Anybody high profile enough, we were way down their list."

CARAS had also introduced new categories for comedy, children's records, and spoken word, bringing the total to twenty-three.

Performing were Claudja Barry, Chilliwack, Nick Gilder, Toulouse, and Quebec chanteuse Ginette Reno, who received a standing ovation for her performance of a medley of songs nominated as top singles.

"That was a knock-'em-dead performance," declares Brian Robertson. "That was one of the major performance highlights in Juno history."

Once again, Cummings and Dan Hill led the list of nominees with four nominations each. Hill was, in fact, named Composer of the Year for the second time in the category with the same song, "Sometimes When We Touch," which had sold more than 75,000 copies after the 1977 Juno voting.

Cummings recalls, "I said something terrible to Dan Hill, and he took it the wrong way. I have been sorry every since. Because he won Junos two years in a row for song of the year. Nobody wins Song of the Year two frigging times in a row. I said to him jokingly, 'Jeez, I heard that song so much I got sick of it.' That was meant to be taken lightly. Just denoting how could you possibly win it two times in a row? And he took it the wrong way."

Competition was quite spirited in the Male Vocalist of the Year category this year, with Lightfoot, Cummings, Hill, and Neil Young edged out by Gino Vannelli, who also won the Producer of the Year award for his co-production (with siblings Joe and Ross) on his *Brother to Brother* album. Another upset was Murray McLauchlan beating out Lightfoot for Folksinger of the Year honours.

Opposite top left: Claudja Barry and a friend celebrate. After two nominations in 1978, the disco starlet won Most Promising Singer in 1979.

Opposite top right: Canadian country music legend Hank Snow was inducted into the Canadian Music Hall of Fame in 1979.

Opposite bottom right: Arnold Gosewich (left) with Liona Boyd and Pierre Trudeau (right).

Opposite bottom left: Don Ferguson, Luba Goy, and Roger Abbott of The Royal Canadian Air Farce picked up the inaugural Comedy Album of the Year award in 1979.

Classical guitarist Liona Boyd was nominated not in the classical category but in the instrumental category, where she beat out pianist Frank Mills, who had topped charts internationally with "Music Box Dancer." Boyd remembers "I thanked my English school teacher . . . who kicked me out of the choir."

Hindemith: Das Marienleben, by pianist Glenn Gould and soprano Roxolana Roslak, was named Best Classical Album. An absent Anne Murray won awards for Female Vocalist and Best Children's Album for *There's a Hippo in My Tub.*

Nick Gilder wasn't, perhaps, surprised to win as Most Promising Male Vocalist, but when "Hot Child in the City," which he performed on the show, won as Best Selling Single, he was certainly taken aback. "What do you say when you win two of these in a night?" he asked.

Ronnie Prophet earned his second consecutive win as Country Male Vocalist of the Year, and Jamaican-born Claudja Barry, home from Germany, where she was living, was named Most Promising Female Vocalist. The Most Promising Group award went to Doucette over heavily favoured Max Webster and Streetheart.

Cummings was quite tickled to pick up the Best Selling Album award for *Dreams of a Child*, which he had produced. "In the seventies I got on quite a roll as a solo artist," he says. "*Dreams of a Child* sold about 380,000 albums in Canada, which

was remarkable. Not that many [Canadian] artists did [sales of] 100,000 at that point."

The evening's highlight was a Canadian Music Hall of Fame presentation to legendary country singer Hank Snow by Prime Minister Pierre Trudeau. "The cultural industries are bigger than steel in Canada," Trudeau noted in his seven-minute speech. "They are bigger than pulp and paper. Some six billion [dollars] a year. It's a big industry."

"Trudeau being there established further credibility for the Junos," claims Robertson.

CARAS' Daisy Falle, however, says that Trudeau's Juno appearance was well calculated. "We would always send an invitation but we would never expect him to come. His appearance was on the eve of an election." The federal election on May 22, 1979, however, resulted in the Liberals' defeat after eleven years in power under Trudeau.

Among those sitting at the table with Trudeau that night were Dan Hill, Ginette Reno, Patsy Gallant, and Hagood Hardy and his wife, Martha. "Trudeau had never heard of me," recalls Hill. "Ginette had recorded 'Sometimes When We Touch' and she kept singing it over and over to Trudeau to convince him that he knew the song. Trudeau was trying to be polite. He had never heard of it. I was dying of embarrassment."

"When the presenters at the table got

up [to go onstage], I was left with Pierre on the other side of the table," remembers Martha Hardy. "I moved over and sat next to him. I couldn't get over Pierre Elliott who picked my brain about who was who in the room, and why was this person winning. I was so impressed with him. He didn't have to do that. He could have sat there like a stone."

The show finished up within a few minutes of its allotted two hours—for the first time. Unfortunately, ratings slipped down to 1,827,000 viewers, perhaps due to the TV broadcast being in a later 9:30–11:30 p.m. time slot.

The timing of the 1979 Junos was a spectacular moment because Dan Hill, Gino Vannelli, Anne Murray, and Nick Gilder had each recently topped charts in both Canada and the U.S., while Rush, Chilliwack, Trooper, and Prism were selling briskly.

"The Canadian music industry started in the mid-seventies," recalls Vannelli. "That's when I could feel the tires screeching a bit. I don't think it really took off until the eighties. For years [Canadians] had a provincial attitude toward recording. They never thought of getting their records released worldwide. The attitude was 'It's good enough for our territory.' Only by the late seventies did that start to change." •

Opposite: The awards show at the Harbour Castle Hilton as broadcast by CBC in 1979.

1970s

1980s

1990s

2000s

As 1980 got underway, I was receiving my fourth consecutive platinum album from Columbia, *Woman Love*. A single surfaced from the album, called "Fine State of Affairs," which garnered tremendous airplay across the country, and I was feeling pretty good about myself. Somehow I had weathered the storm of leaving a group and becoming a solo entity—but before too long my complacency would "disappear in the air like a breath of wind."

Things were about to shift drastically within the record industry. So much so that before long it wouldn't really be called the "record" industry any longer.

In 1983, Alan Thicke and I co-hosted the Junos, and during the opening segment, we held a compact disc up for the cameras. I had never seen or touched one before. Alan explained to the viewing audience that "this was the future": a small, round, shiny disc with a whole lot of zeros and ones on it . . . and absolute silence between tracks. The zeros and ones would be read by a laser, but the disc would never be touched, so it would never wear down, and it would always sound the same. Things didn't exactly change overnight, but that little piece of show-and-tell turned out to be extremely prophetic.

Canada had more of a world presence than ever. No longer was it ever thought of as "that frozen place up there." Sure, there had always been Canadian films, but in the eighties Canada nurtured and developed its first real worldwide power-presence in pop music. Coming of age had nothing to do with it—great songwriting and performances did.

And almost as if overnight, little films were accompanying songs on something called MTV . . . and new elements took new attention . . . and a whole lot of people thought they might become the next Francis Ford Coppola via a four-minute rock song. Show biz is as show biz does. Huge changes came very quickly.

Yeah, it was the eighties now. Machines and videos circled the wagons . . . and music waited till dawn to look more clearly at the lines drawn in the sand.

—BURTON CUMMINGS

THE JUNOS COME

PICTURE the following items: a spiked dog collar, an elephant, and a drag queen.

Now, if you were asked to place them in some sort of context, you might think, "Hmmm, that sounds like a punch line of one of those 'a guy walks into a bar' jokes." What you wouldn't be thinking: 1980 Juno Awards.

Yet, on April 2, 1980, at Toronto's Harbour Castle Hilton hotel, those three elements all made appearances at the homegrown music industry's most prestigious awards show, broadcast by the CBC.

The elephant was probably the easiest to explain: pioneering kids' entertainers

Sharon, Lois & Bram brought their mascot Elephant—a character first introduced on their classic 1978 album *One Elephant, Deux Éléphants*—to "skinnamarink" onstage with them, both as they presented and as they and their producer, Bill Usher, accepted their Juno for Best Children's Album for *Smorgasbord*.

As the actor occupying the elephant skin—trio member Sharon Hampson's fifteen-year-old daughter, Randi—high-fived and hugged everyone within trunk distance to celebrate the win, with Usher commenting on how "most of our fans went to bed two hours ago," there was a sense that this kind of informal whimsy

could only be captured on a Canadian music awards show.

The drag queen and dog collar took on slightly more salacious overtones. "Sparkle," the drag queen, made her debut blowing smoke at the camera during the daring performance of "High School Confidential" by defiant Toronto rockers Rough Trade. The spiked dog collar was the real surprise: it belonged to the show's host, three-time Juno Award winner Burton Cummings.

Worn during Cummings' live-to-track performance of his hit "Fine State of Affairs," and offset by a strangely tacky shirt garishly painted with the American

BY NICK KREWEN

OF AGE

flag, the shocking accoutrement captured the uncertain anticipation and the bold expressiveness promised by the coming decade.

After enduring a disco-and-punk holding pattern for much of the mid to late 1970s, the music industry was experiencing another cultural realignment, yielding options from blue-collar mainstream album-oriented rock (AOR) and earthy *Urban Cowboy*–inspired country to experimental synth-heavy New Wave.

With New Wave in particular inspiring fresh, daring, spiky-haired, pneumatic shoulder-pad glam fashion statements,

one could suggest that Cummings, who had also shaved off his trademark moustache and curly, shoulder-length locks, was undergoing an identity crisis.

"I had a dog collar on . . . it was very strange," he acknowledges thirty years after the fact. "I had been in L.A. for four years, so I guess it wore off. I wasn't trying to make a statement. It was just a big change."

Right: Burton Cummings, seen here in 1980, changing with the times.

Plum Communications Inc.

Clearly the 1980 Juno Awards ceremony was also caught between worlds. Viewers watching the opening montage as a hip assessment of the times would have been sadly disappointed to see disco diva France Joli open the show, especially since the sixteen-year-old Montrealer's "Come to Me" was one of the declining genre's dying gasps.

The only word that can properly describe the show's rollout: "cheesy."

Opening with a dark, high-angle shot of a spotlit glittery disco ball rotating over a red neon-tube Juno, the pre-taped harp strum kicks in and another spotlight reveals a long shot of Joli's face in the centre of the "O."

The camera crane dips under the "O" as the starlet, draped in a black shawl, lip-synchs the slow-mo initial strains of "Come to Me." She finishes the song's intro and as four drumbeats indicate a tempo change, Joli drops the shawl for a view of her backless gold lamé dress. The lights come up to reveal a diamond-shaped, floor-lit stage. The singer sways her hips and then runs off the stage as the opening credits roll.

Once the presenter and performer roll call is complete, Joli jumps onto the main stage to finish her song. Here's where the fromage factor really kicks in: four male dancers dressed in pink and blue unitards accompany her. They have a silver star insignia pasted on their chests and matching silver shoes, and

Plum Communications Inc.

engage in expressionless synchronized choreography that is later marred by a slow-motion sequence.

Unfortunately, the schmaltz doesn't end there: host Burton Cummings–sporting a Vegas-style frilly tux–is introduced, and with seating arranged in dinner-table fashion, glad-hands his way from the back of the Harbour Castle Hilton Grand Ballroom to the stage through a maze of jaded music-industry personnel.

Somehow he resists the temptation to point and wink at numerous movers and shakers, but you can tell it's crossing his mind.

His opening line, as scripted by *SCTV*'s Rick Moranis: "You know, this hotel has one hell of a barbershop."

Rimshot. Please.

For the record, Joli won the first Juno of the decade for Most Promising Female Vocalist–or, as it's known in some circles, "the Kiss of Death," as victory in

this category seemingly cursed certain recording careers into obscurity. Aside from a few future nominations, Canadian disco's coffin had received its final glittery nail.

Ironically, only one Most Promising Male Vocalist nominee, whose sound at the time was immersed in dance, would survive to see another day: Bryan Adams. And he's probably glad he lost the award that night to Montreal-based guitar wiz Walter Rossi.

There were some technical snafus, the most glaring problem occurring when guitarist Kim Mitchell's voice lingered as he pulled back from the mic during Max Webster's performance of "Paradise Skies."

Also missing: an orchestra for 1980 double-Juno-winning pianist Frank Mills. In fact, Mills wasn't even sure the piano was miked for his "Peter Piper" performance.

"I call it 'finger-synchs,' after lip-synching," he laughs from the Bahamas home he bought with the royalties from "Music Box Dancer." "So I invented the finger-synch. It worked pretty well, provided you knew the tune."

Top: Sharon, Lois & Bram with Sharon's daughter Randi in the elephant suit accept the inaugural award for Best Children's Album in 1980.

Opposite: Sixteen-year-old disco diva France Joli opens the show singing her hit single "Come to Me."

Not everything was canned. One of the exceptions was a standout performance from Gordon Lightfoot, who appeared unannounced after a commercial break midway through the show and delved into "On the High Seas" and "If You Need Me." The reason Lightfoot performed a pair of songs? To fill time that would have been occupied by the Canadian Music Hall of Fame induction of Paul Anka, who decided a last-minute Vegas booking held more appeal than the Junos. The public was not made aware of Anka's absence; it was just business as usual.

There was one other no-show. Although Anne Murray's non-attendance at the next five Juno Award ceremonies would become something of a running joke (she boycotted them because she felt they were too amateurish), the Songbird swears she would have been at the 1980 ceremony if not for the death of her father, James, just days before the music industry convened at the Harbour Castle.

But even though the night's biggest winner wasn't there—Murray won Female Vocalist, Country Female Vocalist, Album of the Year for *New Kind of Feeling,* and Single of the Year for "I Just Fall in Love Again"—she did receive consolation in her

mourning from an unexpected source: Rough Trade's controversial performance of "High School Confidential."

The song, a tale of a teenage lesbian high school crush that features the graphic line "It made me cream my jeans when she'd come my way" and the crotch-grabbing antics of leather-bound singer Carole Pope, converted tears of sorrow to tears of laughter for the Murray clan.

"We held my father's funeral the day of the Junos, and we all congregated to watch them that night—my whole family—and we were all very sad and very emotional," Murray recalls. "But when she came on and sang that song, it was so incongruous with the whole day, and the business of 'creaming your pants' and all that—we just howled. It just broke the ice." Murray ended up sending singer Pope a note of appreciation.

k.d. lang was also moved. Watching Rough Trade's performance in the comfort of her Consort, Alberta, living room, the aspiring recording artist also considered "High School Confidential" a benchmark moment.

"The impression of the Junos was strongest when I saw Carole Pope," lang remembers. "And I think maybe the effect of my gayness was speaking to me at that moment. I saw how powerful a nationally televised celebration of Canadian music could be and I think it left an impression on me."

Predictably, the provocative Toronto

band ran into resistance with the CBC censors, although Pope declared that it wasn't the lyrical content that offended them.

"The CBC was always supportive of us," says the True North Records artist, who formed Rough Trade with Kevan Staples in the mid seventies.

"We started doing CBC shows in the late seventies, and they pretty much let us do whatever. I remember doing a song called 'Dyke by Default' on Peter Gzowski's *90 Minutes Live*," she recalls.

"At the Junos, the scandal was that I grabbed my crotch while we were doing the song. We didn't do it during the run-through, but I did it on live TV.

"But I think the CBC was pretty cool about the line 'cream my jeans' as far as I can remember."

Awards show producer Jack Budgell and CARAS president Brian Robertson have different recollections.

Plum Communications Inc.

"The line 'cream my jeans' was a huge problem before the show," Budgell recalls. "I brought that to her attention, and I invited her to substitute her lyrics, because there was a lot of sensitivity about that. Everybody was in a flap about that one—the CBC and CARAS."

Robertson says that CARAS put their foot down and were protective of Pope's right to artistic expression.

"I had huge problems with the CBC with it," Robertson recalls. "They didn't want the number on the show, and if I remember, they wanted some lyrics changed.

"Of course Carole was never going to change the lyrics and her label obviously supported her. Because it was a big hit, it's possible that there may have been some compromise on the airtime. But we supported the record company and the artist. We said, no, this is what people want."

Although known for his excellent production skills—he has commandeered breakthrough albums for Metallica, Mötley Crüe, and Michael Bublé—Bob Rock said the Payola$ Junos that mean the most were Composer and Single of the Year for "Eyes of a Stranger."

"Those two were big for me," Bob Rock explains. "In my mind, that's the art that I love. I would say, even in my production—if you follow my career and got into what I do with whatever artists I work with, it's kind of about the song and it's about radio songs. I always loved the radio. I've always loved music on the radio. And I've always loved songwriting—that's my passion."

Strolling drag queens and unrequited lesbian lust notwithstanding, there was one more water-cooler moment, and it involved the Canadian ambassador to Iran.

On November 4, 1979, Islamic students and militants stormed the U.S. embassy in Iran and took fifty-three hostages.

The prisoner count would have been fifty-nine had it not been for quick-thinking Ken Taylor, Canada's ambassador to Iran, who sheltered six of the intended targets in the Canadian embassy, giving them Canadian passports and shuffling them off to Zurich on January 24, 1980.

The "Canadian Caper" generated a tremendous amount of U.S. goodwill, and CARAS president Brian Robertson remembers that landing Taylor on the Junos was a considerable coup, since everyone wanted a piece of him. When he appeared at the Junos, Taylor, the man of the hour, received a standing ovation from the respectful crowd.

The diplomat humbly soaked it all in, before presenting the final award of the evening, Male Vocalist of the Year, to Burton Cummings.

"I'm still knocked out by this gentleman over here," Cummings exclaimed in his acceptance speech. "This is a wonderful honour. It's great to see the growth of the industry in a country that's becoming more powerful all the time . . . God bless you."

Cummings wasn't blowing smoke: Canadians were indeed making great strides internationally, with domestic rock bands like Rush, Saga, April Wine, and Triumph touring their tails off through endless U.S. arena and soft-seater gigs, album-oriented radio airplay, and a fervent fan base.

With television ratings for the 1980 Juno Awards hitting 1.5 million viewers, Canadians were obviously just as interested in how our musicians were faring both home and abroad.

Over the next three years, Canadians would support the domestic music scene with great relish, with gold, platinum, and multi-platinum certifications (symbolizing shipments of 50,000, 100,000, and multiples of 100,000 albums respectively) doubling from 1980 to 1981 alone.

The notion of a unified groundswell, a breakthrough that would once and for all establish Canadian talent on equal footing with other global acts, continued to infuse our music industry with a sense of hope, promise, and confidence.

Things were only going to get better.

In Canada, music and politics may make for strange bedfellows, but they've always slept with the lights on, with CARAS extending an invitation to the Juno Awards to keep the music industry on the political radar.

Through such arms as the CRTC and, nowadays, the Department of Canadian Heritage, government support has been paramount to the survival of the Canadian music industry.

Top left: The Rovers, seen here performing on the show, were nominated as Folk Artist of the Year for 1982.

Top right: Presenter and Canadian jazz legend Oscar Peterson smiles at the standing ovation he receives from the Juno audience.

Centre: Foil-suited B.B. Gabor performing at the 1982 Junos. It was his second nomination for Most Promising Male Vocalist of the Year.

Bottom left: Chilliwack performing "My Girl (Gone, Gone, Gone)," which was nominated for Single of the Year for 1982.

Plum Communications Inc.

So imagine the delight of CARAS and CBC show organizers when the Right Honourable Pierre Elliott Trudeau—and they don't get much bigger than the prime minister of Canada—agreed to return following a 1979 appearance to induct country music pioneer Hank Snow into the Canadian Music Hall of Fame.

This time he honoured the poetic songwriting of the 1981 inductee Joni Mitchell, as his improvised introductory speech married the importance of the arts to freedom.

"'I don't care who writes your laws, if only I can write your songs,'" Trudeau began. "The poet who said that understood well what makes a country, and how songs and music impacts on its destiny. The essence of living in a country is to promote freedom, so that each man and woman and child can be free to fulfill himself to the utmost.

"And the essence of songs and music is freedom. No great music has been composed where there is repression. Creativity needs freedom. And the songs themselves and music are the freest of all the arts.

"Because once you have heard them, they will live on forever and they can't be suppressed, in your heart and in your soul."

Mitchell, stunning in a taupe dress, her long curly tresses dangling over her shoulders, offered a cryptic response.

"Well, the Hall of Fame makes me feel like Boom Boom Geoffrion," she replied, referring to Montreal Canadiens Hockey Hall of Fame legend Bernie Geoffrion.

Emcee duties for the 1981 Juno Awards were actually divided three ways: first up, veteran *SCTV* comedians Andrea Martin and John Candy—the former playing the role of self-conscious, slightly embarrassed show hostess and the latter offering a riff on his obnoxious Johnny LaRue talk-show host character.

Much of Candy's routine centred on the topics of awards-show hosting excellence, and inappropriate phallic jokes about the metronome-shaped award and U.S. glam rock band KISS. "You know, Andrea, KISS wants to use the Juno. They want to stuff it in their uniforms," Candy quipped.

"Keep it up, and they'll need help finding it in *your* uniform," Martin retorted.

The second set of hosts, pianist Frank Mills and Quebec singing legend Ginette Reno, began their segment with a duet of "The Poet and I," with Mills tickling the ivories of a glass piano, and acquitted themselves admirably as they commanded the next forty minutes of presentations.

The duo had one particularly memorable moment: watching forty-six-year-old trombonist Rob McConnell, leader of The Boss Brass, scrambling up a ladder up from the orchestra pit—where he was moonlighting—to jog to the podium

and accept the Best Jazz Album Juno for *Present Perfect*.

But the most memorable entrance of the evening—and perhaps the entire Juno Awards history—occurred with the third set of hosts: rockabilly legend Rompin' Ronnie Hawkins and country singer Carroll Baker.

"Ronnie was noted for having bought a Rolls Royce with a bag full of cash—that was the rumour in those days," recalls Juno Awards producer Jack Budgell. "So I had him and Carroll driven out in a Rolls Royce convertible when he was introduced. And he ripped his pants on the door on his way out."

The duo climbed into the back of the chauffeured limo and began singing "Hey, Bo Diddley" as the driver drove onto the stage and parked. He then tried in vain to open the locked passenger doors.

Opposite top left: Joni Mitchell (left) is presented with Canadian Music Hall of Fame honours by former prime minister Pierre Trudeau (right) in 1981.

Opposite top right: The Nylons performing at the 1983 Juno Awards. Next year, they would be nominated for Most Promising Group.

Opposite bottom left: "Two hillbillies"—Ronnie Hawkins (left) and Carroll Baker (right)—at the 1981 Junos.

Opposite bottom right: *SCTV*'s Andrea Martin and John Candy at the 1981 Junos.

Loverboy's rise was meteoric: co-founded by Calgary-based former Streetheart guitarist Paul Dean and ex-Moxy singer Mike Reno, the band had only been together a few months when they signed with Columbia Records Canada and recorded their self-titled debut.

Within a few months of release, "Turn Me Loose" and "The Kid Is Hot Tonite" had become album-oriented rock (AOR) staples, with the band selling approximately 500,000 albums in Canada alone before inking a deal with Columbia's U.S. division—and selling another two million albums.

Non-stop U.S. touring with Journey and Cheap Trick, and a six-week break to record the sophomore Get Lucky, continued the momentum with the hits "Working on the Weekend," "When It's Over," and "Take Me to the Top." By March 1982, Loverboy was a bona fide international success story boasting more than 6.8 million album sales.

Hawkins took matters into his own hands: he climbed over the back seat and draped one leg over the back door as he tried to support himself with the front door. The front suddenly swung open; the Hawk lost his balance and ripped a big hole in his tux pants just below his buttocks to his left knee.

But there was another victim.

"The door came back and hit me, and I had a great big hematoma on my leg for a good month and a half," says Baker. "I never told anybody about it, but it was hurting so bad."

Unaware of any injury, the crowd roared with laughter—none harder, apparently than Trudeau himself—and, being the troupers they were, Baker and Hawkins managed to finish the song and save their own chuckles until they reached the podium.

"That was a grand entrance if ever I saw one," joked Baker upon reaching the microphone.

"At least the applause lasted longer than my part in *Heaven's Gate*," cracked Ronnie, referring to his role in the 1980 Michael Cimino film, Hollywood's biggest box-office bomb at the time.

Performers included 1981 Most Promising Male Vocalist winner—and one-hit wonder—Graham Shaw, with "Can I Come Near"; Quebec Félix Award winner and future Female Vocalist nominee Diane Tell; ex-Hometown Band singer Shari Ulrich; and Powder Blues Band, whose hit "Doin' It Right" helped them take home Most Promising Group honours.

In other developments, Toronto husband-wife band Martha and The Muffins' "Echo Beach" tied Anne Murray's "Could I Have This Dance" for Single of the Year; flustered country singer Eddie Eastman flubbed Bruce Cockburn's name when presenting Folk Artist of the Year (the "ck" is silent, Eddie); and TV viewers survived another hideous show intro, which involved a limo pulling up to the O'Keefe Centre entrance, a bunch of fashion-challenged "fans" crowding around non-celebrities for autographs, a forgettable original song called "Make Me a Star," and a disjointed choreography routine.

With a short stroll to the piano and the opening strains of "You Saved My Soul," Burton Cummings returned to the Hilton Harbour Castle Grand Metropolitan Ballroom as host of the 1982 Juno Awards.

Canada was ready to celebrate a banner year. As Cummings noted in his opening monologue, "From New York to Tokyo, from London to Paris, Canadian-made hits have made their way to the tops of recording charts and playlists everywhere." He wasn't kidding. Led by Calgary's Loverboy, who seemingly popped out of nowhere to sell hundreds of thousands of records here at home, and Toronto's Rush, American resistance was finally crumbling.

Opposite top left: Robbie Robertson looks on during Bruce Cockburn's acceptance speech for Male Vocalist of the Year.

Opposite top left: Payola$ Paul Hyde accepting the Most Promising Group award in 1983.

Opposite bottom left: The lovable hosers Bob and Doug McKenzie—the comedy alter-egos of *SCTV* comedians Rick Moranis and Dave Thomas—presenting awards at the 1981 Junos.

Opposite bottom right: Loverboy (pictured here with John Donabie) hit the Juno jackpot in 1982, winning six awards.

Plum Communications Inc.

Plum Communications Inc.

Plum Communications Inc.

And although Loverboy, Rush, Triumph, and April Wine were finally racking up millions of sales, the success wasn't restricted to the rockers: Juno-winning "Hit Me with Your Best Shot" songwriter Eddie Schwartz, Montreal guitarist Aldo Nova, and Bob and Doug McKenzie, the lovable hosers who were the comedy alter-egos of *SCTV* comedians Rick Moranis and Dave Thomas and a Canadian cultural phenomenon, were enjoying Billboard chart and sales success.

Western Canada was also entering a hot streak. A pattern began in 1980 when Trooper had *two* records nominated for Album of the Year (the multi-platinum *Flying Colors* and *Hot Shots*) and won Group of the Year, and Bruce Fairbairn took home Producer of the Year for Prism's *Armageddon*. In 1981, it was Prism's turn to win Group of the Year as Powder Blues Band captured Most Promising Group. It was clear that West Coast talent—especially when it was associated with powerhouse manager Bruce Allen—was on a roll.

In 1982, the West's influence exploded as the quintet of Mike Reno, Paul Dean, Scott Smith, Doug Johnson, and Matt Frenette won six awards: Group of the Year and Album of the Year for *Loverboy*, and Single of the Year for "Turn Me

Loose," which also earned Reno and Dean Composer of the Year. Dean and Bruce Fairbairn captured Producer of the Year for the singles "Working for the Weekend" and "When It's Over," and Bob Rock and Keith Stein won Engineer of the Year honours for "When It's Over" and "It's Your Life" (tying with Gary Gray for Rough Trade's "Attitude" and "For Those Who Think Young").

Paul Dean remembers the band was flabbergasted to win so many Junos. "We figured that after the fifth, that would probably be it: we'd get up and go in the back for a drink. But one of the usherettes came up to us and said, 'Stay in your seats, guys.' And we went, oh, okay, fine."

As for the show itself, some decent performances by a tinfoil-suited B.B. Gabor and a somewhat subdued Rough Trade preceded the show's most hilarious segment—one that almost ended in an arrest.

Dressed in their typical toques and flannel jackets, with a backdrop of the Canadian flag, a Canada-shaped table, and dozens of beer bottles, Bob and Doug McKenzie exchanged "Take offs" and adapted their popular *SCTV* skit to the music business before presenting the awards for Most Promising Male and Female Vocalists and Group.

Then there were the truly bizarre performances inserted by Juno Awards producer Les Pouliot (writer and producer for CBC's *The Tommy Hunter Show*).

One such incident involved poor Ronnie Hawkins, who seemed to be a lightning rod for these escapades.

Accompanied by a horn section and an octet of dancers—the men dressed head to toe in white fringed cowboy suits, their cowboy hats sporting a pimp-like feather in their bands, the women sporting fringed tops and mini-skirts—Hawkins performed John Fogerty's "Travelin' Band" for a few minutes until the song reached a bridge consisting of an extended African drumbeat.

Suddenly, a circular backdrop opened, and for some reason, a tall, slender black woman wearing an ankle-length feathered headdress performed a seductive dance that found her slinking around the stage before disappearing back behind the circle. Hawkins then wrapped the songs following this outlandish thirty-second segment.

At the podium, Most Promising Male Vocalist Juno victor Eddie Schwartz asked for an ale to quench his thirst. His mistake: taking an on-air drink.

"It was real beer," Schwartz recalls. "I had a nice long swig before I started my speech, and then there were two RCMP waiting for me when I got offstage to tell me that that was illegal and that I wasn't allowed to drink beer on national television."

The constables took Schwartz out to the lobby.

"I thought I was going to be arrested, but they just gave me a strong reprimand and I was allowed to go back into the event. In retrospect, I think they were just having fun with the rock musician. He got his nice little award, and now we're going to read him the riot act."

Opposite: In 1982, classical guitarist Liona Boyd won Instrumental Artist(s) of the Year.

One of the following scenarios involving Liona Boyd was almost as peculiar: Boyd gently plucked her guitar as a photo scrapbook of her past was projected on a backdrop. Suddenly, a little blonde girl representing Boyd appeared onstage, as clowns and a small dog danced around her, inexplicably bringing the wonder of the circus to her life.

The dry-ice reverie disappeared, the camera focused back on Boyd concluding her performance, and viewers were forgiven if they felt they'd accidentally walked in on a Fellini film set.

For a career that included fifteen solo albums and membership in the influential Buffalo Springfield and Crosby, Stills, Nash & Young outfits, Neil Young was inducted into the Canadian Music Hall of Fame by Solicitor-General Francis Fox. Dapper in a tux, Young kept his speech short and sweet.

"I'm greatly honoured to receive this award tonight and I'd like to say hello to my family who is spread across this room and also across this country and some other countries in the world. I just have one feeling tonight—I'm proud to be a Canadian. Thank you very much."

Producers could also take comfort in the Junos' ratings growth, with 2.17 million Canadians tuning in, a substantial increase from 1981's 1.88 million viewers.

Between 1982 and 1983, two important developments changed the game forever for the Canadian music business.

In a rare post-Juno Awards wrap-up broadcast on the CBC and hosted by Toronto radio personality John Donabie, Neil Young was a little more outspoken.

Aside from his selective memory assertion than he had never won or been nominated for any awards prior to his Canadian Music Hall of Fame induction (he had been up for a Male Vocalist of the Year Juno three times prior), Young said he was encouraged by what he had seen around him while visiting Canada.

"It feels great to be recognized by my native country and to see how far Canada has come. When I started performing, there were no records and there was very little chance—I had no choice but to leave the country if I wanted to get to the international audience.

"I hate to say it, but at the time, if I hadn't left Canada, I wouldn't be where I am today. It was a chance I had to take. But because of how far Canada has come in the last ten years, these people today like Loverboy don't have to leave like I did. They can stay if they choose to stay, and they can do what they want to do, and Canada can support them. Canada couldn't support me when I needed Canada to make it.

"It has evolved and I think it's a great thing. I like the way the music industry has grown."

Plum Communications Inc.

The first was the establishment of the Foundation to Assist Canadian Talent on Recordings (FACTOR) by CHUM Limited, Moffat Communications, and Rogers Broadcasting Limited in conjunction with the Canadian Independent Record Producers Association (CIRPA) and the Canadian Music Publishers Association (CMPA). The foundation offered Canadian musicians affordable loans and grants to help finance their recordings, an initial $200,000 in invested funding that has since grown to $14 million annually and funded such future Juno winners as Kim Mitchell, Céline Dion, and Rita MacNeil.

More importantly, the 1983 Juno Awards audience was introduced by co-hosts Burton Cummings and actor Alan Thicke to a brand-new music format: the compact disc.

For the first time, music had transformed from analog to digital, and the smaller size of the compact disc would theoretically not only deliver better sound and virtual indestructibility, but greater portability. This technological leap would also allow record companies to market and resell their old catalogues, since everyone would eventually be replacing their vinyl LPs with CDs.

Cummings recalls the impact the glimpse of this digital future had on him.

"That was a brand-new invention, a big milestone for me," Cummings recalls. "Alan held up *Toto IV*, and it was also the first time I held one in my hand. I don't think Alan had seen one before that night. That was the beginning of the digital age—zeros and ones, you know? It felt like 'show and tell,' and it was pretty cool for that to happen on national TV."

There were a few other debuts that night, one being the arrival of Vancouver's Payola$, the music outlet for producer and engineer Bob Rock and singer Paul Hyde.

The duo won three Juno Awards that year: Most Promising Group, Composer of the Year, and Single of the Year for "Eyes of a Stranger," and Rock also captured his second straight engineering Juno for the band's *No Stranger to Danger* album.

Upon accepting the Most Promising Group Award, Hyde—without ever removing his sunglasses—sneered defiantly while cradling the award.

"Somebody told us that to get this award is the kiss-off," he remarked. "Nobody's going to kiss us off."

Hyde ended up giving three acceptance speeches that night, and Bob Rock, who wasn't in attendance because he was busy mixing a Loverboy album, was amused by all of them.

"I always thought it was funny that Paul forgot to mention me," says Rock. "I always tease him about that."

Another person reached a new plateau in 1983: Bryan Adams, whose watershed album *Cuts Like a Knife* earned him his first Juno Award for Male Vocalist of the Year. He was so busy touring in the States that the Kingston, Ontario-born, Vancouver-based singer and songwriter wasn't on hand to accept it, so manager Bruce Allen stepped into the role of surrogate.

"Having Bruce go up there and accept it was perfect. He had done as much as any of us to get there," Adams explains.

Loverboy completed another year of West Coast domination, adding a couple more Junos to the mantel for Group of the Year and Album of the Year for *Get Lucky*.

Award-show producers also learned about the dangers of relying on telephones to entertain live audiences: upon accepting Men at Work's International Album of the Year for *Business as Usual*, the band's manager, Lars Sorensen, attempted to call lead singer Colin Hay at home in Australia.

Hay didn't recognize his manager's voice, resulting in a few minutes of awkward, stilted conversation.

Another 1983 international star presenter was Count Basie, who provided a little background music while co-host Cummings read the Best Jazz Album nominees. Although invited by Cummings to "say hello to the Count," award winners Fraser MacPherson and Oliver Gannon ignored the big band jazz pioneer when they reached the stage.

Also on tap was American Society of Composers, Authors, and Publishers (ASCAP) president Hal David. Better known as Burt Bacharach's lyricist and co-writer of such standards as "Raindrops Keep Fallin' on My Head" and "Close to You," David presented Composer of the Year honours to the Payola$' Hyde.

Kim Mitchell, who had recently launched a solo career after disbanding Max Webster, was named Most Promising Male Vocalist, with Carole Pope and Anne Murray repeat victors, for Female Vocalist and Country Female Vocalist of the Year.

The Canadian Music Hall of Fame inductee was posthumously, Glenn Gould, who had passed away on October 4, 1982, due to a stroke.

In recognizing the man who was globally acknowledged as Canada's foremost classical pianist and a first-rate interpreter of the music of Johann Sebastian Bach, Governor General Ed Schreyer described Gould as "a man whose talent burns so brightly that he transcended all categories of craft and lifestyle, or even nationhood, in the sense that his talent was of international calibre.

"He was one of our greatest cultural gifts to the world." Gould's former manager John Roberts accepted the Canadian Music Hall of Fame honour on behalf of the late pianist's family, and said the normally reclusive musician would have been touched by his induction "because it's the recognition of the sum of his very many accomplishments and of his place in history by his fellow Canadian musicians and the industry as a whole."

Opposite: Neil Young was inducted into the Canadian Music Hall of Fame in 1982.

Plum Communications Inc.

"Your Excellency, ladies and gentlemen, with this award, you not only honour a great musician, a great innovator, a great thinker, and a great man, but someone who I believe will be long regarded as one of the greatest Canadians of the century," said Roberts.

By 1984, CARAS president Brian Robertson had decided he had taken the organization and show as far as he could, and handed over the reins to Peter Steinmetz.

Steinmetz initiated a number of changes. First, he moved the show forward to December to accommodate the Canadian music industry's desire to capitalize on Christmas sales generated by public interest in the Junos. Next, he changed the production team to include Toronto's Concert Productions International, Emmy Award-winning director Rob Iscove, and Garry Blye, a veteran of *The Sonny & Cher Comedy Hour*, with the CBC continuing its co-producer role. A music-industry builder award named after Juno Awards co-founder Walt Grealis was introduced.

The Juno Award itself shrunk from eighteen eye-poking inches to a more-easy-to-handle fifteen-inch statuette,

Ed Schreyer also announced that an intervention had been staged to prevent one of Glenn Gould's pianos to be displayed at the Smithsonian, instead re-routing it to the governor general's residence in Ottawa.

and presenters no longer used twelve-inch albums to announce the winners, reverting to the more standard awards-show practice of tearing open envelopes.

The eighteen-month gap between shows had allowed for plenty of new stars to establish themselves, and the timing couldn't have been better in consideration of one other significant launch: MuchMusic, which debuted on September 1, 1984.

Since MTV wasn't available in Canada, MuchMusic ended up filling a crucial void: for the very first time, Canadians had access to a national, twenty-four-hour music video network that attached faces to the music, allowing them a chance to determine and support their own star system. As a result, the popularity of acts such as Corey Hart, Parachute Club, Platinum Blonde, Gowan, Luba, The Spoons, and many more suddenly exploded.

Accordingly, the impact of MuchMusic resulted in a Best Video category, won

initially by Rob Quartly—who snagged four out of five nominations and was widely regarded as *the* Canadian pioneer in this field—for the Corey Hart hit "Sunglasses at Night."

There was also a major switch-up when it came to hosting duties. CARAS settled on hiring comedians to emcee for the remainder of the eighties. In 1984, the Exhibition Place duties rested on the capable shoulders of *SCTV* veterans Andrea Martin—who had co-hosted a segment in 1981—and Joe Flaherty.

Top: The Spoons gained widespread exposure through the newly minted MuchMusic. In 1983, the band was nominated for Most Promising Group of the Year.

Opposite: Platinum Blonde exploded on the scene with the help of music videos. In 1984, not only were they nominated for Most Promising Group, but their videos for "Standing in the Dark" and "Doesn't Really Matter," both directed by Rob Quartly, were up for awards.

56

"What you have to realize with all of this is, a couple of years before the album *Cuts Like a Knife*, I was a skint musician," comments Bryan Adams. "All I had was Jim [Vallance] enjoying working on songs with me and Bruce [Allen] getting me gigs.

"To suddenly have an album that could pay my record company and management back for all the tour support was unreal."

Adams said that the 1984 Junos offered him and his career a shot in the arm and a night of personal validation that was "more than you can imagine."

"Again, it was the kind of validation we needed to encourage us to keep going, maybe even get to the next step."

The 1984 Juno Awards will be best remembered as the year Bryan Adams came home a superstar.

With the 1983 release of *Cuts Like a Knife*, Adams had found his musical stride and made dazzling inroads into the American market, scoring his first Top-10 hit with "Straight from the Heart" and selling more than 3 million copies of the album in the States and more than 300,000 here in Canada.

The enormous success of *Cuts Like a Knife* garnered Adams five nominations: Male Vocalist; Composer and Single of the Year for both the title track and "Straight from the Heart"; Producer of the Year; and Album of the Year.

The night certainly began on the right foot, with David Foster and Eddie Schwartz handing Composer of the Year honours to the A&M recording artist and his songwriting partner, Jim Vallance.

"Vallance, alright!" Adams shouted as he accepted the Juno on behalf of his absent co-writer.

Opposite: Tina Turner and Bryan Adams after performing the Top-10 duet "It's Only Love" in 1985.

Right: Parachute Club won two Junos in 1984: Most Promising Group and Single of the Year.

"This is the one I really wanted to win. Jim and I have been writing for six years together. Jimmy, we did it! Right on!"

The momentum continued as Adams captured statuettes for Producer of the Year and, for the second year running, Male Vocalist.

Adams was expected to sweep, but CARAS voters had other plans, welcoming The Parachute Club to the fold and surprising them with Most Promising Group and Single of the Year for "Rise Up."

"We were totally shocked," said Parachute Club singer Lorraine Segato. "We were the upstart, alternative, from-the-streets kind of band, who, in fact, hadn't even been looking for a record deal. We just wanted to make a certain kind of music that we thought would be uplifting, but also have a message to it.

"And we were never, ever gunning for mainstream anything. It was shocking because the album [*Parachute Club*] came out and the single came out and just shot up the charts. It was a whole new world we weren't anticipating."

One who wasn't so stunned by the win was Adams.

"I wasn't surprised at all," he said. "It's a good song."

Adams finished off the night by taking home Album of the Year for *Cuts Like a Knife* and invited his entire band to join him onstage to celebrate.

Another highlight of the night was the induction of three pioneering vocal groups

Jim Vallance, who said Adams took his solo win graciously, admits the experience of hearing his name called was peculiar.

"Winning is a strange experience," says Vallance. "They say your name, and it's kind of surreal when you climb the stairs. Your colleagues pat you on the back, you get your picture in the paper. Then the next day, life is back to normal: you're changing diapers and taking the garbage out. That's how it should be."

of the 1950s into the Canadian Music Hall of Fame: The Crew Cuts, The Four Lads, and The Diamonds. Newly appointed CARAS president Peter Steinmetz made the presentation, and surviving members of each group gave brief demonstrations of the vocal chops that earned them recognition: The Crew Cuts sang "Sh-Boom," The Four Lads offered a pitch-strong "Standing on the Corner," and The Diamonds—well, unfortunately, they stormed through "Little Darlin'" plagued by miscues. Still, the standing ovation accorded them by ceremony-goers was a heartwarming, nostalgic Juno moment.

Barry Roden Photography

The only disappointment of the evening for CARAS and the CBC was the ratings, which took a substantial hit with only 1.443 million viewers, well below usual, which Steinmetz blamed on the natural post-November TV viewership drop due to Christmas holiday preparation.

No worries: the Junos would rebound.

If there was a show that marked a turning point for the Junos in terms of professionalism and coming of age, 1985 qualifies as the watershed year.

For the first time, there was something resembling a rivalry as a showdown between Bryan Adams' *Reckless* and Corey Hart's *Boy in the Box* created enormous industry buzz. They were locked in a race to crack the 1-million-unit domestic sales barrier—a Canadian first.

Adams wasn't impressed. "I was aware of it, and it's complete poop, all made up by the press. I suppose it's understandable, because I was from BC and he was from Montreal, but funnily, we never discussed it. I mean how can you? It's nonsense."

The Juno nominations were pretty much neck and neck to capitalize on the excitement: Adams and Hart were nominated for Male Vocalist of the Year, Composer of the Year (Adams with Jim Vallance), Album of the Year, and Single of the Year (Adams for "Run to You" and Hart for "Never Surrender"). Adams also picked up an extra nomination for Producer of the Year.

When the smoke finally cleared, Adams captured three of a possible five awards and Hart won Single of the Year.

"It was nice to finally get one at the end," laughs Hart. "That was my main appearance where I felt I had a chance of maybe winning a few awards. I was certainly happy with the one that I won, because Gordon Lightfoot presented it to me."

Canadians welcomed David Foster and singer Luba to the Juno winners' circle for the first time, as Producer of the Year and Female Vocalist of the Year. CARAS also paid homage to country legend Wilf Carter by inducting him into the Canadian Music Hall of Fame.

Comedic hosts Andrea Martin—back for her third round of emcee duties—and Martin Short provided plenty of laughs to go around, so the 1985 Junos at the Harbour Castle Hilton were top-to-bottom entertaining.

But the two weren't the only comic relief. Composer of the Year award presenter Ian Thomas deliberately ignored the cue cards and launched into his own sidesplitting routine, much to the surprise of co-presenting singer Gary O'.

"There we were onstage—me and Gary O'—with our shoulder pads and our hair plugs—and then the cue cards came up and I thought, let's have some fun for God's sake. It was one of those situations where you look at the cue cards and you go, 'this is not entertaining at all.'"

With a knowing smirk and static intonation, Thomas informed the chuckling crowd that it was he, not any of the other songwriting contenders, who was responsible for the ideas behind every nominated hit.

The story doesn't end there: after returning to his seat, Thomas continued the shtick with a new target: Prime Minister Brian Mulroney and his wife Mila.

"When I came offstage, we were sitting next to the Mulroneys and I said, 'Probably one of my songs was on the radio when you proposed to Mila.' And just kept right on with it, and he laughed, and we had this little bit of a conversation with it. And he was laughing his head off."

The Junos bowed two new categories this year—Best R&B/Soul Recording and Best Reggae/Calypso Recording—and soulful singer Liberty Silver had the distinction of winning both: the first for her rendition of "Lost Somewhere inside Your Love" and the second for her duet of "Heaven Must Have Sent You" with Otis Gayle.

Back at the show, Silver's strong multi-octave rendition of "Lost," as well as stirring songs by Luba, The Box, Kim Mitchell, and The Canadian Brass, led to the first of two show-stopping performances.

k.d. lang stunned audiences with her androgynous look, red velvet Nudie suit, and her energetic showmanship with The Reclines in "Hanky Panky." Later, she

Ian Thomas decided to carry the joke with Brian Mulroney one step further.

"The following week I sent him an eight-by-ten of myself, and it said, 'Dear Bri, if you run into any difficulties in your current office, don't hesitate to give me a buzz. Your new pal, I.'

"I really wasn't a fan, so I sent to him out of a sense of fun, and, I suppose, disrespect," he laughs. "But God love him, he had a great sense of humour. About a week later, a parcel arrives from the prime minister's office. Somebody had taken a picture of the two of us shaking hands, and the PM wrote, 'Dear Ian, if it wasn't for you, I'd still be driving a truck in Baie Comeau. Your friend, Brian.'

"That picture had a hallowed place over the toilet in the downstairs bathroom for a number of years."

shocked the crowd further by prancing up the aisle—in a wedding dress, no less—to accept the Most Promising Female Vocalist award.

Triumph singer and guitarist Rik Emmett, who co-presented the award to lang with Quebec singer Véronique Béliveau, remembers being unsure of what to make of her.

"She comes roaring down the aisle, in that wedding dress and cowboy boots, and she gets up onstage, and she has kind of a buzz crew-cut, men's hairstyle—no makeup—and I go, 'Wow, this is a very strange person.'

"Then she takes the award, and I'm thinking in my own mind, 'Is this a guy dressed up in a wedding dress?'"

Plum Communications Inc.

Plum Communications Inc.

Opposite: Liberty Silver's multi-octave rendition of "Lost Somewhere Inside Your Love" not only stopped the show, it earned her the inaugural Best R&B/Soul Recording. She also won Best Reggae/Calypso Recording, another Juno first.

Top: *SCTV*'s Ed Grimley—Martin Short's alter-ego—asks Mila Mulroney for a post-Juno dance.

Bottom: Canadian country legend Wilf Carter inducted into the Canadian Music Hall of Fame in 1985.

Top right: Toronto Symphony Orchestra conductor Andrew Davis (left), opera contralto Maureen Forrester (centre) , and CBC's *Morningside* host Peter Gzowski (right). In 1986, Davis and the TSO won Best Classical Album: Large Ensemble for *Holst: The Planets*.

Bottom left: David Foster accepting his first Juno for Producer of the Year in 1986.

Bottom right: k.d. lang makes an impression at the 1985 Junos when she won Most Promising Female Vocalist.

Plum Communications Inc.

"We hand her the trophy, and she does her signature kind of dance and then strikes a pose and lifts her back leg while she's spreading her arms. So the wedding dress goes up and I see these cowboy boots, and I think, 'Man, oh man, has she ever got hairy legs!' And I thought, 'Am I ever confused!'"

k.d. lang graciously accepted her award. "First of all, I'd like to promise you that I'm sincerely honoured for your acknowledgment of my determination," she began. "I'd like to promise that I will personally thank each and every one who deserves a piece of this pyramid. I promise that I will work harder next year than I have in the past two years. But most of all, I promise that I will continue to sing only for the right reasons. Thank you very much."

Today, lang says the wedding dress was a deliberate move. "I wanted to make an image or a physical representation of the most promising female and make a splash," she explains. "I think I was aware at that point that the visual impression was a good tool. The Junos presented the opportunity for me to address Canada, and I didn't take it lightly."

Although lang attended some Juno post-show celebrations, she didn't really celebrate her victory until she returned home to Edmonton with an event of her own—a painting party.

"I had some friends over and we painted the statue," she recalls. "It has acrylic dots on it and sort of an acrylic white Dairy Queen–looking crown on top. I still have it—it's at my farm in Vancouver."

The other unforgettable performance: Tina Turner, performing both "One for the Living" and her Top-10 duet with Bryan Adams, "It's Only Love." Perhaps one of the biggest female pop stars at the time, she provided one of the Junos' defining moments. Securing a star of Turner's calibre, enjoying a massive career resurgence with her *Private Dancer* album, was not only a coup but brought some international credibility to the Junos, serving as a turning point to attract global talent to perform on the show in subsequent years.

Adams recalls the duo chomping at the bit during rehearsal to perform the song, which also marked the first time he played on the program. "Tina Turner anywhere is hot, that includes rehearsals.

Neither of us were concerned about product, we couldn't wait to sing the song for everyone. I'm sure it was a defining moment for the Junos: it would be a defining moment for anyone to have Tina on your show."

Notable victories included Family Brown finally snapping The Good Brothers' eight-year stranglehold on Country Group or Duo of the Year; The Parachute Club accepting Group of the Year, but without Lorraine Segato, who had undergone an emergency appendectomy just days before the ceremony; and Luba, beginning her string accepting three successive Female Vocalist of the Year statuettes.

Top: Family Brown broke The Good Brothers' eight-year winning streak to win Country Group or Duo of the Year for 1986.

The year was also remarkable for Canada's involvement with Ethiopian famine relief. Following the success of star-studded efforts by musical communities in the U.K. ("Do They Know It's Christmas") and the U.S. ("We Are the World") to raise money to fight hunger in the underprivileged Third World nation, manager Bruce Allen assembled a Canadian supergroup called Northern Lights that included Gordon Lightfoot, Anne Murray, Neil Young, Bryan Adams, Corey Hart, Joni Mitchell, and Burton Cummings for our country's own contribution: "Tears Are Not Enough." The song—co-written by Foster, Adams, Bob Rock, Paul Hyde, Vallance, and Vallance's wife, Rachel Paiement—raised more than $3.2 million. At the end of the show, Foster presented a supersized Juno to Brian Mulroney as a thank you to Canadians who supported the single with their generosity, and then Juno nominees and winners took to the stage to serenade the crowd in song.

Foster says it wasn't until he was onstage shaking the prime minister's hand that he realized the enormity of the project. "I remember thinking, 'Wow, I grew up on an island, and now I'm standing with the prime minister on stage,'" Foster recalls. "We must have done something really important."

It was one of the Canadian music industry's prouder moments, and more than 2.308 million viewers tuned in to celebrate.

The 1986 Juno Awards welcomed a new host: hyper comedian and Toronto native Howie Mandel. He didn't waste time launching into his semi-slapstick routine: attached to a wire, he soared out over the crowd, and, of course, ran into trouble as he tried to return to the stage.

In what can be described only as perfect comedic timing, Mandel hung upside down in a harness during his opening monologue as he said, "Those who come up to accept their Junos, I know

you'll do so with the dignity that this show deserves."

After Mandel's shtick, the comedian returned to stage in a bright gold suit and introduced the first presenters—Parachute Club's Lorraine Segato and John Oates (minus partner Daryl Hall)—to officially declare 1986 the Year of the Tiger . . . Glass Tiger.

The Newmarket pop rock band won Most Promising Group, its first of three Juno Awards that night, but couldn't accept it: they were onstage getting ready to perform "Someday."

"Some people thought that was intentional, that we might have done a little 'duck and swerve' on that," says keyboardist Sam Reid. "Because it was rumoured that if you won the Best New Artist, it was the kiss of death.

"But I remember us walking out onstage getting ready to perform, and it was a confusing moment because somebody went, 'You guys just won a Juno.' We had our instruments on and were standing in position ready for the commercial break. I did think afterwards, well, does that absolve us from our bad luck scenario?"

Glass Tiger would win more major awards that night—Album of the Year for *The Thin Red Line* and Single of the Year for "Don't Forget Me (When I'm Gone)" .

"This is too much," said singer Alan Frew upon accepting the Juno for *The Thin Red Line*. "Last year, we couldn't even get tickets to the Junos."

After sharing Composer of the Year

honours the past couple of years with Bryan Adams, Jim Vallance appreciated standing on the podium alone for co-writing the Glass Tiger hits "Someday" and "Don't Forget Me (When I'm Gone)."

Another Vancouverite, David Foster, also enjoyed a big year, winning his second Producer and Instrumental Artist of the Year Junos for his work on the film *St. Elmo's Fire*.

Of the two awards, Foster says he treasured the Instrumentalist Award more, for its solo recognition. "Look, I'm a guy who spends his life helping singers realize their dreams, which is great," he explains. "It's a great job, no complaints. But to be able to have a song that was uniquely mine—where I was the artist, the composer, the producer, everything—it was a nice moment."

Corey Hart scored another Juno first by singing his rendition of "Can't Help Falling in Love" from Amsterdam, the first performance via satellite.

"It was 3 a.m. for me when we did the live show," he recalls. "I couldn't hear what anyone was saying and something went wrong in my headphones, so I was basically performing live but not knowing if anyone's hearing me."

Jack Budgell remembers. He was sent to Hilversum in Holland by show producer Garry Blye to direct Hart's performance, and remembers the singer being an intense young man who knew exactly what he wanted.

"He was anxious that I capture the enlarging of the blood vessels on the side of his neck when he was singing," chuckles Budgell. "That was really great, because it really underlined his dramatic interpretation of the song."

To measure just how far the Junos had come in terms of respectability, the ceremony welcomed back an old friend: Anne Murray.

Murray surprised everyone by accepting her award in person for Country Female Vocalist of the Year, and opened with a line that charmed and melted anyone who harboured any grudge for her ten-year absence.

"So this is where you hold this thing," she quipped with a gentle smile.

Opposite left: Cue card for "Tears are not Enough."

Opposite right: Glass Tiger accepting one of three Junos they'd win in 1986.

Top: Behind the scenes with host Howie Mandel in 1987.

Bottom: Anne Murray ends a ten-year absence as she accepts her Country Female Vocalist Juno in 1986. Her appearance was a complete surprise and the audience rewarded her with a standing ovation.

Murray is the first to admit she was extremely nervous when she took those first steps on stage. "I thought I might get booed."

But a standing ovation alleviated any lingering anxiety, a moment that the relieved Murray said was one of the highlights of her life. "I have to say, that certainly was an icebreaker. That was a great moment because I had no idea what to expect. That would probably be at the top of my list, come to think of it."

Murray thanked the crowd for the warm welcome, and mentioned that although she wasn't present to receive the other seventeen Junos from the late seventies and eighties she was accorded, she appreciated them.

"As some of you know, I've won a great many of these and I just want you to know each one . . . I'm proud of every one," Murray said at the podium.

The reason for her return?

"It [the ceremony] got better," she replies. "When I was doing it, they held it in a dinner-theatre kind of format. People just got drunk and disorderly, and I hated it. So when they put it in the proper theatre format and started behaving themselves—and there were good production values in the TV show itself—I decided to go back."

Another inspiring moment was an appearance by Rick Hansen, the Canadian paraplegic athlete and activist whose Man in Motion tour—in which he circled the

globe in his wheelchair—raised more than $26 million for spinal cord injury research.

After thanking David Foster for co-writing the *Billboard* chart-topping hit "St. Elmo's Fire (Man in Motion)," which was inspired by Hansen's trek, the Canadian hero presented the Group of the Year Award to Honeymoon Suite.

Band guitarist Derry Grehan promptly licked the Juno, fulfilling a promise he made to the rest of the band if they ever won the statuette.

Soon it was time for the night's biggest moment: the presentation of the Canadian Music Hall of Fame Award to Gordon Lightfoot.

Murray came out to introduce the man who was going to make the presentation, and announced his name only to be faced with a new dilemma.

There was no Bob Dylan.

After what seemed like an eternity—thirty-two seconds—Dylan ambled out to the stage, ignored the standing ovation that greeted him, and seemed hypnotized by the wall of TV monitors behind him, staring for a good twenty seconds with his back to the audience.

Opposite: Bob Dylan presented Gordon Lightfoot with the Canadian Music Hall of Fame honours in 1986.

Top: In 1989, cellist Ofra Harnoy won Best Classical Album for *Schubert: Arpeggione Sonata*.

Bottom left: Gordon Lightfoot performs at the 1986 Juno Awards, when he was inducted into the Canadian Music Hall of Fame.

Bottom right: Jane Siberry performing at the 1984 Junos, where she was nominated for Most Promising Female Vocalist of the Year.

Plum Communications Inc.

Plum Communications Inc.

Plum Communications Inc.

David Foster was so excited about the possibility of meeting Bob Dylan that he was willing to walk thirty-three flights of stairs to the Sutton Place penthouse to see him, and did, accompanied by NHL hockey legend Gordie Howe.

"I don't take elevators," Foster explains. "And that party was on the top floor. I was hanging with Gordie Howe and he said, 'I'll walk with you.' I was thirty-six at the time, and how old would Gord have been? Fifty? [He was actually fifty-eight.]

"The guy bolted up to the top floor without stopping once. He literally waited five minutes for the rest of us. The guy was an animal."

Even after reaching his destiny, however, Foster was disappointed.

"I never got to meet him. It didn't happen."

CARAS president Peter Steinmetz provided an explanation for Dylan's confusion, citing an unusual entourage that accompanied his arrival.

"I expected a bodyguard and a manager and a publicist—the usual retinue that comes when you deal with stars of that magnitude," says Steinmetz.

"He arrived in a limo with a couple of female handlers who were dressed in leather from head to toe. Those were the days of leather short shorts, and I think the stockings were thin leather stockings and the boots were up to their knees. They were quite striking ladies. It was a lifestyle thing at the time."

When his name was called, Steinmetz said Dylan "was briefly disabled backstage, and then finally got it together."

"He had missed the cue and we had to go searching for him. Then we got him in the direction of the stage and he came out from behind the curtains.

"For a few seconds, I think he was a bit disoriented as to where he was. He then made it to the podium, delivered a somewhat articulate tribute to Gordon, and it was magic for the crowd to see him there."

The icon who redefined songwriting with such profound songs as "Blowin' in the Wind" and "The Times They Are a-Changin'" wasn't too reflective.

"It pleases me to be here to give this award to Gordon," said Dylan, debonair in a sparkling grey jacket, red scarf, and skinny tie.

"I've known Gordon a long time. I know he's been offered this award before, but he has never accepted it because he wanted me to come and give it to him. Anyway, he's somebody of rare talent and all that, and here's a video clip now of his recent and not-so-recent achievements."

Following a video montage of Lightfoot's career, the man of the hour came out and shook hands with Dylan, who then excused himself to return backstage.

Lightfoot delivered a surprisingly candid pre-written speech.

Calling himself "one grateful guy from Orillia," Lightfoot thanked everyone who ever gave him a job, including Art Snider, who hired him as a dancer for the CBC TV series *Country Hoedown* ("I was the guy who do-si-doed when I should have allemande-lefted," Lightfoot joked); Ian & Sylvia, for being the first artists to cover his songs; and even Bob Dylan, who he acknowledged "taught me how to write lyrics." He also recognized his sister Beverley "as one of the people who got me to stop drinking four and a half years ago, for which I am eternally grateful."

"With that I will take it, and proudly wear it," he said, clutching the award. "And to the industry, and everybody here—it's been a great twenty-five years and I'm very much in commission. I feel good, I feel happy, and I'm ready to continue on for an indefinite period of time doing concerts, whatever it is. Thank you very much."

After the show, Lightfoot, Dylan, and actor Matt Dillon, who also happened to be in town, retired to the Sutton Place Hotel for the big post-Juno party.

The 1987 Juno Awards were to be the final fall broadcast. The experiment to capitalize on Christmas sales failed, largely due to the fact that with so much time and energy invested in the awards, record companies weren't able to properly promote their albums for the holiday season.

But repeat host Howie Mandel sent them off in style. For his opening joke, he ran and slid across the stage on his knees and right into the orchestra pit, re-emerging with fake blood pouring down his face.

In 1987, Canadian producers were winning worldwide acclaim and delivering career albums for their clients. The man at the top of his game was Hamilton, Ontario, resident Daniel Lanois, winning Producer of the Year for his work on Peter Gabriel's bestselling *So* (1986) and U2's *The Joshua Tree* (1987), as well as sailing on the momentum of Robbie Robertson's self-titled solo record (1987), Robertson's first since leaving The Band eleven years earlier.

Bottom: Daniel Lanois accepting the Producer of the Year award in 1987.

Plum Communications Inc.

Although Lanois was victorious, he wasn't the only producer enjoying a banner year: Bruce Fairbairn was nominated for the monster Bon Jovi hits "You Give Love a Bad Name" and "Livin' on a Prayer," from their multi-platinum *Slippery When Wet*; Terry Brown helped secure a worldwide hit for Cutting Crew with the chart-topping "(I Just) Died in Your Arms"; Bryan Adams got the nod for "Heat of the Night" from his triple-platinum album *Into the Fire*; and the brothers Vannelli—Gino, Joe, and Ross—were nominated for Gino's gold album *Big Dreamers Never Sleep*. In fact, the field was so competitive that a sixth nominee was added to the usual five: Chris Wardman, for Chalk Circle's gold album *Mending Wall*, an effort so tasteful it was jokingly nicknamed "The Oshawa Tree."

Bryan Adams also received a new award—Canadian Entertainer of the Year—a category that differs in that it's the sole Juno determined by public ballot. Unfortunately, Adams was in the midst of a European tour, although he did accept by satellite, gathered with his band and congratulating his manager, Bruce Allen, for winning the Walt Grealis Special Achievement Award earlier that evening.

For his part, Allen thanked Loverboy co-manager Lou Blair and Randy Bachman, and then had a kind word for Canadian talent. "Some of the best music in the world comes out of this country—

and it can make a job like mine real easy."

There was also a repeat of the Adams-Hart rivalry, but it just didn't generate the same excitement as in 1985. Bryan Adams' *Into the Fire* (300,000 copies) and Corey Hart's *Fields of Fire* (200,000 copies) still sold exceptional numbers, but it was Kim Mitchell's *Shakin' Like a Human Being* that surprised them both as the 1987 Juno Album of the Year.

Nobody was more shocked by the win than Mitchell, who initially had to be persuaded to attend the show. "I remember saying to Tom [Berry, his manager], 'I don't want to go. I'm not going this year,' and he said, 'No, you gotta. *Shakin' Like a Human Being* is nominated for Album of the Year.' And I said, 'It's not going to fucking win, and I don't want to go. I don't want to go this year.'

"And we had a huge blowout as to whether I should be there or not."

While attending the show's afternoon rehearsal, Mitchell may have been accidentally tipped off to his impending victory by Alan Frew and Sam Reid of Glass Tiger, who announced his name during the Album of the Year rundown.

"I remember the guys from Glass Tiger saying, 'Kim Mitchell—Shakin' Like a Human Being.' And I remember the producer saying, 'You're not supposed to say that.' And I thought, well, that was fucking odd."

"And later that night, I won."

Mitchell says a lot of his memory was a blur after his name was announced. "I remember my heart really beating fast, and even though you try to pretend you don't care, you're going 'Wow, would it ever be nice to snag this one!' And when I did, I couldn't even think. I don't even know what I said. I can't remember. I probably made a stooge of myself and said something wrong, but it's really quite a fucking honour to have your peers go, 'Wow. . .'

"It was a really nice moment. It was obviously the highlight of my years at the Junos. What an awesome night that was."

The night wasn't so awesome for Canadian Music Hall of Fame inductees The Guess Who. One of the first rock bands to bring Canada international acclaim, Burton Cummings, Randy Bachman, Jim Kale, and Garry Peterson strolled slowly onto the stage to a standing ovation after a brief recap of their legendary career.

However, the quartet never made it to the podium before the camera cut away for a commercial. The Guess Who believed they never got their proper moment in the sun, and Cummings, for one, wasn't happy about the way things turned out.

"I think I was pretty pissed at the time," Cummings recalls. "As a matter of fact, I think I was fucking furious. But what are you going to do? Television is television. I should know better from the sixties. I did weekly television for the

CBC for two years. So I remember being furious, and then, well, at least we were in the Hall of Fame."

Cummings said it was strange being onstage with Kale and Peterson, because the duo were touring their own version of what the singer calls "the fake Guess Who," while he and Bachman were engaged in a Bachman-Cummings tour and recording project.

"It was really ugly for the four of us to be together."

Also that year, a few new national and international icons entered the fray. Nova

Scotia singer and songwriter Rita MacNeil triumphed over Céline Dion in the Most Promising Female Vocalist category, but Dion performed "I Miss Your Love" and declared her star to be definitively on the rise.

"I remember Céline's performance, and the first time I heard her voice," says Carroll Baker. "That stopped the show."

Top: Rik Emmett (left) and Kim Mitchell (right) present Album of the Year honours in 1989.

k.d. lang had abandoned her cowpunk eyeglass frames and wore a light blue jacket covered in maple leaves to accept her first Country Female Vocalist of the Year award, ending Anne Murray's consecutive string of Junos in that category at seven.

Gino Vannelli returned to play "Wild Horses," his latest hit, and Kim Mitchell remembers being blown away. "He opened the show with 'Wild Horses.' And I remember thinking, 'Holy fuck does this sound good!' Because he always had impressive musicians with him I was getting goosebumps during that song."

There were also a lot of repeat winners: Glass Tiger won their second consecutive Single of the Year, this one for "Someday"; Bryan Adams received his fifth straight Male Vocalist of the Year Juno and second Canadian Entertainer of the Year award; and Jim Vallance won his fourth straight Composer of the Year award, acknowledging Adams in his speech.

Luba also won Female Vocalist of the Year for a third straight time, and announced that this succession of accolades was finally giving her some lasting confidence.

"The first year I thought it was a mistake," Luba confessed. "The second year, I thought it was luck. Now I'm thinking there might be something to this."

At the conclusion of the program,

Howie Mandel ended the show with a touch of slapstick.

He challenged k.d. lang to slap him—and she gave him such a feeble touch that it was obvious she didn't want to engage.

That wasn't the only slap in the face. The ratings were also at their lowest for the decade: only 1.403 million tuned in.

It was time for an adjustment.

Since record companies were now concerned that they couldn't work the Junos and their own records properly during the lucrative holiday season, CARAS decided to move the program back to March, allowing another eighteen-month window for talent to emerge, and scheduled the show for March 12, 1989.

You could say that CARAS wanted to end the 1980s with a good impression, so they hired André-Philippe Gagnon, a Quebec impersonator who made his reputation by accurately mimicking singing voices, to host it.

Gagnon was best known for his precise rendition of every singing voice on "We Are the World," and his gift for mimicry had attracted the attention of Johnny Carson and made him an overnight sensation on *The Tonight Show*.

First time award show co-producers John Brunton and Lynn Harvey also wanted to make a new impression and create a much different vibe for the Junos than in previous years.

The set resembled a city rooftop and tackled the theme of media, setting

up shots so viewers could watch people watching television on television.

It was a hipper approach.

"We kind of felt like previous Juno sets looked like *The Wheel of Fortune* or some cheesy U.S. game show," Brunton explains. "Not to criticize anybody who had done it before, but it had this kind of bright, variety show vibe to it.

"We really wanted to try to bring the show into the next decade, make it edgier, funkier, and little bit more related to what was actually happening in the music scene back then, with the emergence of videos and all those elements."

Brunton and Harvey hired a new designer, Dale Heslip, which helped them transform the visual "into a much darker, more Queen Street West kind of vibe."

The Toronto Queen Street West community was front and centre in 1989, as the rising success earlier in the decade of The Parachute Club, Jane Siberry, Chalk Circle, Martha and the Muffins, The Pursuit of Happiness, Images in Vogue, Handsome Ned, and particularly rock-country hybrid Blue Rodeo offered an exciting new dynamic.

Blue Rodeo, represented by five nominations for Group of the Year, Single and Video of the Year for their signature ballad "Try" (which also netted co-founders Jim Cuddy and Greg Keelor a Composer of the Year nod), and Album of the Year, were particularly embraced by the Canadian masses.

"Eighty-nine was our big coming-out year," remembers singer and guitarist Jim Cuddy, whose band captured Junos for Group and Single of the Year. "I remember we stayed up all night in the office of our manager, drinking champagne. We talked about all the things that had happened, because we never, ever had entrance into that world of success before. It was fun and a pretty sweet memory."

"It's a fluke, because there's a lot of great music out there," singer and guitarist Greg Keelor said during the show, with Cuddy adding, "Thanks to all the people who kept the single alive when it was dying a slow death out there."

But one of the biggest highlights for Blue Rodeo—and one that was marked for potential disappointment—was a surprise performance with The Band of "The Weight" following the induction of Robbie Robertson, Rick Danko, Garth Hudson, the late Richard Manuel, and Levon Helm into the Canadian Music Hall of Fame.

The problems began with a continuing feud between Robertson and Helm over publishing royalties and Robertson's decision to end The Band after filming *The Last Waltz* in 1976.

The bottom line: if Robertson was going to be there, Helm wouldn't attend.

"Robbie had said he was going to need some other musicians to back them up, so I contacted Jim and Greg at Blue Rodeo," says producer John Brunton.

Plum Communications Inc.

"I knew that they were huge fans of The Band and were heavily influenced by their music. I said, 'I'd really love you guys to back up The Band', and to convince them to do it, I said, 'Robbie and the boys would really love you to be involved.'"

Cuddy remembers the invitation all too clearly.

"We were told that The Band were thrilled to do it with us—that was our first TV lie," he recalls.

"When Robbie came into the room, we were all practised. We were going to do 'The Weight' and we all knew everything from the recording. And the first thing he said was, 'Wow, there are too many Indians here. We only need a drummer.'

"Of course, we're shocked—he just fucking dismissed the band."

Brunton corroborates. "Robbie and the boys arrive at rehearsal beforehand, and Robbie looks at me and says, 'Who the fuck are these guys?' And had selective

amnesia about wanting a full band set-up behind him."

According to Cuddy, it was The Band's bass player Rick Danko who stepped in and saved the day. "Rick Danko takes over—he's such a wonderful, gregarious guy, and he says, 'Hey, this'll be fun.' He meets Bazil [Donovan, Blue Rodeo's bass player]. 'Hi Bazil, we'll both play bass. I'll play high, you play low.'"

Cuddy says that, ironically, they had to give Robertson a refresher on the song. "Robbie didn't know the song. He couldn't remember the vocals because he hadn't played it in a long time.

"But the whole rehearsal ended up being great because of Rick Danko. Rick was such a wonderful, wonderful guy."

Top: Blue Rodeo performs back up for The Band during their Canadian Music Hall of Fame induction in 1989.

Opposite: Rita MacNeil performing "Working Man" with The Men of the Deeps at the 1989 Junos.

One of the most emotionally resonant performances of the evening came from Rita MacNeil and The Men of the Deeps, a forty-member coal-miner chorus dressed in coveralls and hard hats who entered the venue with their helmet lamps shining.

After MacNeil sang a verse of "Working Man," The Men paraded in from all sides of the O'Keefe Centre in unison, with everyone present suddenly awestruck at the combination.

"I remember thinking, 'You know, this has nothing to do with the word "hip"—it's just profoundly musical and moving,'" remembers Ian Thomas. "And I was thrilled, because I didn't think that Rita could have been a star anywhere else in the world but Canada. So I was really proud of Canada for embracing Rita and that performance. That was a stunning moment. As a musician and a Canadian, I thought that was one of the most powerful Juno moments."

CARAS president Peter Steinmetz was equally impressed.

"I think that ranks as the most memorable Juno performance that I can recall," he states. "She has such a fantastic voice, and the audience were on their feet to watch this. I don't think there was a dry eye in the house. It was so moving and the applause went on forever. It was really a special moment."

Another spectacular performance was delivered with k.d. lang's "Crying," all the more poignant because her duet partner on the recorded version—Roy Orbison, the song's originator—had suddenly passed away on December 6, 1988.

"There was the feeling that night that when she was singing that song, Roy Orbison's soul was somehow projecting through her," John Brunton recalls. "It was an incredibly powerful performance. She brought the house down that night."

When lang was named Female Vocalist of the Year (she also won her second Female Country Music Vocalist of the Year Juno on this night), she broke into tears, overcome with emotion, held the Juno, and said, "Roy deserves part of this."

Recalling the moment twenty-one years later, lang allows that she "generally feels emotional whenever I'm in front of Canadians."

Plum Communications Inc.

"But I also remember feeling bittersweet about it. I hadn't spent that much time with Roy [Orbison], but I knew that it was a pretty big moment in my life, that singing it with him and sort of inheriting the song was pretty big.

"It was kind of a moment of fate where you recognize that it's going to shift the course of action."
—k.d. lang

72

Plum Communications Inc.

Barry Roden Photograhy

Plum Communications Inc.

Other strong performances came from Canadian Entertainer of the Year winners Glass Tiger in their duet with singer Dalbello (formerly known as Lisa Dal Bello), "Watching Worlds Crumble"; Composer of the Year Tom Cochrane delivering a potent "Big League" with Red Rider; New Zealand's International Entertainer nominees Crowded House crooning "Better Be Home Soon" (they lost to U2); an electrifying performance by Most Promising Male Vocalist nominee Jeff Healey of "My Little Girl"; and guitar slinger and Most Promising Male Vocalist Colin James rocking the joint with "Voodoo Thing."

"What really struck me about watching Colin is how, over the years, you watch it slowly come of age, and part of that coming of age was that Canada was finally kicking out some performers," recalls Ian Thomas.

"In my era [the 1970s], you had people who had a hit single and maybe some radio success, but they weren't necessarily performers."

Cuddy feels that the 1989 Junos marked a noticeable shift in the popularity and acceptance of Canadian music by our home territory. "It was a complete coming out of Canadian music. We've been doing this since '78, so I was aware of how few Canadian bands really took the full national stage, and in 1989, every band that performed at the Junos had double-platinum records.

"It was really such an incredibly successful time for Canadian bands raised, recorded, and released in Canada.

"In fact, the eighties were the perfect storm of audiences ready to hear Canadian music, record companies starting to look at these Canadian bands who were starting to draw crowds, so this was a real turning of the tide."

It seems only fitting to mention that the Junos also came full circle by presenting a Lifetime Achievement Award to Pierre Juneau, the politician for whom the awards show was named.

As the 1980s drew to a close, the Juno Awards introduced and celebrated several stars who would continue to make waves both nationally and globally well into the next two decades: Bryan Adams, Céline Dion, k.d. lang, Blue Rodeo, Tom Cochrane, and many, many others, as well as embracing the enduring talents who still resonate strongly in today's contemporary music scene: Neil Young, Joni Mitchell, Anne Murray, and Gordon Lightfoot.

For producer John Brunton—a constant with the Juno Awards throughout the nineties, two thousands, and the 2010 show in St. John's, Newfoundland—the '89 show brought a realization that the show needed to involve the public.

"One of the big things I took away from that show was that it was in a soft-seat theatre at O'Keefe, and all the guys in the record labels were sitting in the front bunch of rows—and I was struck by what a bad idea that was," Brunton explained.

"I really thought that it was a mistake to celebrate the Canadian music scene and not have any fans in the building. It was one of those things that really stuck with me. I thought that it would really make the performances more exciting."

With a ratings upswing to 1.598 million viewers, it wouldn't be long before Brunton would get the opportunity to realize CARAS' vision. •

1970s

1980s

1990s

2000s

The nineties were indeed a decade of massive musical changes that began to affect the way we listened to, and acquired, our music. The digital world began to explode and we have barely glanced back since. Downloading had begun. Napster entered our homes and offices and with the click of a finger on a button, the tunes began pouring into our greedy little hands. A frenzy of file sharing swept the globe. Who would have thought that ring tones would become one of the biggest money makers for major labels in the past few years? Certainly not me. The nineties exploded with new faces and new exciting music. What was old would become new again. Organic acoustic music ruled right alongside grinding heavy-hearted rock from the American West Coast. Seattle pounded the world with angst and rumours of revolution. "Grunge" became the word du jour.

It was odd indeed that women would have such a dominant role with all this testosterone swirling about. I remember hearing Sinéad O'Connor singing "Nothing Compares 2 U" over and over and over on every radio station I happened to tune in to. I thought, this is 1990's first big superstar. She was the first of many women to hit it big that decade. Céline Dion, Shania Twain, Alanis Morissette, Sarah McLachlan, and a host of other notable women smothered the airwaves with their keen originality and pop sensibility. The fact that they were all Canadian was another interesting part of the equation. These women were responsible for a *huge* part of the music industry's income stream. With things like Lilith Fair hitting the ground running, and Céline and Alanis circling the globe with worldwide tours, the effects of the music economy were staggering. These women opened doors for the hordes of young artists who are making waves today.

The nineties may have dragged us kicking and screaming into the digital world, but there is most certainly no going back. How we listen to music, buy our music, store our music, share our music, make our music were all defined in one little harmless decade.

History will tell us what was good. It always does.

—JANN ARDEN

WAKING UP THE

K.D. LANG slowly rises from her seat when she hears her name called to receive 1990's Country Female Vocalist of the Year Juno. She walks toward the O'Keefe Centre stage with a calm swagger, her demeanour a far cry from the night five years prior when she stormed the podium in a wedding dress to accept her first Juno as Most Promising Female Vocalist. Now, wearing a Nashville-issue rhinestone jacket and faded jeans, she exudes all the charisma of a young Elvis Presley, even giving the television camera a sly glance on her way down the aisle, as if to say, "Get ready for this." Indeed, the audience both in the theatre and watching at home holds its collective breath in anticipation of something scandalous. But lang's straightforward and emphatic message turns out to be everything great Canadian music has stood for, and what it will continue to represent in the decade ahead.

"For me," she says, "it has nothing to do with awards, it has nothing to do with record sales, it has nothing to do with what category I'm in. I love to sing."

In retrospect, lang's statement is laced with irony given that one of the main attractions of the 1990 Junos was a performance by Milli Vanilli, winners of International Album of the Year. Only months before, the duo had been caught lip-synching live on MTV, and by the end of 1990 it would be revealed that neither Rob Pilatus nor Fab Morvan actually sang on Milli Vanilli recordings.

The ensuing uproar from both critics and music fans all over the world suggested that long overdue change was taking hold throughout the music industry. Kids weaned on punk rock and hip hop's founding fathers were now assuming positions of power, determined to drag the music they loved into the mainstream however they could. The gauntlet had been thrown down in Canada by 1990 after bands such as The Pursuit

BY JASON SCHNEIDER

NEIGHBOURS

of Happiness, 54•40, and Cowboy Junkies made the leap from do-it-yourself labels to the majors. By late 1991, as worldwide acceptance of Nirvana's *Nevermind* and the Seattle-based grunge scene grew, there was no doubt that a new generation was boldly leading rock and roll into the future, one in which genre boundaries would eventually become irrelevant.

There were several other signs at the 1990 Junos that a new era was dawning, aside from the confidence at the heart of k.d. lang's speech. Three years into their career, The Tragically Hip were belatedly named Most Promising Group—an award the members declined to accept in person. Conversely, although there was no category yet for Best Rap Recording, Maestro Fresh-Wes and his crew, including Farley Flex and DJ LTD, welcomed the opportunity to perform the hit single "Let Your Backbone Slide," nominated for Best Dance Recording. Kon Kan took home that award for "I Beg Your Pardon," but Maestro's appearance is what most who were there remember, as it firmly asserted hip hop's growing presence in Canada.

Right: Michelle Wright performing at the 1991 Junos. She was nominated for Country Female Vocalist of the Year.

Barry Roden Photography

Maestro, who, after several more Juno-nominated albums, went on to a successful acting career under his birth name Wes Williams, understandably recalls the night fondly. "It felt amazing," he says. "It's like, imagine the first record you put out gets nominated for the biggest award in Canada. It was euphoria, the performance was incredible, but I do remember being very disappointed when we didn't win. It did feel good, though, knowing that the industry was acknowledging me on that level, since at that time the only exposure that hip hop got in Canada was either through MuchMusic or *The Arsenio Hall Show*. Those were the only places where we could get a sense of what other artists were doing."

Williams would be redeemed in 1991 when he won the first Juno for Rap Recording of the Year for his debut album, *Symphony in Effect*, one of five nominations he received that year. "Getting that many nominations meant a lot to me," he says. "I was up for Best Single and Best Male Vocalist against cats like Bryan Adams and Corey Hart. I was probably more nervous that year because I was representing my genre of music. It was such an honour to know that a new category was created just because of my album. But my best Junos memory will always be meeting Quincy Jones for the first time in 1990."

Kim Mitchell also had an enlightening encounter that year with Aerosmith's Steven Tyler and Joe Perry, there to support Bruce Fairbairn, who won the Producer of the Year Juno for his work on their album *Pump*. "I was sitting beside Steven Tyler and he goes, 'Nice pants, man!' After I performed, he and Joe were following me back to the dressing room and Steven says, 'Holy crap, man! Which song is that?' 'Rock 'N' Roll Duty.' 'How is that song not a hit in America? That song rocked our asses off!'" Mitchell adds, "That was a really nice moment. What I should have said was, 'Why don't you cover it?' But you know what? Opportunities like that missed me my whole career."

Mitchell won Male Vocalist of the Year, but the real story of the 1990 Junos was Alannah Myles' long road to international acceptance. "'Black Velvet' was undeniable," is how Myles describes the song that launched her from southern Ontario clubs onto the world stage in 1989. "There wasn't a pore that did not get raised as we listened to it over and over again after the vocal had been completed. That's why the instrumentation was pared down to a minimum; we wanted the vocal to be felt by the listener without reservation." Along with "Black Velvet" earning Single of the Year, and Composer of the Year honours for its co-writers Christopher Ward and David Tyson, Myles was named Most Promising Female Vocalist and her self-titled debut LP won Album of the Year.

With it all coming in the middle of a packed touring schedule—she kicked off the televised broadcast by performing her then-current hit "Love Is"—Myles says she barely had time to catch her breath, or confirm her transportation to the ceremony. "There were a number of very

excited members of my party who made all of the arrangements to have their makeup and hair done, and have their limos booked. I did my own makeup and hair at home while waiting for my limo, which, due to all of the excitement, was never booked. So I had my drummer Jorn Andersen drive me in Christopher Ward's rusted-out Honda, flying like a bat out of hell to get me to the O'Keefe Centre's stage door. There was no red-carpet entrance for this hard-working woman of rock."

Myles capped off her whirlwind ascension when "Black Velvet" won a Grammy for Best Rock Vocal Performance, Female in 1991, a Canadian first. Yet her breakthrough was merely the crest of the wave of female Canadian artists who would come to dominate the charts all around the world for the rest of the decade. It was a far cry from 1971, when Anne Murray and Myrna Lorrie were the only women to be recognized at the ceremony, and emphasizing that advancement, among others, was front and centre when the Junos celebrated its twentieth anniversary in Vancouver.

The change of venue was symbolic of a need to expand the scope of the Junos beyond Toronto, and since Vancouver was home to in-demand producers Bruce Fairbairn and Bob Rock, esteemed managers Bruce Allen and Sam Feldman, and the rapidly expanding Nettwerk label, the West Coast was a natural first choice. With Paul Shaffer hosting, aided at the

outset by his old friend Martin Short, the Vancouver crowd was indeed energized when Courtenay, BC's Sue Medley received the Most Promising Female Vocalist Juno. It was also an impressive night for Regina's Colin James, who took home Male Vocalist of the Year honours, on top of opening the show with his hit "Just Came Back."

Opposite: Maestro Fresh-Wes and crew performing on the 1990 Junos.

Left: Aerosmith's Joe Perry (left) and Steven Tyler (right) present Bruce Fairbairn with Producer of the Year award in 1990.

Right: Alannah Myles' first Juno appearance was a huge success with her winning Single, Album, and Most Promising Female Vocalist of the Year for 1990.

Barry Roden Photography

Barry Roden Photography

But if 1991 was a moment to reflect upon Juno ceremonies past, it also marked the full flowering of an artist who would soon leave an indelible mark on music around the world: Céline Dion. She was already a legend in her native Quebec, the youngest of fourteen children; her unwavering pursuit of her dream to become a singer captured the imagination of the entire province. Throughout the 1980s, her unmatched voice brought international acclaim. There was only one major obstacle holding Dion back from everything she'd ever wanted: she did not speak English. Starting in 1988, she studied for two years with the same zeal she applied to every other aspect of her career, while simultaneously working on the album aimed at introducing her to the English-speaking world. With producer David Foster overseeing the record, it did appear as though *Unison* would either make or break Dion. The album turned out to be an immediate smash in Canada when it was released in March 1990, going on to sell more than 700,000. But it took until that September for *Unison* to reach the U.S. market, propelled by the single "Where Does My Heart Beat Now." The song shot to number 4 on Billboard's Top-100 singles chart, bolstering U.S. sales of *Unison* to more than one million copies.

On the heels of that triumph, Dion was presented with Junos in Vancouver for Album of the Year and Female Vocalist of the Year. Her emotional response to the long-overdue acceptance by the anglophone music industry was entirely genuine, especially in light of

One of the mysteries that dogged the music business had always been: how are the charts compiled? The lack of a definitive answer ultimately put the integrity of music award shows in question as well; that is, until the implementation of Nielsen SoundScan in 1997.

The bar-code technology installed in retail outlets worldwide enabled sales of every album to be tracked, providing a clear picture of a recording's true popularity among consumers for the first time. Prior to this, record companies only had information on how much product they manufactured and shipped, and often less-mainstream genres such as country were underserviced as a result.

The immediate sales feedback that Nielsen SoundScan offered led to a revolution in terms of how labels could target specific markets and listeners. Further statistics came through Nielsen BDS, the radio-tracking system first utilized in Canada in 1996, which allowed airplay numbers from across the country to be tabulated instantly.

All of this precise data allowed CARAS to definitively illustrate that the Juno nomination policy for the major categories was based on sales figures alone, proving once and for all that those artists being honoured were a clear reflection of the music-buying public's taste.

Barry Roden Photography

Barry Roden Photography

the controversy she had generated in Quebec in October 1990 when, on live television, she refused a Félix award (the francophone equivalent of the Juno) as Anglophone Artist of the Year. She says now of that debut Junos appearance, "All I can remember is that I was very, very nervous. But at the same time I was excited to be singing in English, for a national TV audience for the very first time. I knew how important the Junos were, so it was a big moment for me."

The backlash occurring in Quebec over *Unison* was compounded by Dion's deeper concerns over the condition of her vocal cords. The strain she had put them under finally forced her undergo surgery later in 1991, from which she rebounded convincingly with "Beauty and the Beast," her duet with Peabo Bryson for the Disney movie of the same name. It became the song that solidified Dion's international reputation, earning further accolades. She would remain a proud Canadian—and more significantly, a proud Quebecker—throughout it all, but by 1992 she belonged to the world. "It's always an honour and a privilege to win an award, and I never take it for granted," Dion says. "For me, and I'm sure it's the same for a lot of artists, we're doing what we love to do, and we're so lucky for that. So winning those great awards was wonderful, but I don't think it changed me at all. It just made me feel that much more fortunate and grateful for being able to do this for a living."

It's difficult, on the surface, to find many stylistic similarities between Céline Dion and Leonard Cohen, but in some ways the status Cohen achieved as an internationally renowned Canadian artist in the late 1960s blazed the trail that Dion later followed. The Montreal-born singer-songwriter was the 1991 inductee into the Canadian Music Hall of Fame, and the presentation was every bit as stylish, poetic, and darkly humorous as long-time Cohen fans could have expected. The recognition coincided with the release of *I'm Your Fan*, an album of many of Cohen's best-loved songs interpreted by contemporary artists such as R.E.M., the Pixies, and Nick Cave. It was another of the career rejuvenations Cohen experienced each time a new generation of artists discovered his work, something that almost always occurred when his extended periods of silence were broken by the sudden appearance of new material. In 1991, Cohen was still basking in the praise of his most recent album, 1988's *I'm Your Man*, featuring the songs "First We Take Manhattan," "Ain't No Cure for Love," "Everybody Knows," and "Tower of Song."

Opposite left: In 1991, Paul Shaffer hosted the first Juno Awards in Vancouver.

Opposite right: The Vancouver crowd was energized when Courtenay, BC's Sue Medley received the Most Promising Female Vocalist Juno in 1991.

Top left: Céline Dion performs at the 1991 Juno Awards.

Top right: Seen here in 1991, Prairie Oyster built on their success in the eighties, winning Country Group or Duo of the Year throughout the nineties.

Bottom: Leonard Cohen was typically gracious upon his 1991 induction into the Canadian Music Hall of Fame.

Opposite: Tom Cochrane performing "Life Is a Highway," 1992's Single of the Year.

That album was a remarkable display of Cohen's skill at adapting his songwriting to the current zeitgeist, making the choice to induct him into the Canadian Music Hall of Fame seem at once timely but also perhaps slightly premature. Then again, as his friend, broadcaster Moses Znaimer, put it in his eloquent testimonial, "We, all of us, can be glad that we share the same planet with Leonard Cohen." What followed was unquestionably one of the most memorable Juno speeches in the award's history. Cohen, grasping the microphone tightly, admitted that at first he resisted accepting the Canadian Music Hall of Fame honour, as it initially signified to him that his career was over. But upon reflection he decided, "At fifty-six, I'm just hitting my stride and it doesn't hurt at all." Cohen then proceeded to graciously recite the names of all who had earned lifetime achievement distinctions before him. It was a moving tribute to the pioneers of Canadian music, although in typical Cohen fashion he noted that with only two female inductees, "it will be hard for me to get a date in the Hall of Fame." Cohen continued to project humility by next thanking his audience for making his music a part of their lives. From there he

slipped effortlessly into lines from "Tower of Song," lines that proclaimed with little ambiguity that his life's work was far from complete.

Indeed, it wasn't. In 1993, Cohen was back in the public eye with his acclaimed album *The Future*. At that year's Junos he performed a thrillingly raspy version of the album's first single, "Closing Time," and minutes later he was named Male Vocalist of the Year. Standing bemused at the podium, Cohen offered another

immortal line: "Only in a country like this can I get Male Vocalist of the Year." Cohen's Canadian status had never been in doubt, in spite of the fact that he, like most artists of his generation, had to leave Canada in order to launch his musical career. This was taken for granted in the pre-CanCon era, but with so many artists achieving international success by the start of the 1990s, real questions were being raised about CanCon's role within the industry.

George Kraychyk

It came to a head at the 1992 Junos, held once again at Toronto's O'Keefe Centre, with Bryan Adams earning a record seven nominations for his album *Waking Up the Neighbours* and the single "(Everything I Do) I Do It for You," which topped the charts in twenty-one countries. It would have been a cakewalk for Adams, if not for a newspaper article published at the time of the nominations charging that because Adams shared credit as songwriter and producer on the single with his African collaborator Robert John "Mutt" Lange, and American co-writer Michael Kamen, it did not fulfill the CRTC's Canadian content requirements, and therefore should be disqualified from Juno contention. While Canadian broadcasters played the song to death anyway, irate comments Adams made leading up to the Junos over his being deemed "not Canadian," as well as CanCon breeding mediocrity, ignited an intense media debate. Anticipation of the fallout further escalated the minute the first Juno of 1992 was given out to Tom Cochrane's "Life Is a Highway" for Single of the Year.

If anyone was in a position to upset Adams on that night, it was Cochrane. He had established a solo identity with the album *Mad Mad World* after leading the band Red Rider for over a decade. "Life Is a Highway," completed after his first trip to aid refugees in Africa, also symbolized Cochrane's perseverance through his own creative struggles. "I knew it was a

83

special song," he says. "I had written the basic sketch back in the 1980s, but it was never completed. It kept coming back to me like a dream. There was a sense of cathartic relief to finish the song when I did because I needed it. That song became like a pep talk to myself and, consequently to a multitude of other people, I guess. It really is a positive, life-affirming song that resonates with a lot of people."

Cochrane went on to win Male Vocalist of the Year, Album of the Year, and Songwriter of the Year, far and away the most Juno recognition he had ever

received up until then. "It felt incredible," he says. "We had been nominated it seemed like dozens of times as Red Rider and we felt like outcasts. But that was okay, we were comfortable with the underdog tag and never really put a lot of stock in winning awards. Then in '92 it felt a bit like 'this is my party.' But I also remember how humbling it was to be congratulated by people I looked up to, like Robbie Robertson, at the EMI/Capitol after-party. I lived and breathed The Band for a couple of years when I was sixteen or so."

Adams was not completely ignored. He was the fans' choice for Canadian Entertainer of the Year, shared Producer of the Year with Lange, and was given a special international achievement award in recognition of "(Everything I Do) I Do It for You." In explaining the song's origins during his acceptance speech, he pointedly noted that what he heard in Kamen's demo was an "international melody," and closed his comments by thanking CARAS for "putting aside the politics." Although some drew a parallel between Adams's anti-CanCon statements and his poor Juno showing, he stood by his views after the ceremony, saying, "I have no regrets. I think I said the right thing. I don't believe we need [CanCon regulations] in Canada. Canadian music is strong enough and we don't need the Canadian government to tell people what to play."

No one could really argue with those sentiments, and today Tom Cochrane puts it another way. "In the years after [Red Rider] came on the scene in 1979–starting in the late 1980s–it became fashionable for a number of artists that would become Canadian phenoms to proudly embrace being Canadian and to be embraced in Canada first and foremost, regardless of what they did or didn't do in the States or abroad. That is something to be proud of and it shows we were coming into our own as Canadians, confident and proud of our culture. We didn't need to have it validated by another country."

George Kraychyk

Barry Roden Photography

The ubiquitous presence of "Everything I Do" throughout the evening must have heightened the air of romance at the O'Keefe Centre. At least that's something Corey Hart can now attest to. "On the way to the Junos in '92, I was told I was presenting one of the categories alone," he says. "As we were on the way to rehearsal, I got a phone call in the car telling me that they switched it to another category and I'm going to present it with a VJ from MuchMusic. I said I didn't really like the sound of that. It was not the eighties anymore, so somehow I was being relegated to a more minor role of participation. I was nominated for a few awards that year, so I said, 'Fine, I just

won't present.' They were all frazzled and the phone went dead."

Hart continues, "About five minutes later I got a call from Donald K. Donald [Tarlton] and he said, 'Look, we're at the Junos and I want you to present with Julie Masse.' I said, 'I don't know who Julie Masse is.' He explained to me that she's a really popular young singer from Quebec and she's nominated; she wasn't supposed to be on the show, but you're both from Quebec and it'd be a nice thing, so I said okay. We presented that night together, and as we went offstage, her manager grabbed me and said, 'She's going to make an English record, would you work with her? There's a chemistry between the two

Barry Roden Photography

of you.' Prior to doing her record in June 1994 I met her maybe two or three times and talked about what we were trying to accomplish creatively. It was the first time I was going to write and produce someone other than myself. It felt like an interesting challenge and a different thing for me to try at that point in my career. So we did the record in Morin Heights, and we fell hopelessly and madly in love six weeks later. I just couldn't live without her, and her, me. Four kids and fifteen years later, I'm the luckiest guy in the world. It's my stubbornness, because if I had presented with that VJ, I never would have met my angel. It's good to be stubborn."

In addition to the Adams-Cochrane showdown, the 1992 Junos demonstrated how performers who at one time would have been in the margins were now being recognized by the mainstream. Early in the evening, the Most Promising Female Vocalist Juno went to seventeen-year-old Alanis Morissette—then simply known by only her first name—whose early notice as a dance-pop artist came largely through MuchMusic. Loreena McKennitt's worldwide top-selling *The Visit* shared Best Roots & Traditional Album honours with an album of performances from Holger Petersen's popular CBC Radio program *Saturday Night Blues*, and Toronto indie legends Shadowy Men on a

Shadowy Planet were named Instrumental Artists of the Year. Conversely, it seemed enough to have Bryan Adams there to attract viewers; for the first time no foreign star was part of the program.

But it was the induction of Ian and Sylvia Tyson to the Canadian Music Hall of Fame that was the night's focal point. Emotions ran high when the former married couple appeared onstage together again to receive the honour, and performances of their two best-known compositions by a who's who of the current generation of Canadian musicians broadly illustrated the duo's lasting influence. The all-star group, comprised of Blue Rodeo, Jane Siberry, Kashtin, Molly Johnson, and 54•40's Neil Osborne, first played "Four Strong Winds." Then, with Skydiggers vocalist Andy Maize taking control, the ensemble barnstormed through "You Were on My Mind." As Ian said succinctly during his speech, "We did have a sound," and that sound clearly still had special significance in Canada, even as the "alternative" revolution was taking hold.

Opposite left: Corey Hart presenting with future wife Julie Masse at the 1992 Junos.

Opposite right: Seventeen-year-old Alanis Morissette, then only known by her first name, being interviewed after winning the Most Promising Female Vocalist in 1992.

Top: Ian and Sylvia ride the strong winds of lifetime recognition during their 1992 Canadian Music Hall of Fame induction.

The following year, 1993, the televised Junos ceremony acknowledged this in an unconventional way by including clips throughout the broadcast of up-and-coming bands in clubs across the country. These brief, sweaty glimpses of

"I was sitting beside Steven Tyler and he goes, 'Nice pants, man!' After I performed, he and Joe were following me back to the dressing room and Steven says, 'Holy crap, man! Which song is that?' 'Rock 'N' Roll Duty.' 'How is that song not a hit in America? That song rocked our asses off!'" Mitchell adds, "That was a really nice moment. What I should have said was, 'Why don't you cover it?' But you know what? Opportunities like that missed me my whole career."
–Kim Mitchell

The Watchmen, Pure, Change of Heart, and others underscored how crucial the national touring circuit had become in developing new talent. It was hardly a surprise that this subplot culminated with a performance by the most revered live act at that moment, The Tragically Hip, filmed at a tour stop in Australia. That year the band won its second Juno as the fans' choice for favourite Canadian entertainer, and showing The Hip in their natural element proved a brilliant move by the show's producers, considering the band's seemingly ambivalent attitude toward attending previous ceremonies.

Reflecting the growing diversity of Canadian music while simultaneously

making the event more fan-friendly was the top priority of the Juno board of directors by the 1990s, says Stephen Stohn, prominent entertainment lawyer, television producer, and a key member of the CARAS board of directors during that decade. "I became head of the nominating [and voting] committee then, and I'd describe it as a tumultuous time precisely because of all the changes the industry was undergoing," Stohn says. "There was an unjustified fear that the nominating and voting process was not transparent. Fundamental to any awards program is that people have to have trust in the system, and there were certainly elements of the industry and the public that were questioning that trust at that time. So, what we as a committee did was simply go back to basics and ask some core questions about what the Junos should represent. And I'm proud to say on behalf of everyone who was involved that the changes we implemented then really formed the bedrock of the modern Junos."

By 1993, those changes encompassed not only the continual addition of new categories, but also a hard-and-fast rule that nominations in the major categories would be determined by domestic sales, prior to academy members voting on a winner. "For the first couple of years we had intense meetings on a regular basis," Stohn says, "examining whether there would be enough great submissions to warrant all of this expansion we knew was necessary. Along with that came the changes to the voting procedure to make it more democratic, which eliminated those undeserved suspicions entirely. That resulted in two things: people had more confidence in the system overall, and as we were embracing these new musical communities we were coming up with mechanisms to ensure that they were really valued."

Opposite: Led by Ronnie Hawkins, a supergroup of Canadian Music Hall of Fame members from Steppenwolf, The Mamas & The Papas, Blood Sweat & Tears, The Lovin' Spoonful, and Domenic Troiano performing together for the first time in 1996.

Right: Barenaked Ladies clowning around at the 1993 Junos.

Stohn, like everyone else at the O'Keefe Centre in 1993, swelled with pride when Robbie Robertson and Buffy Sainte-Marie announced that the following year's ceremony would feature a Best Music of Aboriginal Canada category for the first time. But what drew the most appreciation were the efforts of host Céline Dion. Although her steadily increasing international profile made her a natural choice to guarantee ratings, organizers were nonetheless taking a big risk based on Dion's still-shaky grasp of English. On top of that, she caught the flu during rehearsals. Whether or not overcoming that setback became her main motivation to silence her critics, Dion surprised many with her charm and self-deprecating humour throughout the evening.

"At first I was very surprised to be asked to host," she says. "I'd never done anything like that before, and it was [a] huge honour. Once again, I was so nervous doing that in front of everybody, and on TV, but in the end, I had a really good time doing it." With so much emphasis placed upon her as host, it was almost an afterthought that Dion had matched Adams' previous year's record-setting seven nominations. At the end of the night, she had four Junos, including Female Vocalist of the Year. Yet the versatility Dion displayed surely won her many more new fans. "I've had great experiences at the Junos, just as I've had at the Grammys, the Félix Awards, and all the other shows. I think they're all so different, and I think my performances have been different each time. They've happened at different times in my career, and I've been able to be as versatile as the songs that were being performed at the time." She adds, "The Junos have been very important to me. I haven't always been able to attend due to my schedule, but I'll always have a special place in my heart for the times that I've been part of the show."

George Kraychyk

Dion aside, the night's truly memorable performance came from Barenaked Ladies, who, prior to surprising some by claiming Group of the Year honours, appeared with each member dressed in an individual clown outfit, a not-so-subtle jab at the band's critics, who still perceived them as a novelty act. "I'll take responsibility for that one," says BNL co-founder Steven Page. "We said, 'You think we're clowns? We'll give you clowns!' Then we launched into 'Box Set,' a scathing attack on the business of selling music. I think it was one of our most exciting performances. The producers had asked us to play 'Enid,' and they had an idea for a stage set that looked like a fifties diner or something. We refused. We were going to play a non-single, because we were young and idealistic—or just difficult—and we knew it would showcase what our band was really about live, more than any of the singles we'd had so far. I can still remember the huge adrenaline rush and the looks of shock, horror, and embarrassment on the audience's faces. Except for Donny Osmond, who was smiling broadly, and later came up to introduce himself and told us how much he loved it."

Page goes on to say that part of the band's motivation was also to do something that people would still be talking about years later, like k.d. lang's wedding dress and Burton Cummings' uncomfortably androgynous performance of "A Fine State of Affairs" in 1981. "The Junos always felt so 'establishment,' and really, to me, they still do. I always have mixed feelings about that—in some ways I want to be part of the club, and in other ways, I love to stir things up a bit. At the same time it seems that awards like the Junos seem to take some of the street cred away, as an artist becomes more accepted by the mainstream. That was never a huge issue for us, as we were happy to have as wide an audience as we did, but I remember some years later reading a quote from Carl Newman of The New Pornographers in which he claimed to not care about winning his Juno because 'that's what they give to Barenaked Ladies.'"

The Ladies really had nothing to lose in 1993; their debut album for Sire Records, *Gordon*, had taken Canada by storm the previous year. It came on the heels of their last independent cassette, *Barenaked Lunch*, which sold eighty thousand copies, enough to earn a gold record in Canada. What they proved was, although there was a vast audience within Canada attuned to the Seattle grunge rock scene, there were just as many (perhaps more) white middle-class suburban kids attuned to BNL's nerdy, oddball approach. This was similarly demonstrated in 1992 when Crash Test Dummies won Group of the Year, largely on the strength of their unconventional hit single "Superman's Song."

It was the first year the Winnipeg folk-rockers had been nominated, and winning such a prestigious award straight out of the gate naturally raised more than a few eyebrows. "Our label at the time [BMG] was pushing for us to be nominated for Best New Group," says front man and songwriter Brad Roberts. "But our manager, Jeff Rogers, said no way, we're going for Best Band. The label wanted the sure thing, but Jeff was confident that we'd made a big enough splash to warrant that award, and he was right." Still, Roberts concedes that timing played just as important a role in the success of Crash Test Dummies as anything else. "Our approach for our first album [*The Ghosts That Haunt Me*] worked for us rather than against us, much to my surprise," he says. "Even though we didn't sound like Nirvana in any way, we were considered 'underground,' which was the vibe that the major labels were looking for. It's a bit funny to think that one of the labels that turned us down said it was because they already had a folky/Celtic-y-sounding band on their roster and signing us meant they would be competing against themselves."

Opposite: Crash Test Dummies perform "Mmm Mmm Mmm Mmm" in 1995.

Kim Cooke, senior vice-president and managing director of Warner Music Canada at that time, agrees that the early 1990s was a "golden era" for Canadian artists at home, especially those with a strong folk element. "All of the major labels were doing huge business with Canadian acts," he says. "One of my proudest Warner signings was Great Big Sea, and they sold 500,000 copies of their debut album. That kind of thing just doesn't happen anymore. We also had Loreena McKennitt, who was selling massive numbers all around the world. Her performance in 1992 with Ofra Harnoy was definitely one of those magic Juno moments that I will always remember."

For George Fox, who in 1993 won his third straight Juno for Country Male Vocalist, it was also a particularly golden era for Canadian country music. While country has been a cornerstone of the Canadian music industry since its earliest days, the late-eighties crossover success of American artists like Garth Brooks, Randy Travis, and Dwight Yoakam led many Canadian major labels to take chances on homegrown acts for the first time. Fox was an Alberta rancher who performed on weekends until Warner Music accepted his demo tape and he released his self-titled debut album in 1988. From there he became Canada's country music ambassador, although he admits he always felt out of place when the inevitable Juno ceremonies came around. "It's like I said in one of my acceptance speeches, it wasn't so long before that a big deal for me was taking one of my cows to see the vet," Fox says.

He still recalls with awe attending after-show parties with Rod Stewart and Quincy Jones, but his most vivid memories stem from 1993, when he found himself on the arm of a certain prominent female politician. "Kim Campbell was set to become our first female prime minister, and needed someone to escort her to the Junos," Fox says. "We had mutual friends, so I was asked, and it was definitely one of the most unique experiences I've ever had. There was so much press there, and I ended up having a lot of responsibility to make sure she was at different places at specific times."

The momentum generated by the new crop of Canadian artists carried over into 1994, when during Canadian Music Week in Toronto, more than 1,300 delegates from around the world got to see 300 acts from every part of Canada. At the CMW awards dinner, *Billboard* editor-in-chief Timothy White said it best to those assembled: "Canada has one of the most exciting talent pools in the world right now, and everybody has their own theories of why this is so. I think it's because Canadian artists stopped looking outward, tailoring themselves to anyone in any way, and instead turned inward—waking up to the fact that their culture, their stories, and their sounds are as special as any others. When you decide that your art deserves to succeed solely on its own terms, that kind of organic passion transcends simple pride. It's honest, it's unselfish, and it's an adventure for all who are drawn to its mystique."

The focus of that mystique had taken a decidedly eastward shift for the 1994 Junos ceremony itself. The host was New Brunswick bilingual singing sensation Roch Voisine, whose classy demeanour set the tone for an evening that on the whole was a full-blown celebration of Canada's folk-based songwriting tradition. That theme was evident from the moment the first award of the night, Best New Solo Artist, was presented to Jann Arden. The Calgary native's road to notoriety had been long and challenging, from the time she released her first independent single in 1980 at age eighteen and hit the Alberta club circuit. Yet, when A&M Records released her debut album, *Time for Mercy*, in 1993, its moody, textured sound, its deeply personal lyrics, and Arden's "everywoman" image immediately connected with a large, mature audience. It was the beginning of her prolonged love affair with the Canadian listening public.

Opposite: Jazz stage show at the 1992 Junos.

92

"When I heard my name called, I honestly felt like someone had made a mistake," Arden says. "I had just turned thirty, so it wasn't like I was some seventeen-year-old kid who expected everything to go her way. I'd been knocking around in bars and really paying my dues, as the old adage goes. So being named Best New Artist did seem like an oxymoron. I was also told that it was a bit of a curse, but twenty years later and I'm still with Universal Records, enjoying a career that I never would have imagined I'd ever have."

Meanwhile, the love affair between Canada and Buffy Sainte-Marie entered a new phase that night when, in what she calls a "dream come true," she participated in handing out the first Best Music of Aboriginal Canada Juno to Lawrence Martin. "I and many other music professionals who happen to be indigenous to Canada had been actively discussing and envisioning the potential for the category, as well as other advancements, since the 1960s," Sainte-Marie says. "Like hearing black music emerge into the mainstream, I always knew the great diversity of aboriginal music styles and artists would be delicious to a wider audience, if people were introduced to it in the right ways. We now have three major aboriginal music awards shows celebrating our artists, our traditions, our producers, record companies, audiences, musicians, and songwriters."

Grant W. Martin Photography

Tom Sandler

It was only fitting, then, that Sainte-Marie was inducted into the Canadian Music Hall of Fame the following year. Although she was raised by her adoptive parents in Massachusetts and launched her career during the Greenwich Village folk boom of the early 1960s, Sainte-Marie's heart and soul always belonged to Canada. She says the Canadian Music Hall of Fame tribute was even more personally moving, considering how she has always credited Canada for supporting her through lean years when her political beliefs led to a concerted effort to stifle her ability to ply her trade in the United States. "From the point of view of the music industry, Canada saved me," she says. "Although I didn't know it while it was actively going on, there was apparently an eight-year period when two U.S. presidential administrations kept me under surveillance and broke my connection to American audiences. But it was a Canadian journalist who first blew the whistle and clued me in, and I feel that the suppression of my career was far less in Canada."

She adds, "Since that time Canada has been very kind to me on all levels. I've been included and honoured by governor generals, universities, museums and galleries, and the entertainment industry. Meanwhile, Canadian indigenous people have always loved and protected me, and I have always felt warmth and good vibes from Canadians everywhere."

While 1994 was a true milestone year in terms of Canadian aboriginal artists being embraced by wider audiences, it was also a significant moment for musicians from the Maritimes, who always sought to bring their regional sounds to national audiences. The groundwork for this had already been laid by artists such as Rita MacNeil, John Allan Cameron, and Figgy Duff, but with the massive success of their 1992 album *Fare Thee Well Love*, Cape Breton's Rankin Family gave the Maritime music scene unprecedented new exposure. The group, composed of five siblings from a brood of twelve, began recording independently in 1989. What had at first been a project intended to help pay for their university educations soon turned into a full-time career once the Rankins' burgeoning East Coast fan base drew interest from Capitol/EMI. The key turned out to be the song "Fare Thee Well Love," which they had originally released in 1990. Its hymnal qualities, accentuated by the group's impeccable harmony, tugged at the heartstrings of listeners the world over, especially those with Maritime roots who had migrated to other parts of Canada. It was hardly surprising that the song also fit perfectly onto the soundtrack of the Disney film *Into the West* after its 1992 major-label re-release.

Top: Buffy Sainte-Marie being inducted into the Canadian Music Hall of Fame.

Opposite: Jann Arden performing "Insensitive" at the 1996 Junos at Copps Coliseum in Hamilton.

Although Arden personally doesn't count herself among the group of female Canadian artists that defined the decade, she still recalls with great fondness an encouraging gesture from one of her peers during her first Juno experience. "Céline Dion was sitting behind me, and I remember her tapping me on my shoulder and saying 'congratulations' in her unmistakable way. I've also kept the clothes I wore that night in a box for safe keeping."

93

"That [song] was a milestone to me because I was recognized as a writer," Jimmy Rankin says. "Back in the day when we were kids playing dances around Inverness County in Cape Breton, I was writing a lot of stuff inspired by traditional music because that's where we were at the time. But I was also influenced by the pop music of the day." The Rankins were by far the big winners in 1994, taking home Junos for Group of the Year, Country Group or Duo of the Year, Single of the Year, and, perhaps most surprisingly, the fan-voted Canadian Entertainer of the Year. The family members themselves didn't seem prepared for the adulation, judging from their giddiness each time they were called to the podium, as well as Jimmy's humble comments to reporters following the ceremony. "I didn't think it'd be such a big deal, but I'm really taken aback by all of this," he said.

For 1994's other major winner, Jann Arden, 1995 would be the year she fortified her place among Canada's musical elite. Each time she came to the stage to accept Junos, for Songwriter of the Year, Female Vocalist of the Year, and Single of the Year for "Could I Be Your Girl," the crowd response was nearly overwhelming. "I'm shocked, I really am, I don't even read music," she said breathlessly to reporters.

That year's ceremony was the crucial moment that Juno organizers had been building up to: allowing fans complete access to the festivities. The site they chose for this bold step forward was Copps Coliseum in Hamilton, Ontario, a short distance from Toronto, and (for some) the symbolic birthplace of rock and roll in Canada, since it was the first city Ronnie Hawkins played upon his arrival from Arkansas in 1958. About seven thousand people paid up to thirty-five dollars a ticket, and the tone of the 1995 broadcast certainly reflected that, for the first time, the general public vastly outnumbered industry attendees. Hosting duties were assigned to the then-cast of CBC's *This Hour Has 22 Minutes*—Mary Walsh, Cathy Jones, Rick Mercer, and Greg Thomey—and their collective comedic experience was required for such a huge audience. As Stephen Stohn, who by then had become executive producer of the show, recalls, "The move to Hamilton truly was a pivotal moment in the history of the Junos. I think everybody who was involved is unabashedly proud of that decision. Part of that also included a shift toward making the show about the fans by putting them on the floor so that the performers could feed off that energy. That strategy worked like gangbusters, and I give full credit to the people of Hamilton and everyone at Copps Coliseum for making it happen."

"At one of the receptions, Sebastian Bach [of Skid Row] got close to her [Kim Campbell] and started yelling something about legalizing pot. It was fun, but it was crazy."
—George Fox

Barry Roden Photography

Top: Country Male Vocalist of the Year George Fox with Juno nominee Lee Aaron presenting at the 1991 awards.

Opposite: The Rankin Family performing on the 1994 Junos where they won four awards.

It was clear by the reactions of everyone who made it to the stage that this was a different Junos ceremony than any before. "I'm very happy that I did my best to stay in the moment that year," Jann Arden says. "I thought this is something I need to embrace because it's not going to keep happening. I was aware too that the awards didn't mean that I was better than anyone else. It was really just recognizing what was to me a very popular trend toward female artists at that time, although I think women have always dominated pop music in Canada. We're just far more interesting."

The night's other biggest ovations came whenever The Tragically Hip's name was called. In many ways the recognition they received as Entertainer of the Year and Group of the Year marked both a creative and a commercial peak for the band. It was a rare case when an artist's most adventurous work to date, in this case The Hip's 1994 release *Day for Night*, connected with an audience that was actually eager to hear them take their sound into uncharted territory. It was unfortunate that the band was not there in person to greet the Hamilton faithful, but they had a good excuse. The night before, they had appeared on *Saturday Night Live* at the behest of a former cast member, Canadian Dan Aykroyd, an equally monumental occasion in the annals of Hip lore.

Opposite: Sarah McLachlan performs at her first Junos, where she, along with director Phil Kates, won Best Video for "Into the Fire."

Left: Susan Aglukark won two Junos in 1995: Best Music of Aboriginal Canada for *Arctic Rose* and Best New Solo Artist.

Right: In 1996, the Canadian Music Hall of Fame inducted guitar hero Domenic Troiano.

Bottom: The Tragically Hip pick up their 1991 Canadian Entertainer of the Year Juno, their second of twelve over their career.

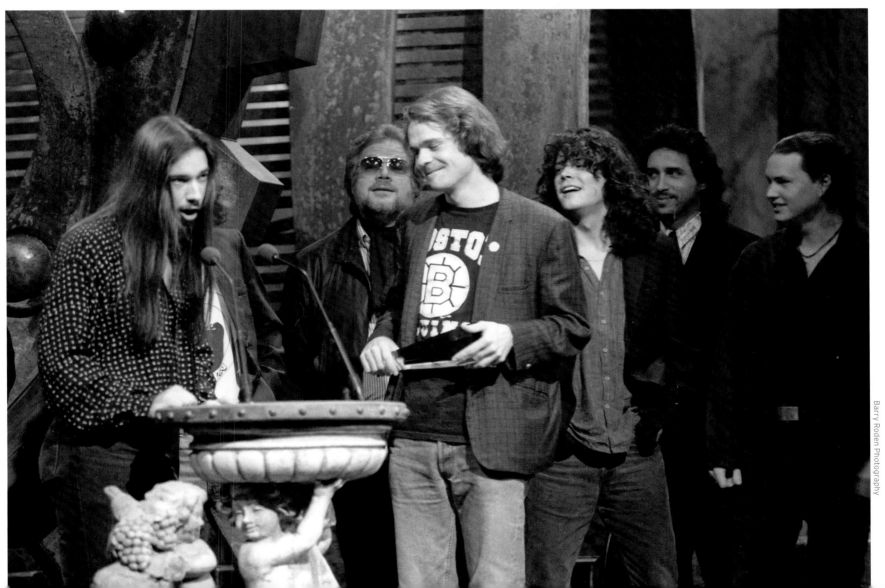

Yet the crowd's excitement only fuelled the indie rock spirit pervasive at that year's event. Vancouver rockers Moist earned Best New Group accolades, and provided one of the night's highlights with a gritty performance of their breakthrough single, "Push." Sarah McLachlan, nominated for Entertainer of the Year, provided another with a stripped-down, sexy version of "Ice Cream." Still, some were left scratching their heads when the first ever Best Alternative Album Juno went to *Shiver* by Rose Chronicles, beating out the arguably more highly touted *Twice Removed* by Sloan, *Naveed* by Our Lady Peace, *Forever Again* by Eric's Trip, and *Project Twinkle* by King Cobb Steelie.

For Sloan's Jay Ferguson, the notion that his band would receive a Juno seemed beyond the realm of possibility anyway, which made it even more surreal when he found himself presenting an award alongside Jann Arden that night.

Tom Sandler

Tom Sandler

Opposite: Vancouver rockers Moist earned Best New Group accolades, and provided one of the night's highlights with a gritty performance of their breakthrough single, "Push," in 1994.

Top: Ghetto Concept accept their first Best Rap Recording Juno in 1995 for *Certified* and would repeat their win the next year for *E-Z on Tha Motion*.

Bottom: The Stoney Park Dancers perform at the 1995 Juno Awards.

George Kravchyk

"At the end of 1994, our band had actually kind of broken up," Ferguson says. "We'd become really frustrated dealing with our U.S. label, so we were basically ready to pack it in after we finished our touring commitments at the start of 1995. When we got the nomination, [CARAS] asked if any of us would like to be a presenter. No one seemed interested, so I decided to do it because I thought this would probably be my only chance to go to the Junos." Ferguson flew to Toronto from his home in Halifax and took a bus to Hamilton but says his strongest memory involves being told by the director to just stick to the script. "She was adamant that if you ad lib, it will be really bad. But Jann Arden was so funny that we ended up ad libbing one little thing, and it worked."

Indeed, so many things about the 1995 Junos worked that there were few doubts the show could not repeat that success in Hamilton the following year for its all-important twenty-fifth anniversary. By the time the 1996 nominees were announced, another strong group of female artists, all of whom could boast international success as well, was poised to clean up. The arrival of Alanis Morissette, Shania Twain, and Deborah Cox that year underscored, in the words of CARAS president Lee Silversides, just how influential the Junos had become over the course of their history. "There's no question that talent from Canada could compete on the world's stage at any time over the past thirty years," he stated at the time. "It was our ability to make the rest of the world aware of the talent that was in our own backyard that took time to mature."

Further marking the occasion was the release of *Oh What a Feeling*, the first comprehensive collection of top-selling Canadian music spanning the previous twenty-five years. It would go on to be certified diamond (1 million total copies sold) and raise $3.2 million for three charities. "[It] was a very exciting time for our industry. We wanted to celebrate our official twenty-fifth anniversary of the Juno Awards by honouring the incredible artists that brought us here to date," says Randy Lennox president and CEO of Universal Music Canada. "We also felt that after twenty-five years, it was appropriate to give back in some meaningful way. We chose to put together a celebration…by bringing seventy-seven artists together to celebrate their music! What we ended up experiencing was just how incredibly difficult it was to actually keep this music contained within just four CDs as the music we listened to for this set was truly the legacy of a country rich with such diverse and world-class musical talent. Two additional volumes were released, bringing the total money raised for Canadian charities to well over $5.3 million."

Unlike the twentieth-anniversary ceremony in 1991, 1996 gave many more obvious nods to Junos past, not the least of which was the multiple Canadian Music Hall of Fame inductions of rock legends David Clayton-Thomas of Blood, Sweat & Tears, John Kay of Steppenwolf, Denny Doherty of The Mamas & the Papas, Zal Yanovsky of The Lovin' Spoonful, and guitar hero Domenic Troiano. But the Junos' milestone was best reflected in the choice of host, the artist with more Junos than anyone else, Anne Murray. She had attended the previous year, to present a lifetime achievement award to her long-time manager Leonard Rambeau, then in the final stage of his battle with cancer. It was perhaps the closest most had ever seen Murray come to being emotionally overwhelmed, so seeing her return to the Copps Coliseum stage with confidence was a reassurance to her legions of fans that she was still committed to them.

It didn't appear to be any coincidence, though, that organizers wanted Canada's most successful female recording artist to play a significant role on a night when the next generation was taking Murray's original breakthrough to previously unimaginable heights. With Shania Twain unable to attend due to illness—her sister Jill accepted the Levi's Entertainer of the Year and Country Female Vocalist Junos on her behalf—the night undeniably belonged to Alanis Morissette, whose *Jagged Little Pill* album was one of the previous year's greatest worldwide successes.

Opposite: Zal Yanovsky (left) of The Lovin' Spoonful performing with his former bandmate John Sebastian in 1996 upon Yanovsky's induction into the Canadian Music Hall of Fame.

Right: Amanda Marshall performing "Birmingham," which was nominated for Best Single at the 1997 Juno Awards.

This was a much different Alanis than the Most Promising Female Vocalist winner of 1992. Now in her twenties and writing emotionally engaging material, such as "Ironic," the song she performed that night, Morissette was the picture of humility as she accepted Junos for Album of the Year, Female Vocalist, Songwriter of the Year, and Single of the Year for "You Oughta Know." "Most people's growth is done in private, while an artist's growth is done in public," she said when accepting her first Juno that night, for Best Rock Album. "I thank Canada, the country, for accepting that in me." *Jagged Little Pill*'s unstoppable momentum was such that "Ironic" won the 1997 Juno for Single of the Year, and Morissette and her chief collaborator, Glen Ballard, shared Songwriter of the Year honours.

With Morissette ruling the rock charts, Twain ruling country, and Dion ruling pop, the Junos made another rare gesture in 1997 to acknowledge this unprecedented feat. Morissette was unfortunately unable to attend that year's ceremony due to touring commitments, but the picture of Dion and Twain jointly accepting their International Achievement award encapsulated for many what Canadian music now represented in the late nineties. "I think it was just coincidence," is Dion's explanation of why so many accomplished Canadian female artists emerged at that time. "Shania and Alanis are amazing, and

there are so many other great Canadian ladies (and men). For such a small population, we've got some of the best talent in the world, and when I travel to other countries, everyone talks about how rich Canada is in talent."

It would not have been inappropriate to include 1997's host, Jann Arden, as part of that International Achievement award as well. Although Morissette's arrival in 1996 prevented Arden from repeating her own triumph of 1995, Arden's second album, *Living under June*, was still attracting new admirers a year later. It would ultimately be certified five times platinum in Canada and gold in the United States, one million copies in total, by far the biggest-selling release of her career. As Arden's fame grew, it also revealed her fun-loving nature to the general public, something that was not readily apparent in her music. It was hardly a shock, then, to see her hosting the ceremony in front of another high-energy Hamilton crowd. Arden had them in the palm of her hand from the opening bit, involving her doppelganger crowd surfing.

"I was absolutely thrilled to be asked to host," she says. "It just seemed surreal, but I also realized that they knew I was funny and could hold my own. So it all seemed to make sense to show my light-hearted side, especially coming off of [her hit single] 'Insensitive.' I didn't watch the show afterward in its entirety, but I think I did a good job. I had great writers, and

they let me run wild with all of their ideas. It was a really fun night."

It did seem like a year where anything was possible, judging from the show's opening performance featuring Instrumental Artist of the Year winner Ashley MacIsaac and his band blasting their way through "Devil in the Kitchen," all adorned in wrestling masks. Unlike prior years, no one artist appeared to be favoured by the selection committee, and in some respects the winners reflected a changing of the guard. This was particularly evident in the country field, as Paul Brandt began his long-running streak of Country Male Vocalist victories and Terri Clark mounted the first serious challenge to Shania Twain's crown, picking up Best New Solo Artist in the process. The Best Alternative Album category was also well represented, with Sloan finally receiving a Juno for its "comeback," *One Chord to Another*, over East Coast peers Eric's Trip and The Inbreds. "Shania presented us with our Juno," says Sloan's Jay Ferguson. "I think we took pictures onstage of that. I still believe it's an incredible honour for an album with drums that were recorded on a four-track cassette."

Opposite: Instrumental Artist of the Year Ashley MacIsaac and his band opened the 1997 Junos.

Grant W. Martin Photography

Although it seemed to go according to script that Céline Dion once again took home multiple Junos, it was also another banner year for The Tragically Hip. Perhaps sensing this windfall—based on the success of the album *Trouble at the Henhouse*—nearly all of the band members were in attendance, and were greeted by fans with the now-familiar chant "Hip! Hip! Hip!" when they were called to the podium to accept Group of the Year, Album of the Year, and North Star Rock Album of the Year Junos. After guitarist Rob Baker made the obligatory thank-yous their first time up, lead vocalist Gord Downie stayed true to form in further illuminating an obscure yet significant contribution to Canadian culture that otherwise would have passed by barely noticed. He dedicated the band's first Juno of the night to that year's Walt Grealis Special Achievement Award winner. The award was given to Dan Gibson, a pioneer in nature sound recording during the 1940s and '50s.

Perhaps the most hotly contested category of that year, though, was Best Rap Recording, which pitted relative newcomers Choclair and Kardinal Offishall against the more established Rascalz and Dream Warriors, the last of whom had picked up where Maestro had left off with their internationally bestselling 1991 album *My Definition of a Boombastic Jazz Style*. The mix of artists clearly showed that Canadian hip hop was steadily gaining

ground within the wider industry, and there were few complaints when Choclair received the Juno for his EP *What It Takes*. Most acknowledged it was additional recognition of Choclair's success with his label Knee Deep Records, which also put out Kardinal's debut single, "Naughty Dread," as well as records by other notable artists such as Saukrates and Jully Black. By the following year, Choclair had signed with Virgin Music Canada, just as Rascalz forged a new partnership with BMG Canada. It all set the stage for what would be a major advancement of Canadian hip hop's maturation.

On the heels of their 1997 album *Cash Crop*, Rascalz put together a single in tribute to the solidarity that Canadian hip-hop artists showed during the 1990s in the face of limited radio exposure. "Northern Touch," featuring guest appearances from Choclair, Kardinal Offishall, Checkmate, and Thrust, had an immediate impact on the perception of Canadian hip hop both at home and abroad. The song cracked the Top-10 playlists of stations in most major markets across the country and scraped into the Top 40 nationally. The song's video also helped launch the careers of two more soon-to-be-familiar Toronto-born names in the hip-hop community, director Little X and model/actress Melyssa Ford.

Top: By 1997, Canadian hip hop was steadily gaining ground within the wider industry, and there were few complaints when Choclair received the Juno for his EP *What It Takes*.

Opposite: Rascalz perform at the 1999 Junos.

"Northern Touch" was released too late to be nominated for the 1998 Junos ceremony, held at Vancouver's GM Place with *Beverly Hills 90210* star Jason Priestley hosting. It turned out to be a night to honour one of the city's favourite adopted daughters, Sarah McLachlan, whose 1997 album *Surfacing*

and that year's inaugural Lilith Fair tour had propelled her to the front ranks of international recording artists. It resulted in her taking home Junos for Female Vocalist, Album of the Year, Single of the Year, and—with her long-time collaborator Pierre Marchand—Songwriter of the Year. In reference to the last, McLachlan said

at the post-ceremony press conference, "This is my favourite one. I came three thousand miles to get this." She added, "I've been doing this for ten years, and it's been a wonderful career. I haven't been an overnight sensation. Perhaps I wouldn't have these four awards tonight if Lilith Fair hadn't happened. It did put me into a completely new place in the industry, and in the public's eye."

Still, all of the good feeling generated by McLachlan's wins was nearly overshadowed by an allegation the Junos had never faced before. Rascalz's *Cash Crop* was nominated in the Best Rap Recording category and most within the scene anticipated it would win handily. This was indeed the case, but no one expected the group to refuse its Juno. They arrived at the arena after the award was presented as part of the pre-broadcast ceremony, and when informed that the rap category would not be a part of the televised Junos, members red 1, Misfit, and DJ Kemo gave a prepared statement saying that they would not accept the award on the basis of the Junos discriminating against urban-music artists. "In view of the lack of real inclusion of black music in this ceremony, this feels like a token gesture towards honoring the real impact of urban music in Canada," the statement read in part.

Other Canadian urban-music industry figures, such as Ivan Berry of Beat Factory Music, immediately backed up the charge.

Grant W. Martin Photography

"Five years ago, when we were fighting to carve out our profile at the Junos, there weren't a lot of [urban music] entries," Berry said. "For the past two to three years, we've had fifty submissions for [Juno] R&B and rap categories. Also, Canadian rap and R&B artists are now starting to scan some decent sales in Canada. How dare [Juno organizers] keep snubbing all of us." That message seemed to be received loud and clear. At the 1999 Junos back in Hamilton, "Northern Touch" won in the Best Rap Recording category and Deborah Cox's album *One Wish* won Best R&B/Soul recording. Both Rascalz and Cox performed on the televised program, hosted by comedian Mike Bullard.

Along with acknowledging the evolution of Canadian urban music, the 1999 Junos also reflected a dramatic shift toward pop aimed at a younger audience than ever before. For the first time, Best Album was expanded to include individual pop and rock categories, with Barenaked Ladies winning the former for *Stunt* and The Tragically Hip the latter for *Phantom Power*. Céline Dion's *Let's Talk about Love* won the overall Best Album Juno and was also named Best Selling Album (Foreign or Domestic). It left fans of that year's teen sensations, The Moffatts, disappointed at seeing them shut out of the major categories, although just having them take part undoubtedly boosted ratings. But for Barenaked Ladies—who appeared on the show via satellite from Australia—it marked

an impressive return to the podium after a six-year Juno drought. The band was also named Best Group and won Best Single for "One Week." "I think our focus on—and later success in—international markets was what sustained us, and what brought us back up to the dais again," Steven Page says. "Although we had continued to make successful records in Canada, I think there was still this perception in the business that we were a flash-in-the-pan or somehow out of favour. When the rest of the world started to take notice, the Junos celebrated that success with us."

Opposite: Deborah Cox at the 1999 Junos, where she won Best R&B/Soul Recording for her album *One Wish*.

Below: Bottom: Céline Dion performs "Let's Talk About Love" in 1999.

Grant W. Martin Photography

Even perennial indie darlings Sloan seemed retooled for the mainstream at the end of the decade, despite their *Navy Blues* coming up short in the Best Rock Album category. The band's performance of the infectious single "Money City Maniacs" did add some much-needed spontaneity to the show. Singer/bassist Chris Murphy even accomplished the seemingly impossible in getting all of the industry representatives, fellow musicians, and also federal Heritage Minister Sheila Copps on their feet and clapping, as an onstage bubble machine went into overdrive. Jay Ferguson recalls, "I think the original idea was to have flash pots on stage, but then whoever was in charge said no, we can't have that. Then of course ten years later when Nickelback played, the stage was basically on fire. So they let us use a bubble machine, which was kind of funny, but also kind of embarrassing as well." Ferguson adds that Sloan have always maintained a lighthearted attitude toward the Junos, using it as a chance to meet musicians they normally would never cross paths with, rather than as an opportunity to subvert the system. "Musically, we definitely felt like the odd band out, but backstage most often, even when we were hanging out with artists whose music we weren't particularly into, we found out that they were great people. So the Junos have always been a great experience for us in that respect."

Grant W. Martin Photography

Opposite: Sloan performing "Money City Maniacs" in 1999.

Left: Philosopher Kings' Gerald Eaton croons his best "Hurts to Love You/Let's Get it On."

It's indisputable that the independent revolution Sloan had played a major role in developing had made an impact on nearly all music made in Canada by the end of the 1990s. In 2000, the Junos would welcome a new crop of indie-informed artists on the rock side, while the next indie wave that produced Arcade Fire, Broken Social Scene, and The New Pornographers gathered momentum. There would be more and daunting growing pains to come, specifically the immense challenges posed by downloading, but Canadian music as reflected by the Juno Awards emerged at the start of the new millennium with its own identity and an ever-increasing level of respect both at home and abroad.

It was also an unquestionable fact that the leading Canadian artists of the 1990s were among the highest selling in the world, and moreover, Canadian writers and producers continued to boost the profiles of artists in the United States and Britain. Yet it was a decade that can be strongly described as the one in which Canadian music fully came of age artistically. A new generation took the lessons of its forebears who were forced out of Canada prior to the 1970s, and used them as primary inspiration in a pursuit to express the realities of life in small towns, inner cities, and suburbs from coast to coast to coast. Through this effort, these artists did more than their share to try to bring an end to the debate over what constitutes a Canadian identity. Yet, each time a new, significant voice chimed in, a whole different set of possibilities suddenly appeared. It revealed that Canada's cultural diversity was deeper than anyone could have imagined, and that our music was now the primary outlet for displaying that diversity. While it was sometimes difficult for some to see themselves in all of it, there was no longer any denying that the rest of the world had taken notice, giving Canada a rightful place on the global stage once and for all. •

1970s

1980s

1990s

2000s

In speaking with many people in different countries over the last few years, I 've noticed the respect, and curiosity, and support that people from around the world feel toward Canadian artists and songwriters. While their humourous question usually involves something about them wondering about what's in the water up here—my answer to them is simple. Canadians are a very passionate and expressive people; who care very deeply, who commune inclusively, who are socially aware, and charitably aware and who laugh very heartily—and that it only makes sense that some of the most profound and conversational music comes from here. My intention in taking part in this show with you tonight is to let you know how deeply grateful I am to have been born and raised in this blessed country, and to honour the brilliance that is birthed from such a place.

—ALANIS MORISSETTE

LONG MAY YOUR

THE AWARDS had been absent from their original host city of Toronto since 1995, but 2000 was a special year. Not just a new century or new decade: it was the new millennium.

The infamous Y2K bug had not derailed the Western world. It was business as usual—but in the music industry, the business model was rapidly changing.

Napster's file-sharing technology allowed people to share MP3s for free and, in 2000, the Record Industry Association of America filed a lawsuit to stop it. The media attention only increased the service's users. Downloading was becoming the single biggest threat to musicians' livelihoods and to the music industry overall. Album sales in the tens of millions previously enjoyed by artists like Céline Dion (200 million), Shania Twain (65 million), and Alanis Morissette (40 million) were becoming relics of the past. In the 2000s, superstars like Nickelback, Avril Lavigne, and Michael Bublé would only come close to Morissette's figures.

Pop band The Moffatts may have walked away from the 1999 Juno Awards empty handed, but the teen brothers, who sold more than 1.5 million albums worldwide, had their hands full with something bigger in 2000: hosting duties. The event was in the largest venue of the Junos' twenty-nine-year history: the Toronto SkyDome (albeit in a tented area that held about fifteen thousand people).

Sam the Record Man, the stalwart record retailer founded in 1937, was a sponsor of the 2000 Junos. (Sadly, the store would be out of business by 2007.) Sam Sniderman was such a familiar face he even had a cameo in the pre-taped Juno Awards opening. Spoofing *A Hard Day's Night*, sixteen-year-old Scott Moffatt and fifteen-year-old triplets Clint, Bob, and Dave were chased by crazed fans through Toronto streets. The band escaped by

BIG JIB DRAW

climbing onto a rooftop, then up into an animated blimp before "falling" through the roof of the SkyDome. It set the tone—the deafening screams of young girls—for the rest of the night. All The Moffatts had to do then was show up onstage.

"CBC tended to have more of a focus in those days on a bit of an older audience," says Stephen Stohn, then executive producer of the show and a CARAS board member. "So sometimes there were some skirmishes not even between the board members but people in the industry saying, 'Can't we get some younger, hotter acts on?'"

That year, they could: with The Moffatts as hosts, CBC and Lynn Harvey could skew the whole show to a younger demographic—the very people that bought the music and went to concerts.

Performers included Barenaked Ladies, rock band Our Lady Peace, rapper Choclair, and even pop act Prozzäk (the animated alter-egos of two members of The Philosopher Kings).

For the first time, the awards ceremony was split into two evenings: thirty-one awards were presented at an untelevised private gala dinner at the Metro Toronto Convention Centre, and eleven were awarded on television. This allowed winners more time for thank-you speeches without the commercial broadcast restraints. As the decade progressed, fewer awards would be presented on air, but the show wouldfeature more live performances.

Another first: CARAS had commissioned Canadian glass blower Shirley Elford to design a new trophy. The award was now a nickel-plated ribbon representing a music staff wrapped around a sleek glass human figure standing on top of the world.

Even the Backstreet Boys recognized the award's importance. The band won the Best International Album Juno for *Millennium,* and Howie Dorough and A.J.

McLean happily accepted—McLean doing a cartwheel onstage. After thanking the usual suspects, Dorough thanked Canada, "because you guys were the first ones to accept us here on the North American continent with open arms."

Later in the ceremony, the pair presented singer-pianist Chantal Kreviazuk with Best Female Artist. She was visibly emotional. "I really can't believe this," she said. "I'm totally overwhelmed right now. I'd like to say the company I'm in is really amazing," referring to co-nominees Céline Dion and Alanis Morissette. The day before, she had taken home Best Pop/Adult Album for *Colour Moving and Still*. These were her first-ever Junos.

Diana Krall also collected her first Juno, the inaugural Best Vocal Jazz Album award, for *When I Look in Your Eyes*. Another first-timer was Julie Doiron and the Wooden Stars, who won Best Alternative Album for their collaborative self-titled recording. This would mark a growing trend toward recognizing independent acts and labels.

There were a number of surprises given the stiff competition. The Matthew Good Band won Best New Group as well as Best Rock Album, for *Beautiful Midnight*. Choclair trumped Edwin, Bryan Adams, Paul Brandt, and Tom Cochrane for Best Male Artist, which spoke volumes about the respect hip-hop artists were earning from the industry as a whole.

Rarely does the Best New Group

Grant W. Martin Photography

honour have such an immediate effect on an act as it did in 2000. Nominees Gob, Len, Prozzäk, and Serial Joe have all since disbanded, but it was award-winning Sky that felt the fabled "Kiss of Death." Antoine Sicotte and James Renald had split weeks earlier when spotlight-shy singer Renald suddenly had enough. By the time the Junos rolled around, Sicotte had a new female singer and planned to continue the band under the same name. "That was the weirdest thing," recalls Sicotte, now a television chef in Quebec. "I was actually there with Anastasia and I ended up receiving the award alone."

The special achievement inductions were emotional, for different reasons.

Producer Bruce Fairbairn, who had passed away at age forty-nine the previous year, was inducted into the Canadian Music Hall of Fame. Loverboy's singer, Mike Reno, recalled how "exactly twenty years and four days ago" the band had gone into the studio with Fairbairn to record its self-titled debut, which became a North American hit. Fairbairn had then gone on to work with some of the world's biggest rock bands, including Bon Jovi, Aerosmith, AC/DC, Mötley Crüe, and Van Halen.

Top: Chantal Kreviazuk accepts her first-ever Juno in 2000.

Opposite: Bruce Fairbairn is posthumously inducted into the Canadian Music Hall of Fame by his widow Julie and sons Scott, Kevin, and Brent. She is holding a photo of Loverboy.

The year 2001 marked the debut of a bright light, Nelly Furtado, whose first album, *Whoa, Nelly!* featuring the single "Like a Bird," was flying up charts around the globe. Her album had been released in October 2000, and Stephen Stohn recalls CARAS having to convince CBC to make her a part of the Junos in March.

"You have to plan the show so far in advance, the thought of bringing on artists that weren't already number 1 on the charts was just something that was a bit of a change from the CBC approach," he explains. "It required, in some cases, a leap of faith, of moving quickly and moving to an artist who the CBC just may not have known was around because they hadn't quite broken yet, but we know this artist is fantastic. By the time the Junos is on, this artist is going to be breaking."

For Furtado's first Juno Awards, she received five nominations, tying veterans Barenaked Ladies for the most nods. She won four: Best New Solo Artist, Best Songwriter, Best Single, and Best Producer, losing only Best Pop Album, which went to Barenaked Ladies for *Maroon*. They would also win Best Group and Best Album.

The 2001 Juno for Best New Group went to Nickelback. During the presentation at the previous night's gala, front man Chad Kroeger joked, "Some people says this is the Kiss of Death award—so thanks a lot."

Alanis Morissette, who won two awards—Best Album for *Supposed Former Infatuation Junkie* and Best Video for "So Pure"—presented the International Achievement Award to Sarah McLachlan. McLachlan had changed the drawing power of female artists in the '90s with her top-grossing Lilith Fair concert festival, which also raised more than $2 million for women's charities.

In 2001, the Juno Awards celebrated its thirtieth anniversary at Copps Coliseum in Hamilton, Ontario. Host Rick Mercer pointed out that Pierre Juneau had introduced CanCon regulations three decades earlier. "Today, it seems that every country in the world has adapted their own CanCon rule," the comedian said. "They play Canadian music because it's the best music in the world." There were plugs throughout the evening for the second *Oh What a Feeling* box set: "a vital collection of Canadian music" which raised nearly $2 million for various charities.

A lot had changed in the span of a year, Mercer noted. "Remember back in the old days, before Napster, when you had to buy your music at a thing called a record store in exchange for a thing called money?" The courts had since shut down the service. "They say consumers have to stop ripping off the artist and leave that to the agents, the way it's supposed to be," he joked.

Page 116: The matching Moffatts sing and dance.

Page 117: Barenaked Ladies mount an attack.

Opposite top: An urban music tribute performance in 2001 including Snow, Maestro Fresh-Wes, jacksoul, Deborah Cox, Kardinal Offishall, and Jully Black, among others.

Opposite bottom: Gordon Lightfoot and Dr. David Suzuki induct Bruce Cockburn into the Canadian Music Hall of Fame in 2001.

To keep its younger viewers, the show included performances by The Moffatts, Furtado (who was introduced by Joey Fatone and Lance Bass of 'N Sync), treble charger, and soulDecision.

An amazing tribute celebrated fifteen years of the Junos' urban music categories, including R&B/Soul and Rap. The Philosopher Kings' Gerald Eaton and Tamia introduced the "pioneers and the poets" of urban music, among whom were Michie Mee, Kid Kut from Baby Blue Soundcrew, Snow, Dream Warriors, Maestro Fresh-Wes, jacksoul, Deborah Cox, Ghetto Concept, Rascalz, Kardinal Offishall, and Jully Black.

Heritage Minister Sheila Copps presented the Best New Solo Artist Award to Nelly Furtado. In accepting her award, she said, "The first thing that came across my mind just now, as I was watching this urban tribute, is that Canada is indeed a multicultural country, and that's what this [the award] represents. That's what it represents to me, anyway."

Latin music singer-guitarist Alex Cuba couldn't agree more. In 1999, he and his twin brother moved to Canada from Cuba and formed a band, the Puentes Brothers. A year later they were nominated for Best Global Album. It didn't matter that they lost to Jane Bunnett and the Spirits of Havana Ensemble (for *Ritmo and Soul*), as Cuba explains. "Even though we didn't win, it was our introduction to Canada. For me, it had a lot to do with the fact that I come from another country and the most important music award is recognizing me." It kind of made it official: he was now a bonafide part of the Canadian music scene.

Swollen Members won Best Rap Recording, beating frontrunner Kardinal Offishall as well as Baby Blue Soundcrew (featuring Kardinal Offishall), DJ Serious, and BrassMunk. The award would take the Vancouver group from the underground to the mainstream as fast as Prevail's rhyming skills. They would win that category for three consecutive years and again in 2007.

Another Vancouver-based group that was getting some mainstream recognition was indie collective The New Pornographers, who took home Best Alternative Album for their debut *Mass Romantic*. Their Juno marked the growing impact of enterprising labels such as Mint, Arts & Crafts, Last Gang, and Paper Bag, and their ability to break acts domestically and internationally.

Gordon Lightfoot and Dr. David Suzuki provided one of the highlights of the show when they inducted Bruce Cockburn into the Canadian Music Hall of Fame. They were the perfect choices to present the honour, symbolizing the way Cockburn's musical, environmental, and humanitarian work influenced and complemented one another. Sarah Harmer performed his "Waiting for a Miracle" solo. A video tribute followed with well-wishes from the likes of Bono, Jackson Browne, and Midnight Oil's Peter Garrett. Then, live from Prince George, Barenaked Ladies covered "Lovers in a Dangerous Time," which had been their first Top-40 hit, in 1991.

Cockburn's speech was articulate, moving, and thought-provoking, just as one would expect. "Over the years, there has been a wonderful flowering of creativity and spunk in our music scene, paralleling, often reflecting, other currents flowing around us," he said. "This spirit has developed into a widespread embracing of each other's music and cultures."

One other highlight of the show was a performance by The Guess Who, which prompted a standing ovation from young and old alike.

Over the next few years, the Juno celebrations would change dramatically, expanding in size and scope to match the remarkable domestic and international success of Canadian artists, including Nelly Furtado, Avril Lavigne, Michael Bublé, and Nickelback.

Meanwhile, there was cod to be kissed.

Grant W. Martin Photography

During Juno Week in St. John's, Great Big Sea's Séan McCann became the city's de facto host. "We were so proud," he says. "We took it very seriously. Everyone was looking for advice: 'Where should we eat? Where should we drink? Where should we go?'

"Junos previous to St. John's, driving was a big deal," he points out. "People would drive to Hamilton from Toronto. Just to get from venue to venue, everything in the big cities was so spread out. People were hiring limos and it all became a pain in the ass. So for St. John's, my Toronto buddies contacted me: 'We need a driver. We need this.' 'No, you don't. You don't.' 'Well, our hotel is here.' I'm like, 'You can hit the venue with a rock.' They couldn't wrap their head around it.

"We knew the city could handle it because it's not a big industry. It's a couple of hundred people, crazy people, all looking for a party. It's not a bunch of hedge fund managers or bankers; it's music heads. So they come to St. John's where there's lots of music and tons of bars and they're looking for exactly those two things."

At the legendary Ship Inn, Toronto singer-songwriter Ron Sexsmith played what he describes as "a little set." In the audience was legendary producer/musician Daniel Lanois. "Apparently, he was shushing people," laughs Sexsmith. "I always have my eyes closed [onstage] so I didn't know he was there until afterwards."

Grant W. Martin Photography

Grant W. Martin Photography

Grant W. Martin Photography

"Good luck to all the Juno nominees onboard," the Air Canada pilot said as his plane landed at St. John's International Airport, Newfoundland and Labrador, in April 2002. An unusual announcement, to be sure, and one not likely heard upon arriving at Toronto Pearson International.

The Juno Awards, like the musicians it celebrated, was hitting the road.

The idea had been brewing for some time, says Stephen Stohn. "CBC was going through, as it always is, tremendous budget restraints. The amount of money that they could provide as a licensee of the show was going down, not up, and taking the show on the road is a more expensive proposition.

"So there was this: Should we take the show on the road? Would it work? It was going to be an experiment. Of course, it ended up working beyond our wildest

dreams, but CBC at that point just didn't have the license fee that would enable us to move forward. CBC did a great job, but we wanted a fresh approach."

The CARAS board negotiated with CTV "for months and months," with the network offering a high level of sustained license fees "and all these wonderful ideas," explains Stohn.

"They didn't own MuchMusic at the time, but they did have other specialty channels and they had the ability to promote the Junos through a broader range of programming and a younger range of viewers than CBC had. So all of a sudden, you started to see ads in major American televisions shows for the Junos, which helped drive the audience. But the key difference was moving to St. John's in that first year, which was a leap of faith."

Most touring musicians skip St. John's. Because it's on an island (and is Canada's most eastern point), travelling there is simply cost prohibitive. So, in the spring of 2002, having major acts such as Nelly Furtado, Nickelback, Sum 41, Diana Krall, and American artist Shaggy on "The Rock" generated a street buzz more effective than any television commercial. From local cab drivers to shopkeepers to waiters to pilots—everyone knew the Junos were in town.

In the lead-up to the event, CTV had rolled out a splashy, pumped-up publicity campaign with tidbits and exclusive

announcements each week. It wasn't just the host city that was gearing up for the festivities; Canadians coast to coast to coast knew when and where and what the Juno Awards were.

Opera tenor Ben Heppner, working in a totally different music world, recalls sitting next to "an American rapper" at the Saturday-night gala dinner and awards, held at the St. John's Convention Centre for more than a thousand music-industry and political figures. Shaggy? "Shaggy, yes," he says, memory jogged. "I didn't know who he was. I had heard their [sic] name, but I wasn't familiar with their music. I came home and I told my kids, 'Shaggy sat next to me,' and my older son said, 'What on earth could you possibly have to talk to with Shaggy?'"

His son was right. "We didn't have any conversation," Heppner laughs. "He was concentrating on those to the right of him and I was concentrating on those to the left. More than pass the salt, I don't think we really spoke."

Besides revealing the nominees, presenters, performers, and emcee, the St. John's Host Committee added three special components to engage the audience: Juno Fan Fare, a meet-and-greet event featuring Juno nominees; a weekend-long JunoFest with national talent and regional up-and-comers playing in the local clubs; and the Songwriters' Circle, a stripped-down afternoon concert by a handful of notable songwriters who shared the inspiration behind their songs.

It didn't take long for the artists and music-industry types to fall in love with the city, the people, the traditions, and the brogue. The menus boasted cod tongues, fish and chips with stuffing and gravy, fish and brewis, and scrunchions. The most welcoming tradition of all was getting "screeched in:" repeating a short toast that includes the words "long may your big jib draw," downing a shot of Screech rum, and kissing a cod. After these ceremonial rites, you were an honourary Newfoundlander. This would be a Junos like no other.

Opposite left: Shaggy accepting the award for Best Selling Album in 2002.

Opposite right: Best Classical Album winner Ben Heppner acknowledges the crowd.

Left: Dance Recording nominees Boomtang Boys give it their best shot.

Great Big Sea multi-instrumentalist Séan McCann, a native son, half-jokes that it was "a bit silly" for them to participate in Juno Fan Fare there because everybody knew them. "Literally, 'Hey Séan, I'm your cousin,'" he quips. But Great Big Sea—local heroes who have sold about a million albums throughout Canada—ruled the music community in Newfoundland.

So when Barenaked Ladies were asked to host the 2002 Juno Awards, singer Ed Robertson quips, "I did feel very self-conscious and slightly embarrassed. Nothing says Newfoundland like Barenaked Ladies, all of our jigs and reels and fishing songs." He admits that "I was actually mortified at the thought, initially, that we were hosting in their [Great Big Sea's] hometown, but they opened the show, so they were looked after."

The performer lineup was top notch: Sum 41, Alanis Morissette, Nickelback, Diana Krall, Swollen Members with Nelly

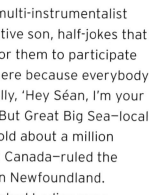

Shaggy, the Jamaican-born American reggae star who was performing on the Sunday show and was up for Best International Album, found "a pretty surreal kind of vibe" in St. John's that weekend.

"Here's a little town that's obviously not used to this kind of event, but people are making parties at the simplest places. You go to this little hole-in-the-wall and it's jamming with all these big stars so it kind of humbles you," Shaggy says, not able to recall names. "The glitz and glamour goes out the door and it just goes down to the natural you just having fun.

"It's really good because it puts a lot of those small towns on the map, even for one night. Not only that, when the Junos come to a particular city, you get a whole perspective on the city. They give you the history. Like Newfoundland, what do they do there? I think it's codfish. They do things like that where they tell you the whole nine yards, what they're famous for. It's an educational experience."

Grant W. Martin Photography

Furtado, Shaggy, Great Big Sea, Amanda Marshall, and the hosts themselves.

Barenaked Ladies had been working hard preparing for the Sunday gig. With the audience of 6,000 settled into their seats, the 2002 Junos opened with a hilarious clip the guys had filmed in and around town—beginning with them emerging from the ocean wearing wet suits. "For me, the great thing about that hosting role was that they actually let us do the stuff we wanted to do. It took convincing," says Robertson, who assured producers they would keep it funny *and* respectful.

There were plenty of BNL shenanigans over the next two hours, including a quirky live skit in which their drummer, Tyler Stewart, was afflicted with "Compulsory Drumming Syndrome (CDS)." Stewart drummed on the stage floor, stairs, Steven Page's and Robertson's backs, even his own head, until comedian Seán Cullen (dressed as "the Lobster of Healing") came to the rescue. Obviously, the gang had had too much Screech.

David Usher seemed genuinely surprised to win Best Pop Album for *Morning Orbit*. "I thought Leonard [Cohen] was gonna take it," he admitted. Glenn Lewis won Best R&B/Soul Recording for "Don't You Forget It" and thanked Denise Donlon and MuchMusic for starting to support homegrown R&B.

The country had already supported the international acts. Shaggy's *Hot Shot* CD, eight times platinum (800,000) in Canada at the time, was the number one sales territory in the world. Shaggy got the crowd jamming with his performance of "Wasn't Me." No surprise, he beat out U2, Backstreet Boys, Limp Bizkit, and Destiny's Child for Best Selling Album (Foreign or Domestic).

Despite not winning any awards, Sum 41 came out rocking with its song "Fat Lip," then donned metalhead wigs for "Pain for Pleasure." They must have impressed Nickelback's Chad Kroeger, who said, when his band won Best Group, "We're gonna share this with Sum 41, if

that's cool." Nickelback were big winners that year, taking home Best Rock Album (*Silver Side Up*) and Best Single ("How You Remind Me").

Diana Krall also took home three awards, including Best Artist. Krall, in accepting the award, revealed it was also her first time in St. John's, and praised the proceedings: "This is the best awards–most musical, best music–I've heard in a long time."

Concert promoter Michael Cohl was presented with the Walt Grealis Special Achievement Award for his many years in the music business. He was given a standing ovation after his tribute clip, which included congratulations from Neil Young, members of the Rolling Stones, and U2.

Daniel Lanois was inducted into the Canadian Music Hall of Fame for both his music and his production work. Among

his well-wishers were U2, Peter Gabriel, Willie Nelson, and Emmylou Harris–all artists he'd produced. Lanois came out onstage with his guitar. "What I have to say is pretty much wrapped up in this little song," he said, before singing "Sometimes."

Nickelback capped the stage performances with more pyrotechnics than the Junos had ever seen. (There would be more to come over the decade, as well as other Juno performances, as the band increased in popularity.) Robertson introduced the band by referring back to their 2001 win for Best New Group: "They have turned that award into a Kiss in Your Genital Regions."

The Junos was certainly now its own travelling roadshow. Municipal governments in different provinces were putting together bid committees to lobby the CARAS board of directors to host the

awards show and companion events in their city. The 2003 awards would take place in Ottawa, followed by Edmonton in 2004.

"What originally some people had thought would be very expensive, moving the show from one city to another, actually became a source of revenue for the program because all the cities and provinces across the country wanted the show to come to their town," explains executive producer John Brunton. "So all these cities were revved up to welcome the Junos."

Opposite: "Lobster of Healing" Seán Cullen (right) cures Tyler Stewart (left) of his Compulsory Drumming Syndrome.

Top: Great Big Sea bring the ceilidh to the Junos.

Page 124: Prozzak, The Philosopher Kings' side project, gets animated.

Page 125: Our Lady Peace performs "Is Anybody Home" at the 2000 Juno Awards at the Skydome in Toronto.

Grant W. Martin Photography

Grant W. Martin Photography

So what makes a successful bid?

"One is the desire to have us," says Melanie Berry, who became CARAS president in 2002. "We've been lucky that, since going on the road in 2002, host cities have been approaching us. Then, the key is having infrastructure in place to accommodate the events and people, from the hotels and all the cars right down to the suppliers and making sure that there's enough power to draw electricity. It's challenging to get all the pieces in place, but the benefit of moving city to city far outweighs any challenge because it adds a great new flavour every year."

While the appeal in St. John's was the quaint locale, people, pubs, and parties, the million-plus population of Ottawa-Gatineau wouldn't have the same vibe in 2003. The venues were quite spread out, with the main awards held at the Corel Centre in suburban Kanata, Ontario, and the gala dinner at Lac Leamy in Hull, Quebec. But CARAS expanded on the idea of taking the music to the fans and exposing the Juno brand. "It was a different model in St. John's, a much smaller version of Juno Fan Fare, JunoFest, and Songwriters' Circle," says Berry. "Ottawa really kicked it up a notch." More than 120 acts were showcased at local clubs for JunoFest, giving exposure to indie and developing artists not yet recognized by the Junos.

The year also marked the debut of the now-annual Juno nominee compilation album, *JUNO Awards 2003*, assembled by all five major labels—BMG, Sony, EMI, Warner, and Universal. The CD featured fifteen hits by artists such as Shania Twain, Avril Lavigne, Céline Dion, and Nickelback. A CD would be released every year thereafter, with each major label (now down to four) taking turns distributing and marketing with proceeds going to MusiCounts.

Since the majority of the Canadian music industry is in Toronto, 450 kilometres away, CARAS chartered a Via Rail train to shuttle about five hundred musicians and industry reps to

Ottawa. Some artists, like rapper red 1 of Vancouver's Rascalz and Montreal rocker Sam Roberts, chose this interesting option. When the April 4 departure date rolled around, many discovered they had made the right choice. Severe winter weather forced the cancellation of all flights out of Toronto. Some people decided to drive, battling the snow and icy roads.

The weather prevented many people from attending the gala dinner the next evening. Among the no-shows were Sum 41, who won Group of the Year, and Diana Krall, who received Vocal Jazz Album of the Year for *Live in Paris*, as well as Our Lady Peace, who took Rock Album of the Year for *Gravity*.

Broken Social Scene made it in to pick up Alternative Album of the Year for *You Forgot It in People*.

Undeterred by the snow, sax player Richard Underhill (formerly of The Shuffle Demons) showed up for his first Juno nomination and win: the Contemporary Jazz Album of the Year for his solo debut *Tales from the Blue Lounge*. Underhill then made the three-hour drive to Oshawa, Ontario, to play with Blue Rodeo. They would all be back in Ottawa the following day to perform the band's hit "Bulletproof" on the Junos complete with a horn and string section.

Opposite left: Singer-songwriter Ron Sexsmith courts the press on the Juno train.

Opposite right: The Juno train awaits departure from Toronto's Union Station.

Record business pioneer and Nettwerk Music Group CEO Terry McBride received the Walt Grealis Special Achievement Award at the gala. He delivered an eloquent speech, in which he briefly digressed to state his view on the Iraq war, a subject everyone else had ignored. "We are a country. We are a nation. War is being waged. The thing I want most is peace," he said.

It was hockey, not war, that host Shania Twain wove in and out of her script during the Sunday ceremony. Six custom-designed outfits emblazoned with different Canadian hockey team logos kept up the theme. She opened the show wearing a sequined Montreal Canadiens crop tank, jacket, and track pants, singing her single "Up!" while walking through the crowd slapping hands. She later donned an asymmetrical Edmonton Oilers dress and, a sleeveless Ottawa Senators dress, and braved the wrath of 12,900 people when she put on a sparkly Toronto Maple Leafs turtleneck—the only time she was booed.

Kathleen Edwards and Glenn Lewis presented the first award, Single of the Year, to Avril Lavigne for "Complicated," which beat out Céline Dion, Our Lady Peace, Blue Rodeo, and Sam Roberts. This was one of four Junos Lavigne would win this year, making up for her shutout at the Grammys six weeks prior. "I smile every time I see this video because it feels like ten years ago," she laughed. "We all look like little kids."

As artists and members of the music industry assembled in Toronto's Union Station to board the Juno train to Ottawa on a wintry April day, Snow could be found indoors as well. He got the party started with a performance in the bustling Great Hall, as travellers queued at the ticket wickets or hurried to their trains. "Playing in front of everybody getting their tickets and all the artists looking up, 'Hi, Snow,' and walking by, was pretty fun," the rapper recalls.

"The Juno train was either a public relations blessing or nightmare," says Roberts, now a six-time Juno winner, then a first-time nominee up for two awards, New Artist of the Year and Single of the Year for "Brother Down."

"We [he and his bandmates] were really still pretty wet behind the ears in all respects and I remember showing up at Union Station and [my publicist] came up to me while I was standing in line to get on this train and said, 'Your time in the press car is between this time and that time.' I was already three sheets to the wind.

"That's how we did everything in those days. Our mentality was 'This is probably all gonna disappear tomorrow so let's just live it to the fullest while it's happening," he explains. "When I got on the train, there was this wild raging party going on all around us and we were kind of in the thick of it.

"It was our little version of Festival Express for a couple of hours," he concludes, referring to the 1970 train across Canada taken by Janis Joplin, The Band, and The Grateful Dead, except there has been no Juno Express documentary made about all these goings-on.

Grant W. Martin Photography

Grant W. Martin Photography

In a brief but charitable aside, a short pre-recorded piece was shown of Alanis Morissette's and Jann Arden's visits to schools that benefitted from MusiCounts Band Aid Musical Instrument Grant program, which provides grants to elementary and secondary schools to replace old or broken instruments.

Then Arden introduced a performance by four-time Grammy nominee Remy Shand, the young multi-instrumentalist who would soon retreat from the spotlight, never to release another album. But in 2003, even he thought he'd be back. "We'll see you at the Junos in '05," he said after winning 2003 R&B/Soul Recording of the Year.

Sarah Slean and Jarvis Church (the solo stage name for The Philosopher Kings' Gerald Eaton), presented Songwriter of the Year to Nickelback. When accepting the award, guitarist Ryan Peake said, "This is supposed to be Avril's night." And it was: besides Single of the Year, the Napanee, Ontario, resident would take home awards for the New Artist, Pop Album, and Album of the Year for *Let Go*, beating Twain, Céline Dion, Our Lady Peace, and francophone singer Daniel Bélanger in that top category.

Swollen Members were presented with Rap Recording of the Year at the gala dinner, then performed on the show the next night–and were paid a surprise visit by Shania Twain. In one of the evening's funniest moments, she walked up to the

group in the stands, leaned forward to say hello to Morissette, and in a perfectly set-up joke, said, "Sorry about my butt there, guys. I would take a seat, but I wouldn't dare sit on a Swollen Member."

Presented by Doritos, the Juno Fan Choice Award was handed out by an "ultimate fan" contest winner and Theory of a Deadman to Twain, who would later win Artist and Country Recording of the Year awards for "I'm Gonna Getcha Good!" Theory of a Deadman would return to the stage to accept the New Group of the Year honours.

Sam Roberts gave his usual rousing rock 'n' roll all, ordering viewers at home "Off the sofa!" as the band kicked into

"Brother Down." k-os joined Roberts waving a white flag to the camera that read "No War," the only televised reference to the recent U.S. invasion of Iraq.

Shifting from politics to pop, Twain related the story of her first meeting with Avril Lavigne during a talent contest. Lavigne then took to the Juno stage to perform "Losing Grip." It led nicely to a performance of "Sk8er Boi."

Opposite top: The Ennis Sisters sing resplendent in white.

Opposite bottom: Remy Shand makes his first and only Juno appearance.

Top: People come out in droves to Juno Fan Fare, a free autograph-signing event.

Then Ottawa Senator captain Daniel Alfredsson and singer Molly Johnson presented the International Album of the Year to Eminem.

One of the highlights of the 2003 Juno Awards was Tom Cochrane's induction into the Canadian Music Hall of Fame. Blues guitarist Jeff Healey did the honours, reading his script in Braille. The tribute clip covered everything from Cochrane's days with Red Rider and his monster solo album, Mad Mad World, featuring "Life Is a Highway," to his humanitarian work with World Vision. The singer-songwriter received a standing ovation as he walked to the stage to the sound of "Big League."

Alanis Morissette won Jack Richardson Producer of the Year, beating Shand and long-established professional producers, such as Richardson's son, Garth, Arnold Lanni, and Bob Rock.

Jack Richardson describes that eponymous award as "an honour." "It's a physical manifestation of what's somebody's been doing over a period of time and it's nice to see people appreciate it."

As the show neared the end, Twain had proved herself a likeable, endearing host, plunking down cross-legged on the stage to sing "Forever and for Always." Tom Cochrane, along with Red Rider, then gave the 2003 Juno Awards a send-off with his biggest hits, including "Life is a Highway," joined at the end by Twain.

From the nation's capital, in 2004 the Junos headed west to Edmonton, taking with it Ottawa's own Alanis Morissette as host. The singer-songwriter—known for her serious side—turned out to be a talented showman with a definite sense of humour.

Another fan event was added to the Juno festivities, one that today many artists couldn't imagine the weekend being without: the Juno Cup. Jim Cuddy of Blue Rodeo (and Rockers team captain) founded the hockey game between the NHL's all-time greats and "a very ragtag group of Gretzky-wannabe rock stars," with all proceeds going to MusiCounts. The chance for these hockey hobbyists to play

with their hockey heroes made coming in early for Juno weekend an easy sell.

"One of the reasons that we felt that it would be a good idea is that it would encourage people to come to the Junos," says Cuddy. "Ten or fifteen years ago there wasn't a lot of enthusiasm for people to attend the Junos. Certainly, when they started travelling that was a big deal and they incorporated more communities and encouraged more people, but the idea of getting people there on the Friday night to play in a hockey game against NHLers, the party is better and it's more successful because there are more musicians there."

With fewer trophies awarded at Sunday's big show—which was becoming more of a best-of concert featuring fifteen performances—the gala dinner stretched to four hours. Some of the off-camera wins went to Michael Bublé for New Artist of the Year, Holly Cole's *Shade* for Vocal Jazz Album, Shania Twain's *Up!* for Country Album, and Buck 65's *Talkin' Honky Blues* for Alternative Album of the Year. "A Juno award is a Juno award and it's every bit as important on Saturday night as it is Sunday night," says CARAS' Melanie Berry.

Top: Wearing one of six custom-made hockey-themed outfits, Shania Twain holds a photo of Avril Lavigne holding a photo of her.

Bottom: Avril Lavigne sings her smash hit "Complicated."

Opposite: Diana Krall jazzes up the Junos.

Grant W. Martin Photography

Grant W. Martin Photography

Shania Twain's and Avril Lavigne's 2003 appearances and trophy triumphs in Ottawa's Corel Centre were extra special. In 1999, Twain gave the then-unknown Lavigne a rare break in this very arena. "I organized a talent contest in every city we visited," Twain recalled. "The winner in each city got to join me onstage and sing one of my songs...So on opening night...guess who rocked out to a packed house full of confidence?" She held up a photograph of Lavigne, with shoulder-length hair, wearing a blue V-neck shirt, holding a photo of Twain.

"I remember that Shania was onstage holding a picture of me, and in that picture I was holding a picture of her when I was fourteen years old," Lavigne wrote in an email for this book. "It was from when I had won a contest to sing on stage with her in Ottawa. Also, I remember Shania had invited me to her hotel room for tea the year she hosted. I was so young that I don't recall what we had talked about, but I do remember her being really nice."

The Sunday show at Rexall Centre featured a set by Insight Production's designer Peter Faragher, who came up with three stages that gave maximum visibility to the more than 16,000 ticket-holders. "I loved the set in Edmonton," says John Brunton. "It was very pure and simple, but really yin and yang. It was basically two stages on either corner and another stage in the middle of the arena. It allowed us to do performance after performance without a break because you didn't need to do a band changeover. I thought that was unique design."

Morissette's mischief as host began with a pre-taped segment of the singer trying to get past security but being refused entry to the festivities because her trademark bum-length hair had been cut short, making her unrecognizable.

Trying to get a ticket from a scalper, she tells him her name—and he sarcastically tells her he's Burton Cummings. So she grabs the ticket and runs off. With that, the thirty-third annual Juno Awards opened with a pyro-popping performance from Alberta natives Nickelback, now one of the world's biggest rock bands, with their hit "Figured You Out." Sarah McLachlan immediately emerged on another stage and went straight into the more subdued "Stupid," accompanied by members of the Edmonton Symphony Orchestra.

After a commercial break, Morissette got serious: "My intention in taking part in this show with you tonight is to let you know how deeply grateful I am to have been born and raised in this blessed country and to honour the brilliance that

is birthed from such a place." Then her silly side peeked out as she went to a clip of the host selection process. Sitting in a waiting area with just one other contender, a basset hound, Morissette is called in to impress Brunton and Johanna Stein with her various hidden talents: baton twirling, playing the triangle and the sitar, and a hat-toss (copied from *A Chorus Line*) that whacks Brunton in the face. The clip reveals that she gets the gig because k.d. lang is a "no" and the dog has a conflict.

The skits and performances made it easy for viewers to forget that it was an awards show. Nevertheless, the honours were doled out, with Nickelback receiving Group of the Year and Nelly Furtado took Single of the Year for "Powerless," from her second album, *Folklore*.

Next, Avril Lavigne performed "Don't Tell Me" from her second album, *Under My Skin*. Then, in another pre-taped clip, a fan runs up to Lavigne and asks to take a picture. The singer—who famously mooned the camera at a MuchMusic Video Awards ceremony—replies, "Why don't you take a picture of these babies," and lifts her shirt to reveal a T-shirt of two babies. "This one's Matt and this one's Evan," she says, referring to her bandmates Matt Brann and Evan Taubenfeld.

CARAS//Photo Inc.

Left: Measha Brueggergosman plays for The Rockers in Juno Cup.

Sarah Harmer never imagined she'd be able to say she was roughed up by hockey great Doug Gilmour. Seems preposterous. Even for Sam Roberts, who plays on a local hockey team, to be given a hard time on the ice by Tiger Williams seems something out of dream. But the Juno Cup has made it possible.

"If you call head-butting somebody and compressing a few vertebrae of their spine and then spearing them in the stomach with the butt-end of their stick a hard time, yeah, he gives me a hard time," laughs Roberts.

For some of the musicians who take part in this annual charity hockey game between The Rockers and the NHL Greats, it's better than any Juno nomination or win. "It's a highlight of the whole weekend, absolutely," says Roberts.

Hockey nuts George Canyon and Kevin Parent will actually fly in for it, even if they aren't nominated for a Juno. "The hockey game for me has always been the coolest part because awards shows make me nervous," says Canyon. "But hockey, just bringing all the acts together from all the genres, you still celebrate the music of Canada, even though you're playing hockey.

"The first Juno Cup I ever played, I took Gilmour out at the blue line. I didn't mean to, but he was in the way and I didn't see him and I slammed right into him and he went flying. I felt so bad, but since that time I've gotten to know Doug and he was in a Christmas special of mine."

Besides Gilmour, among the former NHL players whom CARAS has flown in for the game are Paul Coffey, Lanny McDonald, Mark Napier, Wendel Clark, Russ Courtnall, Brad Dalgarno, and the late Bob Probert. Many go to the awards too.

"The NHL Alumni have been really good," says Cuddy, the co-founder of the Juno Cup. "Mark [Napier], he runs the Alumni and he's been a great supporter and has really upped the game since we became involved with him because they know how to put on a bit of a show, so it's made a difference.

"They certainly understand how to put on these events and entertain the audience. Paul Coffey once did the accuracy shot blindfolded and actually hit a target which is further amazement, so I had to spin him around to make sure he wasn't facing the net. That kind of stuff is very entertaining for people."

To date, the Juno Cup has raised close to a million dollars for MusiCounts, via gate receipts, sponsor funds, and a silent auction. "That charity has benefitted a lot, not necessarily from raising money but because people know about it and more schools apply," says Cuddy. "And every community, we always have a former recipient band come and play the anthem. That's a really sweet thing."

The idea for the game grew out of another musicians-versus-NHLers charity game that MasterCard president Walt Macnee asked Cuddy to put together for the Bobby Orr Equipment Drive. "We did that at St. Mike's and it was a fun game, but the equipment drive didn't need a game. It took place in all the CHL rinks already so rather than disband the game, I proposed it to the CARAS board," says Cuddy.

"Music and hockey is such an easy marriage and we can do it as a profile thing for MusiCan. MasterCard was willing to be the sponsor for a couple of years, but then we were lucky to bring in the Keg. They have restaurants in the cities. It engages the local populace and tries to get people from the locale that have played in the NHL to play in the game. There's always a bit of regional pride and everybody feels sorry for the musicians."

Although Cuddy, who is team captain for The Rockers, says there are "no standards whatsoever," that doesn't seem enough to entice some musicians to hit the ice with pros.

"Not everybody wants to play in front of a crowd and be embarrassed. Being able to play hockey is not a requirement at all. In fact, some people who have come out, Kathleen Edwards and Measha Brueggergosman, they've been the most fun because they really didn't know how to play hockey.

"Measha in Halifax was such a gamer," Cuddy laughs. "She couldn't really skate and, well, just imagine trying to find a helmet to go over that hair, this big huge 'fro, but she got the audience's heart. So if an NHLer takes the puck from her or does anything that makes her fall down, they get booed, the NHLer, and the NHLers don't like that because they're used to being heroes. So, in this case, they're close to being villains; the more poor the musicians are, the more we're supported."

Harmer was one of the first women to participate. It was in Saskatoon and she even got her own dressing room. "I went out and got gear and played with some of my friends who play pick-up games and got myself ready a month before the big game," she reveals. So

were the boys kind to her? "Doug Gilmour and a couple of the NHL guys totally triangulated me," she laughs. "They completely roughed me up so I got a penalty shot opportunity. Nah, they were nice to me. It was fun—and Doug complemented me on my 1976 Guy Lafleur skates that I still wear."

Classified says that the Juno Cup is a definite highlight for him. "Since I was seventeen, eighteen years, that was my life, hockey," he says, "so when I had a chance to play against some NHLers—I always wanted to play in the NHL in my life and if that wasn't going to happen—this is the next best thing."

As one can imagine, the former NHLers always beat the musicians—except for one time in Vancouver. "They made a tactical error," says Cuddy.

"They wanted to win the game in dramatic fashion in the last minute so they allowed us to tie it up and I was the beneficiary of that. I was skating with the puck and I realized that the defencemen were skating away from me, so I went in and scored and tied the game.

"Then, they were going to send Lanny McDonald through the middle, bang, score a goal, which they did, and they wanted it to end like that 12-11. But there was still quite a bit of time left and with all the fooling around that happened after that, we went down again and tied the game and then we legitimately won in a shootout."

The score was 13-12. "It was hilarious," Cuddy says.

And yes, the scores are usually that high. "They score legitimate goals. We score penalty shots and we win something in the skills competition that's usually a cheat. Honestly, the difference between them and us, it's as if we're not even the same species. They could score at will. They felt that they could spot us 25 goals. They could start out 25-nothing for us, and they could win. So that's how confident they are."

Roberts says it doesn't matter what kind of hockey background you have, a passion for hockey is a must, "but once you are on the team, there is no joking around.

"So even if you are a plumber, a grinder on the fourth line, you still have to toe the line. You're playing against these NHLers, which puts you in this Harlem Globetrotters/the Washington Generals realm, the team they beat like a 150-2. So we're like the Washington Generals of the Juno Cup, but we're serious. We don't joke. People aren't smiling. Practice is intense. No sex—like the Italian soccer team."

As the night progressed, it appeared there would be no big winner *per se*. Céline Dion, a quadruple nominee, would be shut out completely, and Sam Roberts would emerge with the most awards—three—winning every category in which he was nominated. The rocker beat Nickelback, Sum 41, Billy Talent, and Danko Jones for Rock Album of the Year for his first full-length effort, *We Were Born in a Flame*, and was called up twice more, for Artist of the Year and Album of the Year. On his second trip to the podium, Roberts gave a shout-out to The Dears, Broken Social Scene, and The Constantines: "Whether you've heard of

CARAS/iPhoto Inc.

them or not they're out representing you in the best possible way." On his third, he alluded to *Lord of the Rings*: "This has been an extraordinary evening for our band. The second album, all of a sudden, feels as heavy as the ring on poor Frodo's shoulders. I don't really know what we're gonna do from here."

Nickelback may have lost Rock Album of the Year to Roberts, but the band scored the coveted Juno Fan Choice Award. Onstage, Kroeger said that he dedicated the win to "the fans who haven't met Nickelback yet," after having watched a girl on the news who was upset that she didn't get a chance to meet the band at the Juno Fan Fare autograph event at West Edmonton Mall.

Billy Talent was named New Group of the Year and had to go up minus a member. "We don't know where our guitar player is and I'm not kidding," said front man Ben Kowalewicz, as Ian D'Sa came running up. Sarah McLachlan won two of the five awards she was nominated for: Songwriter and Pop Album of the Year for *Afterglow*.

The highest recognition of the evening went to producer Bob Ezrin, who was inducted into the Canadian Music Hall of Fame by none other than Alice Cooper. A filmed tribute included congratulations from Peter Gabriel, Lou Reed, and film director Terry Gilliam. "I owe everything to this country," Ezrin said. "I'm so grateful to have been able to play

some small part in the cultural history of Canada." He then made a plea to the public, touching on the "dramatic cutbacks" to music in the schools and citing statistics on the benefits of the arts. "Keep music education alive in our schools," he implored.

One of the night's highlights—providing photos that were readily picked up by the media—was Morissette in a flesh-toned body suit with ridiculously exaggerated false pubic hair and nipples. It was her statement on her recent "little problem" in the U.S., where the first line in her song "Everything" was censored by American radio. Overjoyed to be back in the "True North strong and censor free," she removed her robe to reveal her "naked body." An assistant director, part of the shtick, told her, "You can't do that, Alanis. You can't show nipples." So she simply pulled off the velcroed private parts. Later, when she closed the show with "Everything," true to character, she sang the first line as it was meant to be: "I can be an asshole of the grandest kind."

She can also be very funny.

For the 2005 Juno Awards at Winnipeg's MTS Centre, the Juno Awards decided to go with comedian Brent Butt, star and creator of CTV sitcom *Corner Gas*. It would be the first time since CTV had taken over that a non-musician had hosted the show.

The announcer's introduction to the two-hour Juno ceremony centred on what

made Winnipeg special, and, in this case, relevant—the music. "Its musical history is legendary: home to The Guess Who, Neil Young, Bachman-Turner Overdrive, Lenny Breau, Crash Test Dummies, Remy Shand, Doc Walker, The Watchmen, Chantal Kreviazuk, The Weakerthans—tonight the legend continues."

Montreal pop-rock band Simple Plan kicked off the show, imploring everybody to "get up" as they ran through their hit "Shut Up." The camera pans of the darkened audience dancing and clapping showed an evening that was more a rock concert than an awards ceremony.

Brent Butt came out wearing a KISS-style black and silver one-piece and platform boots, playing a double-neck electric guitar. He admitted he looked foolish and soon changed into a tuxedo. Only eight awards would be given out on air, in between performances that included Feist; k-os; k.d. lang with the Manitoba Chamber Orchestra; Billy

Talent; Kalan Porter; Sum 41; and Burton Cummings and Randy Bachman joined by The Wailin' Jennys, Nathan, Fresh I.E., and The Waking Eyes.

Jann Arden, host of the non-televised gala event, honoured pioneering radio entrepreneur and philanthropist Allan Slaight with the Walt Grealis Special Achievement Award, which had been presented the night before. She joked that the non-televised awards were "all nude" but her contract allowed her to wear pasties—but she misread it as "pastries" and stuck on two cinnamon Danishes.

The most memorable moment from the gala was George Canyon's win for Country Recording of the Year for *One Good Friend*. Having nothing prepared, Canyon pulled out his cellphone onstage and called his wife, Jennifer, who had stayed home with their children in Okotoks, Alberta.

The televised awards would have some emotional moments too. While many top

acts were absent, one notable person was missing: Neil Young. The Winnipeg-raised rock legend was supposed to make his first Juno appearance in nearly twenty years, but in mid-March he had been diagnosed with a brain aneurysm. He had been treated in hospital earlier in the week and advised not to travel.

k.d. lang stepped in last-minute to replace Young and delivered two songs, the first a jaw-dropping rendition of Leonard Cohen's "Hallelujah," for which she was given a minute-long standing ovation. Prefacing the second song, her version of Young's "Helpless," lang called the honour "bittersweet" and described Young as "an artist who has maintained his integrity and his uncompromising vision and purity." She dedicated the song to him, saying, "Heal fast, my friend."

Other performances left their mark. Feist, who had won Alternative Album of the Year the day before, came out on a small stage solo to sing "Mushaboom," and experienced technical problems with her guitar. She knelt down at one point to talk with a stage tech as the audience cheered her on. Handling the moment with absolute grace, she continued and held her arms up in victory at the end of the song.

Opposite left: Host of the 2005 Junos, Alanis Morissette—a "bare-naked lady" flashes Edmonton.

Top: Sam Roberts won three Junos in 2004 for Album, Rock Album, and Artist of the Year.

Australia's Keith Urban was also on hand in Winnipeg, to banter via satellite with Sam Roberts, who was in Australia recording his next album. "Is the weather good?" asked Urban. Turning to look at the Sydney sky, Roberts replied, "Not really" and asked Urban about Winnipeg. Urban said it was balmy. "You're probably the first person ever to use the word 'balmy' to describe the Winnipeg weather in April," Roberts said. "It's gonna get a hell of a lot hotter," Urban segued, and Roberts introduced k-os, who had been nominated for a Grammy for his work with The Chemical Brothers. k-os then performed "B-Boy Stance" and "Crucial" from *Joyful Rebellion*, for which he snagged three Junos: Single of the Year for "Crabbuckit," Rap Recording of the Year, and Video of the Year (with Micah Meisner) for "B-Boy Stance." k-os smiled and said "Thank you" when he accepted his awards, but that was it.

Sarah Slean, jacksoul's Haydain Neale, and Burton Cummings had the privilege of handing out Songwriter of the Year to the much-respected and often overlooked Ron Sexsmith. The Toronto-based singer-songwriter had been nominated in this category in three previous years but had never won. "I knew if I kept showing up every year they'd have to give me one of these things," he said. He also thanked his muse, musician Colleen Hixenbaugh of By Divine Right.

Feist thanked Broken Social Scene

CARAS/iPhoto Inc.

and Apostle of Hustle for their inspiration when she won New Artist of the Year. "The most exciting part of this moment for me," she said, "is that I'm on the same stage with k.d. lang."

The Tragically Hip—one of the country's most inspirational and inspired bands—received its much-deserved induction into the Canadian Music Hall of Fame in 2005. Fellow Kingston, Ontario, musician and friend Sarah Harmer did the honours. "When I was sixteen, I spent a summer in bars across small-town Ontario watching one of the best bands in the world," she said. "The Tragically Hip had the magic then and they have it now." The rock band, which had by then sold 7 million albums, collected eleven Juno Awards, landed thirty Top-10 hits, been given a star on Canada's Walk of Fame, and even performed before Queen Elizabeth II, received videoed congratulations from an esteemed and assorted bunch including: hockey great Wayne Gretzky;

golfer Mike Weir; Rush's Geddy Lee and Alex Lifeson; Prime Minister Paul Martin; filmmaker Atom Egoyan; figure skater Kurt Browning; news anchor Peter Mansbridge; *Hockey Night in Canada*'s Ron MacLean; and environmentalist David Suzuki. Bypassing the usual speeches delivered by other inductees, The Hip did what they do best—they *performed*, but not just a by-rote TV-style performance: they ripped into smoking versions of "Fully Completely" and "Grace, Too," delivering one of the most intuitive and spontaneous performances in the show's history.

Billy Talent performed "River Below" and soon returned to the stage to pick up Album of the Year for their self-titled debut. Ben Kowalewicz made a point to give a shout-out to a ton of up-and-comers, including Death from Above 1979, Stars, and Arcade Fire. "We have so many amazing bands in this country," he commented. The band also took Group of the Year.

Sum 41 won Rock Album of the Year for *Chuck*, which had been named after UN peacekeeper Charles Pelletier. Pelletier had escorted the band members to safety after fighting broke out while they were travelling with War Child Canada in Bakavu, Democratic Republic of Congo. Sum 41's Juno performance of the ballad "Pieces," featuring a string section and front man Deryck Whibley on grand piano, included a backdrop of photographs from that humanitarian mission.

Avril Lavigne, Whibley's girlfriend at the time, was the top winner that night, taking the Juno Fan Choice Award, Artist of the Year, and Pop Album of the Year for *Under My Skin*. Lavigne, however, was unable to attend the ceremony because she was touring in Southeast Asia.

A curious new award was added in 2005: Adult Alternative Album of the Year, for which Sarah Harmer, Ron Sexsmith, Matt Mays, Rufus Wainwright, and Sarah Slean were nominated. Presenters Matt Dusk and Measha Brueggergosman didn't have a clue about the difference between adult and adult alternative. "We both have no idea what it means to be an adult alternative act," said Dusk. "So I looked up adult alternative on the Internet," said Brueggergosman, prompting audience laughter. "Do not do that, especially in front of your kids or at work." She then quipped, "If that is what adult alternatives are, then all these nominees deserve a prize." Harmer won without mentioning the strange category, saying, "I want to thank the songs, first of all."

The show ended with a raucous rendition of "Takin' Care of Business" with The Wailin' Jennys, Nathan, Fresh I.E., and The Waking Eyes joining Cummings and Bachman before going into The Guess Who's "Share the Land."

The love-in continued at the Junos' thirty-fifth anniversary in 2006. Returning the ceremonies to Atlantic Canada, Halifax played host and, with its population of

380,000, the excitement was just as tangible as it had ever been.

Actress Pamela Anderson, who was born in British Columbia, was tapped to host the main event at the Halifax Metro Centre. Quick witted and self-deprecating, she displayed a keen understanding of her public perception, often playing that up. But controversy started brewing even before the awards began when Anderson, a vocal animal-rights activist, spoke out against the regional seal hunt. She asked for a one-on-one with Prime Minister Stephen Harper but was refused, then faxed a second request at her own press conference on the Saturday. She warned the media her views were "bound to come out" on the broadcast.

The Saturday-evening gala dinner hosted by Jully Black was a straightforward affair. Winners included Daniel Powter for New Artist of the Year; Corb Lund's *Hair in My Eyes Like a Highland Steer* for Roots & Traditional Album of the Year; Neil Young for Jack Richardson Producer of the Year for "The Painter"; and K'naan's *The Dusty Foot Philosopher* for Rap Recording of the Year.

Opposite: Feist recovers from a technical guitar flub to win over the adoring crowd.

Top: Juno host Pamela Anderson shows off her high heels to the Halifax audience.

Bottom: Comedian Brent Butt channels his inner KISS at the Winnipeg awards.

137

Right: Sum41 poses on the red carpet.

Opposite top: Coldplay performs "Talk" in Halifax.

Opposite bottom: Black Eyed Peas perform "Pump It" on the 2006 Juno Awards.

Bernie Finkelstein, True North Records founder and Bruce Cockburn's long-time manager, was given the Walt Grealis Special Achievement Award. Finkelstein started out in the late sixties managing bands like The Paupers and Kensington Market. His label, founded in 1969, is the oldest in Canada and has released records by acts such as Murray McLauchlan, 54•40, and Blackie and the Rodeo Kings.

Cockburn himself received the first-ever Allan Waters Humanitarian Award "for his selfless participation in lending his passionate voice and music to social and political causes around the world." His activism includes poverty, peace, human rights, and the environment.

Helping Anderson emcee the televised event—and getting a kiss on the lips at the end as a reward—was rapper Buck 65, who provided the flow in between Anderson's sporadic appearances. The guy who rhymed the iconic Nova Scotia "Bluenose" with "Junos" listed off names of the upcoming presenters and performers, and, even if they didn't rhyme, his gravelly speaking voice sounded oh so cool. Not only did he announce the gala winners' names as they flashed onscreen before the commercial breaks, he also announced his own for Video of the Year ("Devil's Eyes") without a hint of self-awareness.

The stage set resembled a regular concert setting. The crowd was on its feet at the foot of the stage, surrounding the walkways and second stage. There would be ten performances, including Nickelback, Bryan Adams, Michael Bublé, rising pop-rock band Hedley, and indie-label acts Divine Brown, Massari, Bedouin Soundclash, and Broken Social Scene. The remaining coveted spots were given to Coldplay, from Britain, and The Black Eyed Peas, from the U.S.—a major coup from a broadcast perspective, but somewhat to the chagrin of some who felt the spots should have gone to Canadian artists.

Coldplay's front man Chris Martin recalls the event: "It was wonderful. It's very seldom that you get to go to places that end in the letter 'X.' As a band, that was a first for us. And we were very thrilled.

"It was also one of the only times we've ever done the red carpet anywhere. I have fond memories, but we were only there for about three hours though." Most acts wouldn't bother for such a short stay, but Martin explains, "On a very cheesy level, we feel very grateful to people in Canada who listen to our music. It's always been a place where we've had a good time and we've always felt like the audiences there are fantastic."

Anderson came out in a simple but revealing black spaghetti-strap dress and got right into the coy and playful sexual innuendo. "Bryan Adams and Chris Martin were tearing through catering, looking for vegan buns—well, right here, boys," she said, lifting the back of her dress. A little later on in her speech, she was even more obvious: "The Canadian music scene is bursting at the seams," she said—looking down at her chest.

As expected, she did not waste any time before slamming the seal hunt. "Unfortunately though, one of my favourite artists couldn't be here tonight —Seal. He was afraid he might get clubbed

CARAS//iPhoto Inc.

to death," she joked, and was awarded her first boos. A Vancouver Canucks fan, she mentioned, "But, as you know, I don't even mind a little blood on the ice—when it's a hockey rink. I hate seeing blood on the ice from baby seals." More boos. "I can take it. I got high heels and they dig in deep," she egged.

She then turned to another personally passionate topic, "sexy rockers," and introduced Nickelback, who led the 2006 Juno contenders with six nominations and had already won two the previous night, for Group of the Year and Rock Album of the Year for *All the Right Reasons*. The band tore into "Savin' Me," complete with a string section and the customary flashpots that erupted into impressive fireballs.

Bublé proved the year's big winner, taking a total of four awards: Album and Pop Album of the Year for *It's Time*, and Artist and Single of the Year for "Home." When presenting Artist of the Year with jazz singer Sophie Milman, Kardinal Offishall joked that he was going to give the award to himself, "seeing as they never give me a Juno." Bublé, with dramatic silliness, said, "I desperately wanted to win. Artist of the Year... I hoped that you liked my music, but to win Artist of the Year is to know that you actually love my paintings." Later, in picking up the award for his single "Home," he told the crowd: "This song was about every single Canadian. This song is about home, baby."

CARAS//iPhoto Inc.

Bedouin Soundclash performed its hit "When the Night Feels My Song" and then came back onstage to collect New Group of the Year. Singer-guitarist Jay Malinowski made a point to tell everyone that the trio had been together four years and it had been a "long trip" to get to the Junos.

Coldplay followed up by ripping into "Talk," during which Martin asked an audience member for a cellphone and sat down to mess with the keypad. Broken Social Scene—all sixteen members including Feist—delivered an equally strong performance of "Ibi Dreams of Pavement,"

with singer Kevin Drew yelling at the end, "Fight for better music, Canada! Fight for better music."

Martin had one more duty: inducting Bryan Adams into the Canadian Music Hall of Fame. It was also the first time he'd ever presented an award. "Bryan's a legend so it was nice to do that," he says. "But I'm a singer. There are certain things that when you join a band you're not told you're going to sign up for, like red carpets and inaugurating people." Going off-script, Martin rattled off some of the singer-songwriter's accomplishments, goofing around that he had performed in seventy-

two countries for over "eight people—oh, over 88 million people" and mistakenly calling him an "Officer of Canadian Customs, oh no, Officer of the Order of Canada."

Out of his entire catalogue, Adams played "18 'Til I Die," a song that epitomized his commitment to rock and roll, not to mention his eternal youth. "Being here tonight is really about the effort and time devoted by many people behind the scenes. It's not just the singer," Adams began. He proceeded to thank his family and everyone from every facet of the music industry who had helped him

CARAS/iPhoto Inc.

CARAS/iPhoto Inc.

Left: Simple Plan accepts their 2006 Juno Fan Choice Award.

Right: Broken Social Scene crowds the stage to accept Alternative Album of the Year.

Opposite top: Juno host Nelly Furtado flies like a bird in Saskatoon.

Opposite bottom: jacksoul's Haydain Neale accepts his Juno in 2001.

get where he is, most notably his manager of thirty years, Bruce Allen.

It was a good night for newer acts too. Dave Desrosiers and Jeff Stinco of Simple Plan picked up the Juno Fan Choice Award, and Arcade Fire won its first Juno for Songwriter of the Year. There was a new respect shown by the mainstream industry for the less mainstream artists. Broken Social Scene won Alternative Album of the Year for its self-titled recording, and the award was actually presented on-camera. So many band members went up to accept, people lost count. "We're an army, ladies and gentlemen; we're an army of friends," said Kevin Drew, a beer bottle in his hand. "Is there gonna be a change in Canadian music?" he said, adding, "Enjoy your lives!"

The Black Eyed Peas then took the stage to perform "Pump It." They had tied for International Album of the Year with Coldplay. Martin, the perpetual joker, gripes that they spent two hours looking for a saw to split the trophy. "We couldn't find one so they took the actual trophy themselves so they still owe us half of it. Those fuckin' bastards are still walking around with half of our Juno."

For 2007, the Juno Awards moved from the ocean back to the Prairies, specifically Saskatoon. Host Nelly Furtado, a bright, charming personality with an infectious laugh, was up for anything. So the show's directors did just that, dropping her from the rafters wearing a black glittery tutu with giant feathers on the

CARAS/iPhoto Inc.

141

back, a feather cap, and knee-high boots, "flying like a bird," of course, over the crowd at Credit Union Centre. From there, Furtado glided into some ribbons of fabric and pretended to lose her balance, frantically doing a kind of airborne breaststroke to propel herself. "Hey, don't look up there," she yelled to the people below looking up her skirt. "Put me down, please. Down. Down. Please," she said in mock frustration.

Once on solid ground, and her ruffled feathers smoothed, Furtado rhymed off a list of hometown musical heroes, such as Buffy Sainte-Marie, Wide Mouth Mason, and Joni Mitchell. "We may be on the Prairies, but there's nothing flat about our first performers. They're nominated for five Junos tonight," she said, introducing Billy Talent. The rockers broke into "Devil in a Midnight Mass," on a creepy set with two stark trees as props and a projected church background. For this Junos, the crowd on the floor was general admission, standing up against the security barrier, just like a rock concert.

Impresario Donald Tarlton, also known as "Donald K. Donald," was presented with the Walt Grealis Special Achievement Award. Tarlton started out as a concert promoter, but in 1969 he formed the Montreal-based record label Aquarius, which went on to sign April Wine, Corey Hart, and Sum 41.

Blackie and the Rodeo Kings handed out the first on-air award for R&B/Soul

CARAS/iPhoto Inc.

Recording of the Year, which went to jacksoul's singer Haydain Neale's first win since 2001. Neale looked snazzy when he accepted the award, dressed in a black three-piece J. Lindeberg suit.

The announcer ran through the winners from the previous night, then k-os took the stage to play his single "Sunday Morning." He was joined by dancers dressed in either long white dresses or cheerleading outfits, and a string section was positioned on a set of stairs in the stands. Partway through the song, as if it were part of the lyric, he sang, "This is not me. This show is propaganda." Most people probably missed it—and then at the end of the performance he smashed his guitar. It was one of those things that came and went, but his friends and people in the industry knew something was up.

k-os admits he doesn't know if his actions are "explainable." In a nutshell, he says, "It was more of an existential crisis about me being in the music industry. When I smashed the guitar and said the Junos is propaganda, it was a much deeper statement for how I felt about my life and my relationship to pop music at the time. It wasn't really just about the Junos. It was about wanting to having accolades but not caring at the same time; wanting to have songs that everyone could sing and penetrate, but then being scared of what happens when it does occur."

Furtado swept all the categories in which she was nominated: Single of the Year for "Promiscuous." Album of the Year for *Loose*. Pop Album, Artist, and Juno Fan Choice. Colin James and Rick Hansen presented Single of the Year. Hansen was famous for his 1985 Man in Motion World Tour, pushing his wheelchair more than 40,000 kilometres through thirty-four countries and raising $26 million for spinal cord research.

One of the show's funniest pre-taped skits featured Furtado, dressed as her "Tia Maria" (aunt) in a gaudy blouse and spectacles, with Michael Bublé. She was supposed to interview the crooner but kept raving about her fantastic niece. "You jealous," she says in an accent. "Have you ever hosted the Junos?" Tia Maria mentioned the duet Furtado and Bublé sang together, "Quando Quando Quando." According to Bublé, he did the duet because "I think she's sexy and I

142

thought maybe I could score with her." She whacked him repeatedly with her purse. Finally, the picture cut out as the "passion" between the two became too much. Later in the show, the audience saw the pair in bed, wearing silky nightwear, enjoying boxing on TV and a playful pillow fight. Tia Maria even stood on Bublé's back—still in her matronly shoes.

After a quick rundown of some more winners, Tom Jackson was honoured with the Humanitarian Award for his "unwavering support to Canada's hungry and underprivileged." Jackson had founded various benefits and raised millions of dollars for food banks, family services, and disaster relief.

Sticking to the charitable theme, Sam Roberts introduced living proof of what can be achieved when youth are exposed to quality music education, and demonstrated the immediate need for a national charity such as MusiCan, now known as MusiCounts: twelve-year-old local singer-guitarist Stephen Fischer. The kid showed off his skills with The Guess Who's "American Woman."

"That was heavy duty, Stephen," said Roberts, before turning his attention to up-and-comer Patrick Watson and his "dreamy cinematic approach to contemporary rock music." The Montreal pianist played "Luscious Life," which likely prompted more than a few viewers to take a mental note to check out his music.

You're either a red-carpet kind of person or you're not. It has nothing to do with worthiness or albums sold. It's a personality thing.

One would think multi-platinum sellers Coldplay would be pros at the custom by now, but front man Chris Martin denies it: "We don't really like talking to people in that situation. We're not very good with flash blubs and all that kind of thing. So unless we can provide our own lighting then we're very loath to do anything—I'm only half-joking."

Broken Social Scene's Brendan Canning has almost as much trouble with the red-carpet deference and media circus as Martin. The indie-rock collective used the fact it was performing on the 2006 Junos to come in a back entrance and avoid it altogether. "We're so not that band. I would really feel too silly, I think.

"I definitely felt like it was silly having all of us being interviewed and they take you in, 'Do press here; do press here,' and we're talking to Ben Mulroney and Tanya Kim [of eTalk]. Meanwhile, I'm thinking, 'Well, this is Broken Social Scene and despite the fact that people think we're this hip band or something, we're still under the radar when it comes to all the other kinds of artists, your Nickelbacks, your Célines.'"

But Deryck Whibley of Sum 41, a band that has sold millions of albums worldwide, also isn't into it. "I always feel a little, well not a little, a lot uncomfortable on red carpets. I prefer not to [do them]," he says. "I guess it's great for everybody else, but for me it's really uncomfortable. I never really know quite what to do and the second you get out there, there are so many people; there are so many other artists, I always feel uncomfortable to wave because I'm like, 'Well, they're probably not waving at me; I feel kind of stupid.'"

Classified, however, was proud to walk the red carpet. The rapper had been under the radar for years, but was starting to penetrate the mainstream in 2006. He had already put out ten albums by the time he received his first-ever Juno nomination for Rap Recording of the Year—and the event happened to be taking place in his hometown of Halifax.

"I ended up buying about thirty-five tickets for the show. I think we had the biggest entourage in the whole place," he laughs. "My entourage wasn't your average entourage. Mine was filled with mothers and fathers and aunts and uncles and brothers and sisters, so it was more of a family thing.

"Like we said, the Junos decided to come to Halifax so the fact that I was involved with it made it that much more exciting for friends and family. They all wanted to come. And Coldplay played that year. A lot of people were psyched to see that.

"For me, it was just great to get my name out there," adds Classified who three years later had a deal with Sony Music Canada. "It was my first time doing the red carpet, first time being on *Entertainment Tonight Canada* and *eTalk*. Definitely, it takes you to a new audience who normally wouldn't listen or even check for Canadian hip hop."

Opposite: k-os smashes his guitar at the 2001 awards.

Below: Tanya Kim and Ben Mulroney of CTV's *eTalk* host the red-carpet coverage.

When Billy Talent won Group of the Year in a tough category that included Alexisonfire, Hedley, The Tragically Hip, and Three Days Grace, Kowalewicz made a point to "share" the award with Alexisonfire: "We've been good friends with them and they've toured with us and we know how hard they work." Later they won Rock Album of the Year for *Billy Talent II*.

The Tragically Hip were there to induct Bob Rock into the Canadian Music Hall of Fame, but first they rocked out with him on guitar and piano for a version of the band's "Yer Not the Ocean" from *World Container*, which Rock produced. After

the performance, there was a short break before the induction. Gord Downie then emerged to give a lyrical, concise, literate speech, as only he could. Calling the esteemed producer "the rock 'n' roller, the fan star, the sound tiger, the self-imposed rock 'n' roll exile, the warm and interested and alive man of the world beyond guile," The Tragically Hip poet spoke fiercely and passionately about Rock. "He makes you want to sing your punk rock heart out and play your drums into the ground." With that, a tribute clip pulled together all Rock's accomplishments from his days with Paul Hyde in the bands Payola$ and Rock and Hyde to his production hits for

Mötley Crüe, Metallica, Bryan Adams, Our Lady Peace, and Simple Plan. Rock received a standing ovation and then thanked a ton of people.

New Artist of the Year went to Hamiltonian Tomi Swick, a musician whose name wasn't on the tip of most Canadians' tongues until his win.

The show closed with newcomer DJ Champion and his pumping, soulful dance track "No Heaven," which featured singer Betty Bonifassi—who would later move on to become one half of the electronic music duo Beast.

In 2008, Calgary, Alberta, got its long-awaited turn at hosting the Junos, a charge it could no doubt handle. Back in 1988, it had been the first Canadian city to host the Winter Olympics.

This celebration was a laidback country affair, reflecting the oil town's cowboy traditions; indeed, Calgary is often referred to as "Nashville of the North." Ironically, the Juno show at Pengrowth

Saddledome was hosted by Brampton, Ontario's Russell Peters, a man who couldn't be any less country.

The Canadian comedian of East Indian heritage had built a nineteen-year career making sharp observations on race, culture, and stereotypes. In 2007 he sold out two unprecedented performances at Toronto's Air Canada Centre and one at New York's Madison Square Garden. It was a brave move by CARAS and CTV; Peters would not play by the rules, but he definitely would be funny.

Performers were also decidedly more adult-leaning than some of the more recent Junos choices: five country artists (Gord Bamford, Aaron Lines, Johnny Reid, Shane Yellowbird, Paul Brandt); opera singer Measha Brueggergosman; Anne Murray with Jann Arden and Sarah Brightman; Michael Bublé; and the younger set—Avril Lavigne; Hedley; Feist; Finger Eleven with Mount Royal College Conservatory Calgary Youth Orchestra; and Jully Black.

Some of the nominee categories were the strangest in years. Pop Album of the Year pitted Feist against Murray, Bublé, Céline Dion, and Bedouin Soundclash.

The show opened appropriately with a five-star performance of Paul Brandt's "Alberta Bound," as footage of horses and hay bales flashed on the screen in the background. But on the stage was an opposing image: a mound of empty oil drums that Peters called a

"post- apocalyptic theme."

"We'll let a brown guy host, but the world has to end first," he quipped. The comedian then took swipes at everything from Nickelback's Chad Kroeger, for his recent drunk driving arrest ("They're gonna have to change the name from Nickelback to 'Get your licence back'"), to the Juno Awards itself.

Corb Lund and Suzie McNeil presented the first award, Single of the Year, to Feist. She would end up sweeping the awards, winning all five categories in which she was nominated.

Peters made some off-the-cuff remarks about how tiny Lavigne was and having a crush on her. Against the pink and black setting, with her blonde hair streaked pink, Lavigne—up for five awards—performed the buoyant "Girlfriend," a Canadian-flag hanging down across her butt.

Legendary singer-songwriter Ian Tyson presented Brandt with Country Recording of the Year for *Risk* before a list of the winners from the gala was announced: Arcade Fire for Alternative Album; Alex Cuba for World Music Album;

Blue Rodeo for Adult Alternative Album; and Jully Black for R&B/Soul Recording of the Year.

When rapper Belly and Deborah Cox took the stage to present the next award, Cox took the time to send her prayers to jacksoul's Haydain Neale. He had been hit by a car while riding his Vespa scooter in August 2007, and was still recovering from the crash. "Best wishes on your remarkable road to recovery," Cox said from the stage. Belly, a hip-hop artist through and through, joked that he "was actually listening to Anne Murray on the way here" and blew her a kiss. Pop Album, however, would go not to Murray but to Feist, who was overwhelmed and on the verge of tears.

Opposite top: The Tragically Hip perform "You're Not the Ocean" with Bob Rock, who produced the album.

Opposite left: Billy Talent won two awards in 2007—Group and Rock Album of the Year.

Opposite right: Bob Rock is inducted into the Canadian Music Hall of Fame in 2007.

Left: Measha Brueggergosman and Jully Black share a laugh.

Right: Russell Peters hosts Calgary.

CARAS/iPhoto Inc.

Belly also took home, from the gala, a glass statuette for 2008 Rap Recording of the Year for *The Revolution*. "It meant the world. As a Canadian artist, I say it time and time again—that's your stamp right there. That's your certification," he says.

Michael Bublé arrived onstage to talk about MusiCan and introduce three young jazz musicians: Ryley Bennett, Josh Crowhurst, and Elliot Cudmore, who had all benefitted from the program. Opera powerhouse Measha Brueggergosman, winner of the Classical Album of the Year: Vocal or Choral, then performed, capping a musical segment of styles that don't often get showcased on the Junos.

Media mogul Moses Znaimer was acknowledged for the Walt Grealis Special Achievement Award he had received at the previous night's gala dinner. Znaimer began his broadcasting career at the CBC, after which he founded CityTV and later created MuchMusic.

The next award was the Juno Fan Choice, which was presented to Bublé. "I'd like to thank Doritos for making such tasty treats," he said of the award's sponsor. "Seriously, sometimes when I eat them, my fingers, they go orange, but it's worth it." Then, after thanking the proper people, the always hilarious singer closed with, "This is for all those people that said that I couldn't vote for myself enough times to win."

Then it was time to acknowledge another legendary act, one that helped

CARAS/iPhoto Inc.

define the whole arena rock genre in the '70s and '80s: Triumph. Tom Cochrane did the honours, talking about how Triumph "showed the world time and again how to give bigger-than-life live performances." A retrospective video tribute backed this up, talking about their "unrivalled" pyro and laser light show, and their philosophy of "overkill."

This year, live performances took precedence over pre-recorded skits: the only one showed Arden giving Peters pointers on how to win over the Calgarians. When Peters was seen live following the clip, he was wearing a full cowboy get-up from hat to belt to boots. Of course, he gave it his own twist: "This cowboy thing is irritating," he declared, unzipping his pants and removing the stuffing in his crotch. "Now maybe Paul Brandt will hang out with me."

This segued into announcing Brandt's Allan Waters Humanitarian Award "for all the great charity work he does for others." The country singer raises money for children's hospitals and is also involved in the campaign against the trafficking of women and children.

The next award was given out by two Canadians who had won awards at the gala: Cuba's Alex Cuba (World Music Album of the Year) and Russia's Sophie Milman (Vocal Jazz Album of the Year), plus a third, World Music Album of the Year nominee Jesse Cook, who was born in France to Canadian parents. The three presented Group of the Year, a diverse category with Arcade Fire, Finger Eleven, Hedley, Kain, and the winner, Blue Rodeo. "This is stunning. I don't think we really expected to win," said co-leader Jim Cuddy.

Cuddy and Greg Keelor took a moment to acknowledge one of this country's most remarkable talents and music aficionados, Jeff Healey, who had passed away from cancer just weeks earlier. They then got down to presenting the last award of the evening: Album of the Year, to Feist for *The Reminder*. She thanked her "human shield," then turned to Cuddy and Keelor. "I recorded some of my album at Blue Rodeo's studio and I played guitar through their amplifiers and it is a very wonderful thing to receive this award from these boys right here."

With that, Peters introduced Jully Black to end the historic evening, singing her hit "Seven Day Fool." And just to get the last laugh, he ran up and put his arm around Black, and said, "This is the first time the Junos ever ended in brown and black."

Peters was so funny and irreverent that he was invited to emcee the 2009 Junos at General Motors Place in Vancouver, the third time the city would host the event. This time, he took everything up a notch.

For Nickelback's opening number, "Something in Your Mouth," Kroeger debuted a Swarovski Austrian crystal Gibson Les Paul Custom, designed for his Juno appearance by artist Amanda Dunbar, who hand placed six thousand individual crystals on the guitar as part of her Precious Rebels Collection.

"She took the logo from the cover of the [*Dark Horse*] album and put the crystals all over it," says Kroeger. "The design is just fantastic. It's very Vegas."

After that glittery display, Peters burst onstage with equally dazzling Bollywood dancers. Making his best attempt to join

in, he showed his true colours and break-danced. From the second he took the mic, his whole shtick was elevated from the previous year. Looking at the stage design—oversized multicoloured leaves and foliage—he quipped, "I know this is Vancouver but what's with the grow-op on stage? . . . Do you know what the street value of this stage is right now?"

"Pete [Faragher's] design was like a trip through psychedelia," says Brunton. "It had a bit of an Alice in Wonderland feeling to it."

Opposite left: Triumph's Rik Emmett, Gil Moore, and Mike Levine relish their Canadian Music Hall of Fame induction.

Top: Blue Rodeo accept Group of the Year honours in 2008.

Bottom: Nickleback's Chad Kroeger rocks the Junos with his dazzling guitar.

The Walt Grealis Special Achievement Award had been given the previous day to broadcasting veteran Fred Sherratt, whose sixty-year radio career began in Truro, Nova Scotia, and who later became an executive at CHUM Limited. CARAS and CTVglobemedia established a scholarship in his name to be awarded to eleven outstanding post-secondary graduates of Canadian music education programs.

Nickelback led the nominations with five, Sam Roberts came in next with four, then Hedley and Céline Dion with three. Other nominees included Michael Bublé and Kardinal Offishall who won Single of the Year.

Dallas Green won the first award of the night, Songwriter of the Year. The musician began his acceptance speech by thanking "anybody who's ever tried to write their own song."

Nickelback won Group of the Year for the fourth time. Obviously friends with the presenters, Hedley, it was a big hugging love-fest onstage with the two bands. "We should just get some chairs and crack some beers. It's been a while, fellas," said Kroeger. "We'll start smoking some of the stage. It'll be fantastic."

Right: Kathleen Edwards accompanies Bryan Adams for "Walk on By" in Vancouver 2009.

Opposite: Jacob Hoggard from Hedley performs "For the Nights I Can't Remember" on a red Baldwin piano.

A list of some of the winners from the gala dinner was then announced, including The Stills for New Group of the Year, Sam Roberts for Rock Album of the Year, Alanis Morissette for Pop Album of the Year, Kardinal Offishall for Single of the Year, and Serena Ryder for Adult Alternative.

Sarah McLachlan received the Allan Waters Humanitarian Award for her philanthropy. Not only has she raised millions of dollars for women's charities with Lilith Fair, but she has also established foundations to support music and arts education for youth in underserved communities.

Deborah Cox, Sarah Slean, and Kreesha Turner presented Rap Recording of the Year to Kardinal Offishall, who was in Europe and accepted by a pre-recorded video message. He said that there should be "90 per cent hip hop and 10 per cent lifetime achievement awards to Nickelback. You can only give them so many awards."

Following McLachlan's performance of "U Want Me 2," there was a hilarious pre-taped battle of words between Bublé and Peters in the dressing room, where the pop singer proved himself a worthy comedic foil. In the skit, Bublé assumed he was performing on the show because he did last year, and Peters had also returned. "We don't have time to fit you in," Peters said. Bublé shot back, "Maybe if your monologue wasn't so long, Russell, or you didn't do the waste of time with the dance number or you didn't harass the celebrities, maybe there'd be a little time for Bublé man?"

One of the highlights of the night was pop singer LIGHTS' win for New Artist of the Year. "It's really amazing that someone can do something independently and be recognized on such a massive scale," she said.

Move from rising star to legend, Loverboy was inducted into the Canadian Music Hall of Fame in front of a hometown

crowd by a fellow Vancouverite, producer Bob Rock, who had recorded the band's very first album twenty-nine years before at Little Mountain Sound when he was "a no-name engineer." The band had massive hits with "Working for the Weekend" and "Turn Me Loose," and sold more than 20 million albums worldwide. Singer Mike Reno, guitarist Paul Dean, keyboardist Doug Johnson, and drummer Matt Frenette were all on hand to thank their families and business colleagues, and made sure to speak of their late bassist Scott Smith for "his gift of music, humour, and eloquence" and to acknowledge his wife and sons in the audience.

The Juno Fan Choice Award went to Nickelback. "This is the good one," Ryan Peake said. "This is why we didn't get a real job. This is why we still don't have a real job."

After Bryan Adams' duet with Kathleen Edwards—a smouldering country-tinged version of "Walk on By"—it was time for another award. Feist, described as "last year's Queen of the Junos," and Jim Cuddy presented Artist of the Year to Sam Roberts, who beat out Bryan Adams, k.d. lang, City and Colour, and Serena Ryder for the award. "We are Sam Roberts," he said, "myself and my bandmates," and brought them up onstage with him as he always does.

Vancouver's Diana Krall and her husband Elvis Costello, who called the city his "family hometown," gave out the final

award of the night. An eclectic assortment of artists were nominated for Album of the Year—including Nickelback, Hedley, Simple Plan, and two francophone artists with retro cover discs, Sylvain Cossette's *70's Volume 2* and The Lost Fingers' *Lost in the 80s*. Few were surprised when Nickelback took the trophy. "The press are gonna have a field day with this one," quipped Kroeger.

Post-Junos, it was party time. Ron Sexsmith remembers Vancouver as particularly "star-studded," and one of the hottest invites was to Adams' bash at his studio, The Warehouse.

"I met [producer] Bob Rock on the curb waiting for our car to take us to the party," Sexsmith says. "Then he did my new record so that was kind of fateful, and at the party I'm sitting on the couch between Bryan Adams and k.d. lang. It just felt [like] I didn't really belong there." He also got up onstage and sang "Don't Be Cruel" with Bublé.

It's those types of magical moments that happen long after the two-hour Juno Awards shows are over.

After nine years, eight cities, and more than 27,000 kilometres, the biggest night in Canadian music returned to St. John's for the 2010 Juno Awards. The city was abuzz with excitement, particularly parents of young daughters trying to get Justin Bieber's autograph. The teen heartthrob was up for three awards and slated to perform on the show. Not bad for kid who hadn't even been on the radar.

The nomination list was a mix of the familiar and the new. Leading the pack was Bublé with six, followed by Billy Talent, Johnny Reid, and another newcomer, hip-hop artist Drake, with four each. In fact, this Juno Awards would see ninety-four first-time nominations, including Bieber, Drake, Carly Rae Jepsen, Danny Fernandes, Shiloh, Arkells, Down with Webster, Stereos, Ten Second Epic, and The New Cities.

CARAS founding board member Ross Reynolds was presented with the Walt Grealis Special Achievement Award. In 1969, Reynolds was president of GRT Records, holding the position for ten years and signing such acts as Dan Hill, Ian Thomas, and Moe Koffman. He would later become Universal Music Canada president and chairman emeritus.

Along with the many new artists embraced by the Junos, digital downloads of their performances would be for sale for the first time after the show, with proceeds going to MusiCounts. To shake things up even more, an outside, ticketed licensed stage on George Street was added to the televised event. Native Newfoundlanders Damhnait Doyle and Kim Stockwood hosted the outdoor festivities, while the indoor event would do without a host altogether. Juno Fan Fare, JunoFest, the Songwriters' Circle, and Juno Cup would continue now bigger than ever.

Everything seemed to be going smoothly, ready to welcome the Canadian music industry once again—until the notoriously thick Newfoundland fog set in on the Thursday prior, preventing planes from landing. Then, as if fog weren't enough, ash from a volcano in Iceland grounded all flights in Europe and the U.K. Many artists experienced long and frustrating delays, and a few couldn't make it at all.

Nevertheless, the show must go on, and those who could make it in, did.

CARAS/iPhoto Inc.

Thousands of ticket-holders filed into Mile One Centre and poured onto George Street. And what better cut to kick off the awards ceremony than Classified's "Oh . . . Canada" from his Juno-nominated album, *Self-Explanatory*.

From the arena, Bublé launched into his hit "Haven't Met You Yet." Just as it had over the last nine years, the ceremony retained its concert vibe, with people on the floor standing, close to the action, and artists and industry reps in the stands. Bublé made the most of it by walking through the cordoned-off pathway, slapping hands, on his way to a smaller stage. Confetti streamed down: the Canadian music celebration had begun.

Eight-time Juno winners Barenaked Ladies then took the stage, with drummer Tyler Stewart feigning the belief that the group was back hosting again, as it had in 2002. When told by Ed Robertson that nobody was hosting, Stewart said that "makes no sense."

"Tonight is a party, it's a chance for musicians to celebrate their own in the most musical city in Canada," Robertson explained. "We don't need some comedian or actor to come in and steal our thunder."

"What, Russell Peters couldn't make it because of the volcano?" mocked Stewart.

The group then talked about the "big battle" for Album of the Year, with Bublé up against Bieber—noting that if he won, the elder pop crooner would have the "dubious honour of crushing the hopes and dreams of a child."

The first award, Single of the Year, was then presented to Bublé. The normally confident singer said, "I'm nervous. I don't get nervous usually."

Next up was Justin Bieber, who was introduced as the youngest male solo artist to have two albums on the Billboard Top 200. He then performed to screams reminiscent of those commanded by The Moffatts back in 2000. Singing "Baby," with acoustic guitarist Dan Kanter and some male backing vocalists, he was soon joined by Drake, who draped his arm across the sixteen-year-old's neck and rapped.

Depending on the artist, different images were projected on the backdrop: for Bieber, there were multi-coloured stars and hearts; for Billy Talent, icebergs.

"I loved the set," says John Brunton, whose team includes producer Louise Wood, production designer Pete Faragher, supervising producer Lindsay Cox, lighting designer Alex Nadon, and director Joan Tosoni. "I thought it really had an ethereal feeling to it, like a Group of Seven painting, and it could turn into a spectacular, beautiful, modern-looking iceberg to a volcano. It was really versatile. We pushed our technology to the limit with this set. We've never done projection. We had, I think, sixteen projectors in the hall to try to create the look, so, in fact, a lot of times it looked like lighting that was changing, but to get that 3-D effect we used projectors."

Group of the Year, a solid category with Metric, Blue Rodeo, The Tragically Hip, Hedley, and Billy Talent, was given to Metric, the band's second win for these Junos.

Danny Fernandes and a contest winner presented the Juno Fan Choice Award, a cross-genre assortment of nominees including Bublé, Maxime Landry, Nickelback, Johnny Reid, and Ginette Reno. Bublé took this one too, and, in a slight variation on his 2008 Doritos comment, he said, "I would like to thank the sponsor, Pepsi. Pepsi tastes great in a glass, but in a Slurpee it completes me." On a more serious note, he added, "This is the best one. I mean, because we talk about our managers and our companies and all of that stuff but we don't talk about you enough—the fans. Without you, none of this happens. From the very West Coast to the East, black, white, rich, poor, gay, straight, thank you so much for supporting Canadian artists."

Somali-born K'naan was Artist of the Year at the gala and presented Bryan Adams with the Allan Waters Humanitarian Award. A tribute clip aired detailing Adams' lifelong philanthropy for causes such as whale preservation, Ethiopian hunger relief, breast cancer research, and poverty issues. Grounded in London due to the volcanic ash, Adams delivered a videotaped message from the U.K.

Opposite: Michael Bublé is the Juno Fan Choice for 2010. He also won Album and Pop Album of the Year for Crazy Love and Single of the Year for "Haven't Met You Yet."

Right: Drake (right) gets Justin Bieber (left) fever during an inspiring duet in 2010.

CARAS/iPhoto Inc.

Top left: World Music Album nominee Alex Cuba performs in St. John's.

Top right: K'naan won two awards in 2010 for Artist and Songwriter of the Year.

Bottom: Group of the Year Metric bask in their 2010 Juno victory.

"It's humbling and I'm honoured to receive this award, but I want you to know that it's a bit odd for me to be recognized for what countless people do around the world every day—people giving to other people with needs greater than their own. What I hope for in accepting this is it will inspire people to get out and get involved with what moves them."

LIGHTS and Dallas Green then presented what is always an important award for many of the nominees, Songwriter of the Year, which K'naan nabbed. "Last night, I won one of these things at the ceremony, for Artist of the Year, and I'm just as baffled as I was then," K'naan said. "Honestly, there is no greater dream than the one that comes true in the way of a song. I feel like you couldn't really write my story any better. K'naan here, and really appreciate you, Canada."

Despite not having a full-length album out yet, Drake won New Artist of the Year and dedicated the award to his mom. "She's responsible for not only the artist I am but the man that I am."

There were lengthy rundowns of the Saturday gala winners, including Billy Talent for Rock Album of the Year; Arkells for New Group of the Year; Joel

Plaskett for Adult Alternative Album of the Year; Bublé for Pop Album of the Year; Johnny Reid for Country Album of the Year; and Broken Social Scene's Charles Spearin for Contemporary Jazz Album of the Year, a category he was surprised to be in.

Hometown gal Amelia Curran, who won Roots & Traditional Album of the Year, also took the stage on Sunday to talk about the gala wins and gave due respect to Ross Reynolds for his "tremendous contribution to Canadian music." jacksoul's Haydain Neale won a posthumous award for R&B/Soul Recording of the Year. He had passed away from lung cancer in November 2009.

Of course, a Junos in St. John's could not go by without hometown heroes Great Big Sea, whose members introduced a performance by Blue Rodeo, the first band to take them on tour.

The induction of April Wine into the Canadian Music Hall of Fame was presented by the band's mega-fan Dave Cameron and Three Days Grace guitarist Barry Stock, who used to work for the group and played on its 2001 album, *Back to the Mansion*. Since the seventies, the rock band's legacy includes sixteen studio albums and such enduring hits as "Roller," "Say Hello," and "Just between You and Me." Myles Goodwyn and Brian Greenway accepted the honour.

The final award, Album of the Year, was a diverse category featuring Michael Bublé, Billy Talent, Diana Krall, Johnny Reid, and Justin Bieber. The award was given out by the Olympic freestyle skier Alexandre Bilodeau, the first Canadian athlete to ever win a gold medal on home soil. When Bublé went up to collect the statuette, he said, "This is amazing to receive an award from a real champion."

But there were still more champions to close the 2010 Juno Awards. K'naan began his song "Wavin' Flag" from behind a baby grand and then stood up as the band came in and the people in the audience waved theirs arms to the music. He was joined onstage by artists such as Drake and Bieber. During the 2010 Vancouver Olympics, more than fifty Canadian musicians assembled to record the song for charity with producer Bob Ezrin, under the banner of Young Artists for Haiti.

"It was certainly a shout-out to people across Canada to hold their hearts and think about giving," says Brunton, who doesn't recall that happening before at the Junos. "None of those international tragedies happened close enough to the Junos that it altered our content for the show to any great extent."

No matter what is going on in the world, music always has the power to lift and comfort, and Canadian music has never been more prominent. The Junos have come such a long way since their humble beginnings at the St. Lawrence Hall in 1970 with just 250 people in attendance (especially compared to the 16,000 to 18,000 expected at the 2011 Juno Awards in Toronto to celebrate the awards' fortieth anniversary).

"There was a time when the Junos were seen just as a cute little show in Canada," Brunton reflects, "and from this year's Junos, there are photographs in *Rolling Stone* magazine and *People* magazine and people refer to the show all over the world. So what we really tried to do is become a world-class show.

"When I first stared doing the Junos, even popular Canadians didn't want to do the show. Now, acts like Coldplay, Black Eyed Peas, some of the very biggest acts in the world, want to be associated with the Juno Awards because it seems to be one of the great awards show in the world, and our music scene in Canada is a scene that everybody around the world respects and would like to be a part of."

It's been eleven years since Canada's biggest city hosted Canada's biggest music awards celebration, and as the show moved from coast to coast, in many ways, it left a lasting impression, an imprint. Now, in many ways, it doesn't matter where the broadcast is from: Canadians have made the Junos theirs.

"It makes Canada feel more of an all-inclusive country," says Hedley's frontman Jacob Hoggard. "Not only did it start opening it up to an entirely different audience, but really started to give people that feeling of national pride. Sometimes, when everything comes out of Toronto, this big mystical city where most people haven't been, you don't feel included. When the Junos come to your city and you get to be the host city, it really makes you feel a part of the whole thing. From that point on, people are a lot more interested."

So when the Junos come rolling into Toronto, it won't be this big mystical city; it will be a big *musical* one—and everybody's invited. •

MUSICOUNTS

EXTENSIVE research on the subject of music education confirms that students who participate in school music programs derive immense benefit. "Music education is not just about putting an instrument in a student's hands," explains Steve Cranwell, executive director of MusiCounts. "Research proves it enhances cognitive development, fosters a positive attitude towards school and academics, lowers school dropout rates, and it gives the student the opportunity to take pride in being in a music program. We know music education can really transform kids."

This realization is at the very heart of the work of MusiCounts, the music education charity associated with the Canadian Academy of Recording Arts and Sciences (CARAS). The origin of MusiCounts (or MusiCan, as it was first known), dates back to 1997, when CARAS committed itself to music education in Canada by establishing a charitable organization dedicated to that cause. CARAS' share of the proceeds of the sale of the twenty-fifth-anniversary Juno Awards commemorative CD box set, *Oh What a Feeling*, fuelled the Band Aid grant program.

Through Band Aid, elementary and secondary schools across Canada have received $5,000 and $10,000 grants to replace old, borrowed, and broken instruments, thus ensuring continued growth in their music programs. As Melanie Berry, president and CEO, CARAS and MusiCounts, reports, "Students from all walks of life, low-income, socio-economically disadvantaged, and culturally diverse backgrounds have been given the chance to play music and further explore their own creativity."

The numbers chalked up by MusiCounts and Band Aid since their inception are now quite staggering. The program has revolutionized music education across Canada. "At the end of the 2010 school year, we will have raised $4 million, and that means over 265,000 students have now benefited from our Band Aid grants," says Cranwell.

Anne Turner, music teacher at Vanier Catholic Secondary School, Whitehorse, Yukon, can testify to the positive impact of Band Aid. Her school received a grant in 1999, something she says "made the students very excited and proud." In 2005, she took a class to Cuba, and the following year her Adult Senior Jazz band competed at the prestigious Lionel Hampton International Jazz Festival in Moscow, Idaho, taking home the Outstanding "B" Band trophy.

Success also comes in less tangible forms, as Doug MacLean, music teacher at Coast Tsimshian Academy, a school in a remote First Nations community in BC, explains. "The Band Aid grant provided instruments. The instruments provided opportunity. When an instrument could play nice music, the achievement then becomes quite personal. Parents, elders, students, and community could appreciate you. As a result, today our students are caring, courteous, respectful, and motivated. What a difference!"

In 2004, it was time for CARAS' music education program to shift into a higher gear. the program had grown to dozens of Band Aid grants per year, in addition to annual scholarships awarded at the post-secondary level. Srinka Wallia was hired as the executive director of MusiCounts and within just a few short years of her arrival, the charity enjoyed an explosion of activity. Several new initiatives were created, while the impact of the existing programs was increased considerably. It is safe to say that Wallia's vision and hard work is one of reasons for MusiCount's success today.

She recalls that, upon assuming her position, "I could sense there was an opportunity to bring the cause more into the limelight. There was fantastic good

Bruno Wong

will from the industry, so it became about getting everyone thinking, contributing, and participating. The groundwork had been laid, and it was upwards from there. It was hugely satisfying and gratifying to see the impact one had."

Sums allocated to Band Aid grants continue to be substantial, with sixty grants and more than $500,000 being dispersed in 2009. As Steve Cranwell observes, "It is absolutely essential for schools across Canada that we are available to assist them to not just keep their music programs going but to help them flourish."

Recent initiatives by MusiCounts have helped increase its profile and brought more attention to the issue of music education. In 2005, the MusiCounts Teacher of the Year Award was instituted to recognize the dedication of music teachers in keeping music education available to young Canadians.

The winning teacher receives a $10,000 cash award and a hand-crafted statuette, while an additional $10,000 goes to the school's music program. The prestigious nature of this award is exemplified by the superstar status of those artists presenting the award: Anne

Murray, Céline Dion, Michael Bublé, The Rolling Stones, and The Tragically Hip.

When Bublé presented the 2006 Award to Anne Turner, he noted, "I'd have loved to have been around a teacher as supportive as Anne, though I'm sure I'd have driven her nuts! It is scary what you can accomplish when you have someone who builds you up and makes you believe in yourself."

Since 1989, CARAS and (now) MusiCounts have been awarding scholarships to exceptional graduates enrolled in post-secondary music industry arts programs. Students enrolled in twelve partner colleges across the country receive these $1,000 grants annually. One such student, jazz pianist/singer Laila Biali (Humber College, 2000 to 2001), has gone on to become a multiple National Jazz Awards winner (including the 2005 SOCAN Composer of the Year Award). Nik Kozub (Grant MacEwan Community College, 1997 to 1998) and his band Shout Out Out Out Out were nominated for the 2007 Juno Alternative Album of the Year (*Not Saying/Just Saying*).

In 2007, the MusiCounts Fred Sherratt Award was established in partnership with CTVglobemedia. This annual scholarship is named in honour of Canadian broadcasting pioneer Sherratt, and recognizes the achievements, talent, and leadership of twelve outstanding post-secondary graduates of Canadian music programs. Recipients receive a cash prize of $3,500, a special certificate, and a unique opportunity to spend an educational day at CHUM radio and MuchMusic. Together, the MusiCounts Scholarships and the Fred Sherratt Award have been presented to more than two hundred graduates from coast to coast to coast.

In 2009, MusiCounts forged a partnership with the Polaris Music Prize. Half the gate receipts from the gala awards night went to MusiCounts, while an auction of ten limited-edition prints from the Polaris nominees brought extra funds.

Another new initiative is the annual Baldwin Piano Prize, launched in 2010 in conjunction with Baldwin Pianos. Previous recipients of Band Aid grants are eligible to compete for the much-coveted prize, a baby grand artist piano valued at more than $40,000. "This is a nice way for MusiCounts to reconnect with past Band Aid-awarded schools," says Cranwell.

A key date on the MusiCounts calendar every year is Juno weekend. The biggest celebration in Canadian music is a perfect opportunity for MusiCounts to get its important message out, while two Juno-related events have become significant fundraising tools. Proceeds from the always-popular Juno Cup (presented by the Keg Steakhouse and Bar) celebrity hockey game and Songwriters' Circle (presented by CMPA and SOCAN) go to MusiCounts, as do proceeds from sales of the annual Juno nominees CD.

Enlisting the support of the Canadian

Robin Hart Hiltz

music industry and its artists has never been an issue. All have rallied to the cause with real enthusiasm, and their commitment has strengthened over the years. "The artists have been incredible," says Cranwell. "Everyone we've worked with fully believes in the charity." As Michael Bublé has said, "MusiCounts will never have problems finding musicians who want to give back. I'm a lucky duck to be in this position."

Many of the schools that receive a Band Aid grant are subsequently visited by a leading Canadian artist, who can directly observe the students' playing the

new instruments. Check this out for just a partial star-studded list of those who have participated in the celebrations: 54•40, Alanis Morissette, Great Big Sea, Gregory Charles, Hawksley Workman, Jann Arden, Jim Cuddy, Barenaked Ladies, Jimmy Rankin, Jully Black, Kathleen Edwards, Nickelback, Remy Shand, Sam Roberts, Sarah McLachlan, Sarah Harmer, Serena Ryder, and Shania Twain.

Opposite: Sarah McLachlan performs for Multiple Band Aid Grant recipient schools in Vancouver, 2008.

Top: Youth Ambassador for MusiCounts, Nikki Yanofsky poses with students from Centennial Regional High School at Montreal, January 2010.

Fast-rising teenage jazz-pop singer Nikki Yanofsky is another true believer, as Cranwell explains. "We have just started a new program of Artist Ambassadors, and Nikki is officially on board as our MusiCounts Youth Ambassador. She will speak on behalf of MusiCounts whenever and wherever she can, and there'll be a mention of MusiCounts in the CD booklet of her new album. She did a wonderful Band Aid celebration in January at Montreal's Centennial Regional High School."

One of the dedicated volunteers assisting MusiCounts is Margaret McGuffin. She helps review the grant applications every year, a task she finds quite moving. "We always joke that we need to bring a tissue box to the meeting, she says. "The stories of how music programs change students' lives is energizing." McGuffin witnessed the impact directly when she attended a MusiCounts presentation at Driftwood Public School in Toronto's Jane-Finch area. "Jully Black made the presentation. She talked about growing up and the importance of music education in her life, and then the kids surrounded her and sang 'O Canada' at the top of their lungs. I cried! Music can change lives."

In her six-year tenure at MusiCounts, Wallia attended every presentation. "Each one was unique as we went from big metropolitan areas to small and remote communities," she recalls. "One enduring memory is of a presentation at Greenwood

Academy in remote Campbellton, Newfoundland, with Rex Goudie and Melissa O'Neil. It was a remarkable event, and as I was leaving a young boy came up to me and said 'Thank you for the best day of my life.' That was incredibly moving."

EMI Music Canada president Deane Cameron, the first vice-president on the CARAS board of directors and a MusiCounts Advisory Committee member, is justifiably proud of the way in which the Canadian recording sector has supported MusiCounts. "It has been amazing to see how the industry has gathered under this initiative. I can honestly say this has been one of the most rewarding parts of my career, as you really do feel you are significantly returning something to the community."

Former president of Sony Music and now general manager, CBC Radio

Denise Donlon was there at its creation and remains a passionate support and MusiCounts Advisory Committee member. She stresses that "all the existing empirical research supports the fact that having a solid music education in schools is better for young people in literally every way. It improves your socialization skills, your maths, it makes you a team player. Music education makes better Canadians."

Another longtime advocate for MusiCounts is record-label veteran, former CARAS chairman, and Advisory Committee member Ross Reynolds. In his view, "all of us who owe music for giving us a living feel it is important that there be an appreciation of music on a wide level. All the indications are that making music makes you smarter, so our programs extend deeper than just creating the next Juno Award winner."

Bob Ezrin, legendary producer, Canadian Music Hall of Fame inductee, and MusiCounts Advisory Committee member has perhaps said it best when it comes to the impact and importance of music education. "Music education in Canada is at risk. Our programs across the country are continuing to be cut because of budgetary restraints. Music is no longer a core subject in most provinces. We are losing a connection with our children that is deep, meaningful, and very important, not so much because want to grow the next Glenn Gould or Geddy Lee, but because through music education, through learning to play in groups, to focus, to take direction, to imagine and create things, through learning to experience true joy from accomplishing something, we are growing Canada's next leaders, our workforce for the future. We're growing our economy. It makes good sense to us as a country to ensure that we support music education in every way we possibly can."

Music does indeed count.

MusiCounts relies on your continued generous support of its valuable work. Donations can be made via www. musicounts.ca or www.musicompte.ca.

Opposite: Barenaked Ladies celebrate a Band Aid grant at Alexander Muir/Gladstone Public School in March 2010.

Left: Student from Band Aid Grant recipient school, Ernest Morrow Jr. High School in Calgary.

Laura Pedersen

ACKNOWLEDGMENTS

IT'S NO EXAGGERATION to state that this book has been forty years in the making and celebrates great music, amazing accomplishments, and unforgettable memories, none of which would have been possible without the dedication of a remarkable group of people. First, of course, a huge thanks to the millions of fans whose passion and loyalty to Canadian music makes it all worthwhile. We must also thank our dedicated Board of Directors, members, and staff, whose support of this project made it all possible.

To our artist contributors Anne Murray, Burton Cummings, Gordon Lightfoot, Jann Arden, and Alanis Morissette: a tip of the hat to you for all of your personal contributions. Thanks to all those artists and members of the industry who gave of their time to be interviewed for this book. A special thank you to Jim Cuddy, who honoured the book with such an eloquent foreword; a previous CARAS Board of Directors member, Jim continues to be an icon and mentor in Canadian music.

Further, thanks to our talented writers for taking us on a journey through time: Karen Bliss, Nick Krewen, Larry LeBlanc, and Jason Schneider. Your insight and recollections from Canada's musical past were as colourful as the artists who fill these pages.

A picture is worth a thousand words (or lyrics) and the stories could not be complete without all the photos that captured that perfect moment in time from our collective past. A special thanks to Bruce Cole for cataloguing and storing these memorable shots for forty years. Thank you to Barry Roden, Grant Martin, iPhoto Inc. (Alex Urosevic), George Kraychuk and Tom Sandler, for sharing their passion with us and being part of such a great collaboration.

To our partner, Key Porter Books, and the team of Carol Harrison, Tom Best, Michael Mouland, Martin Gould, Katherine Wilson, and Sonya V. Thursby, among others: a special thanks to you for your expertise and commitment to make sure it was perfect.

We would like to give a heartfelt thank you to the dedicated team of Jill Primeau and Kathryn Hamilton who have worked tirelessly on this book.

Thanks to our broadcast partners CTV and CBC, who have brought the best in Canadian music to a nation far and wide. Special thanks to our current publicity team Holmes Creative Communications Inc. and to our past teams of Andree Joffroy, Barb Fraser, Carol Marks-George, Chart Toppers, Creative Arts Company, Gino Empry Public Relations, Group of Four, Jane Harbury Productions, Joanne Smale Productions, NextMedia, Planet3 Communications Ltd., Richard Flohil, The Music Breakers, The Publicity House, and The Raleigh Group. Special thanks to our current production company Insight Productions and to our past teams of Maurice Abrahams, Jack Budgell, Bob Bowker, Cynthia Grech, Lynn Harvey, Rob Iscove, Judith Kangas, Jack McAndrew, Ron Meraska, Les Pouliot, Perry Rosemond, and Paddy Sampson.

Last and certainly not least we would like to thank you the reader, for wanting to share in all of our many accomplishments. We are so very proud to be able to present this to you.

Robin LeBlanc

LARRY LEBLANC thanks his family, wife Anya and their children, Robin and Sean; Kathryn Hamilton and Jackie Dean of CARAS; Juno co-founders Walt Grealis and Stan Klees for hiring me in 1965 as a trade writer; Marlene Palmer; Anne Leibold; Nick Krewen; and Carol Harrison of Key

Porter Books. Thanks to Ron Scribner and Tommy Wilson for introducing me to Canadian music. Thanks to John Bassett Jr. for "After Four."

NICK KREWEN: They say no man is an island. Here are my personal flotation devices for this project: Many thanks to Margaret Spence Krewen, CARAS, Jill Primeau, Carol Harrison, Jackie Dean, Kathryn Hamilton, Melanie Berry, Karen Bliss, Jason Schneider, Nicholas Jennings, Marlene Palmer, Lorne Saifer, Burton Cummings, Brian Edwards, Anne Liebold, Ngoc Huang, Gail Lagden, John Beaulieu, Steve Waxman, Joanna Dine, Sam Reid, Jessica Moore, Jennifer Mitchell, Richard Flohil, Michael Barclay, Kerry Doole, photographer Robert Nowell, *Niagara Magazine*, and the many participants interviewed within, including Mike Reno, Murray McLauchlan, and Sharon Hampson. Finally, I'd like to dedicate this chapter and offer a very big thank you to my fellow author Larry LeBlanc, for his lifelong sage advice, and encouragement, and for giving me my real start in this crazy business twenty-seven years ago.

JASON SCHNEIDER dedicates his chapter of the book to Dan Achen. He would also like to thank Wendy Rofihe, Dave Bidini, Céline Dion, Stephen Stohn, Wes Williams, Jann Arden, Tom and Kathleene Cochrane, Alannah Myles and Christian Michaels, Buffy Sainte-Marie, Steven Page, Brad Roberts, Jay Ferguson, George Fox, Kim Cooke, Jimmy and Mia Rankin, Cynthia Barry/SRO-Anthem, Joanne Setterington, Sony Music Canada, Bruce Allen Talent, Melinda Sutton/Epitome Pictures, Michelle Szeto/Paquin Entertainment, and Mary Mill/Maplemusic Recordings.

KAREN BLISS would like to thank her friends and family for putting up with her hibernation while she worked on this chapter. As well, thanks to Jill Primeau, Melanie Berry, Kathryn Hamilton, Brenna Knought, Jackie Dean, and Chris Topping at CARAS; and Carol Harrison at Key Porter Books. To all the publicists, managers, and artists who came through with interviews, no matter where they were in the globe: Anastasia Saradoc, Jo Faloona, Prevail, Louis Thomas, Chantal Kreviazuk, Cristina Fernandes, red 1, Coalition Entertainment, David Tysowski, Dave Spencer, Eggplant Entertainment, Sarah Fenton, Darren Gilmore, Dawn Dwyer, Jessica Zambri, Christina Rentz, Antoine Sicotte, Andres Mendoza, Maple Music, Strut Entertainment, Michaela Neale, Steve Waxman, Joanna Dine, Sean Cordner, Tina Kennedy, Sander Shalinsky, Manny Dion, Tyson Parker, Sol Guy, Snow, Charlotte Thompson, Amanda Persi, Suzie McNeil, Starfish Entertainment, Joanne Setterington, Joanna Dine, Sandy Pandya, Matt Attfield, Ron Kitchener, Carla Palmer, Jeff "Kue" Esposito, Anya Wilson, Stephen Stohn, Insight Productions, Jack Richardson, Chris Nary at Red Light Management, and Elaine Tennyson. I would also like to thank my sounding boards Nick Krewen and Larry LeBlanc, as well as David Farrell for giving me my first trade paper gig, which helped shape my interest in the business side of music. To Linux Caffe for letting me escape my house to work for hours and hours. And, lastly, to all the musicians who, quite frankly, make my life's "work" so much fun. I dedicate my chapter to the shining star Haydain Neale and the one and only Jeff Healey.

APPENDIX

JUNO AWARD WINNERS 1970–2010

Note: Winners are listed by show year.

1970

Dianne Leigh..Top Country Female Artist
The Mercey Brothers ....Top Country Instrumental Vocal Group
Tommy Hunter..Top Country Male Artist
Ginette Reno...Top Female Vocalist
The Guess Who ....Top Vocal Instrumental Group
Andy Kim..Top Male Vocalist
Gordon Lightfoot..Top Folksinger (or Group)
Which Way You Goin' Billy–Poppy Family.......................Best Produced Single
Quality Records......................................Top Canadian Content Company
Capitol Records.................Top Record Company in Promotional Activities
RCA Records...Top Record Company
CKLG Vancouver...................Special RPM Radio Award For Community Activities
Saul Holiff..................Canadian Industry Music Industry Man of the Year

1971

Myrna Lorrie... Top Country Singer Female
The Mercey Brothers ....Top Country Instrumental Vocal Group
Stompin' Tom Connors .... Top Country Singer Male
Anne Murray.. Top Female Vocalist
The Guess Who ....Top Vocal Instrumental Group
Gordon Lightfoot.. Top Male Vocalist
Gene MacLellan......................................Special Award: Canadian Composer
Bruce Cockburn .... Top Folk Singer (or Group)
Brian Ahern–Snowbird by Anne Murray.........................Best Produced Single
Brian Ahern–Honey, Wheat & Laughter by Anne Murray.......Best Produced MOR Album
Quality Records...Top Canadian Content Company
Capitol Records.......................Top Record Company in Promotional Activities
Capitol Records.....................................Top Record Company
Standard Broadcasting ....Broadcaster of the Year
Dave Boist–Montreal Gazette.......................... Music Journalist of the Year
Pierre Juneau....................................Music Industry Man of the Year

1972

Myrna Lorrie...Female Country Singer of the Year
The Mercey Brothers ....Country Group of the Year
Stompin' Tom Connors ....Male Country Singer of the Year
Anne Murray..Female Vocalist of the Year

Ginette Reno....................Outstanding Performance of the Year, Female
Lighthouse ....Outstanding Performance of the Year, Group
The Stampeders .... Vocal Instrumental Group of the Year
Gordon Lightfoot.................................Male Vocalist of the Year
Joey Gregorash.............Outstanding Performance of the Year, Male
Rich Dodson....................................Composer of the Year
Bruce Cockburn ....Folksinger of the Year
Mel Shaw–Sweet City Woman by The Stampeders.............Best Produced Single
Brian Ahern–Talk It Over In The Morning by Anne Murray....Best Produced MOR Album
GRT of Canada ....Canadian Content Company of the Year
Kinney Music of Canada....................Record Company in Promotional Activities
Kinney Music of Canada.................... Record Company of the Year
The CHUM Group ....Broadcaster of the Year
Ritchie Yorke.................................. Music Journalist of the year
George Hamilton IV ....Special Juno for Contribution to Canadian Music

1973

Shirley Eikhard ....Female Country Singer of the Year
The Mercey Brothers ....Country Group of the Year
Stompin' Tom Connors ....Male Country Singer of the Year
Anne Murray....................................Female Vocalist of the Year
Ginette Reno.................Outstanding Performance of the Year, Female
Edward Bear ....Outstanding Performance of the Year, Group
Lighthouse .... Vocal Instrumental Group of the Year
Bob McBride.................Outstanding Performance of the Year, Male
Gordon Lightfoot.................................Male Vocalist of the Year
Gordon Lightfoot.................................Composer of the Year
Bruce Cockburn ....Folksinger of the Year
Valdy.................Outstanding Performance of the Year, Folk
Gene Martynec–Last Song by Edward Bear ....Best Produced Single
Brian Ahern–Annie by Anne Murray .... Best Produced MOR Album
Capitol Records................................Canadian Content Company of the Year
RCA Ltd. ....Promotion Company of the Year
WEA Music of Canada Ltd......................... Record Company of the Year
VOCM, St. John's, Newfoundland ....Broadcaster of the Year
Arnold Gosewich ....Music Industry Man of the Year
Peter Goddard .... Music Journalist of the year
David Clayton-Thomas.............Outstanding Contribution to the Canadian Music Scene

1974

Danny's Song—Anne Murray	Pop Music Album of the Year
Bachman-Turner Overdrive	Contemporary Album of the Year
To It And At It—Stompin' Tom Connors	Country Album of the Year
Shirley Eikhard	Best Country Female Artist
The Mercey Brothers	Country Group of the Year
Stompin' Tom Connors	Country Male Vocalist of the Year
Anne Murray	Country Female Vocalist of the Year
Lighthouse	Group of the Year
Terry Jacks	Male Vocalist of the Year
Farmer's Song—Murray McLauchlan	Country Single of the Year
Farmer's Song—Murray McLauchlan	Folk Single of the Year
Seasons in the Sun—Terry Jacks	Contemporary Single of the Year
Seasons in the Sun—Terry Jacks	Pop Music Single of the Year
Murray McLauchlan	Best Songwriter
Old Dan's Records—Gordon Lightfoot	Folk Album of the Year
Cathy Young	Most Promising Female Vocalist of the Year
Bachman-Turner Overdrive	Most Promising Group of the Year
Ian Thomas	Most Promising Male Vocalist of the Year
Valdy	Folksinger of the Year
Dave Nichol	Most Promising Folk Singer of the Year
True North Records	Independent Label of the Year
GRT of Canada	Canadian Content Company of the Year
A&M Records	Record Company in Promotional Activities
WEA Music of Canada Ltd.	Record Company of the Year

1975

Bart Schoales	Best Album Graphics
Not Fragile—Bachman-Turner Overdrive	Best Selling Album
Band on the Run—Paul McCartney	Best Selling International Album
The Night Chicago Died—Paper Lace	Best Selling International Single
Seasons in the Sun—Terry Jacks	Best Selling Single
Paul Anka	Composer of the Year
Anne Murray	Country Female Vocalist of the Year
The Carlton Showband	Country Group or Duo of the Year
Stompin' Tom Connors	Country Male Vocalist of the Year
Anne Murray	Female Vocalist of the Year
Gordon Lightfoot	Folksinger of the Year

Bachman-Turner Overdrive	Group of the Year
Gordon Lightfoot	Male Vocalist of the Year
Suzanne Stevens	Most Promising Female Vocalist of the Year
Rush	Most Promising New Group of the Year
Gino Vannelli	Most Promising Male Vocalist of the Year
Randy Bachman	Producer of the Year

1976

Bart Schoales	Best Album Graphics
Four Wheel Drive—Bachman-Turner Overdrive	Best Selling Album
Greatest Hits—Elton John	Best Selling International Album
Love Will Keep Us Together —The Captain and Tennille	Best Selling International Single
You Ain't Seen Nothing Yet—Bachman-Turner Overdrive	Best Selling Single
Hagood Hardy	Composer of the Year
Anne Murray	Country Female Vocalist of the Year
The Mercey Brothers	Country Group or Duo of the Year
Murray McLauchlan	Country Male Vocalist of the Year
Joni Mitchell	Female Vocalist of the Year
Gordon Lightfoot	Folksinger of the Year
Bachman-Turner Overdrive	Group of the Year
Hagood Hardy	Instrumental Artist(s) of the Year
Gino Vannelli	Male Vocalist of the Year
Patricia Dahlquist	Most Promising Female Vocalist of the Year
Myles & Lenny	Most Promising Group of the Year
Dan Hill	Most Promising Male Vocalist of the Year
Peter Anastasoff	Producer of the Year
Michel Ethier	Recording Engineer of the Year

1977

Michael Bowness—Select by Ian Tamblyn	Best Album Graphics
Beethoven Vol. 1-2-3—Anton Kuerti	Best Classical Album of the Year
Nimmons 'n Nine Plus Six—Phil Nimmons	Best Jazz Album
Neiges-Andre Gagnon	Best Selling Album
Frampton Comes Alive—Peter Frampton	Best Selling International Album
I Love to Love—Tina Charles	Best Selling International Single
Roxy Roller—Sweeny Todd	Best Selling Single
Gordon Lightfoot	Composer of the Year

Carroll Baker ....Country Female Vocalist of the Year
The Good Brothers ....Country Group or Duo of the Year
Murray McLauchlan ....Country Male Vocalist of the Year
Patsy Gallant ....Female Vocalist of the Year
Gordon Lightfoot ....Folksinger of the Year
Heart ....Group of the Year
Hagood Hardy ....Instrumental Artist(s) of the Year
Burton Cummings ....Male Vocalist of the Year
Colleen Peterson ....Most Promising Female Vocalist of the Year
The T.H.P. Orchestra ....Most Promising Group of the Year
Burton Cummings .... Most Promising Male Vocalist of the Year
M. Flicker ....Producer of the Year
Paul Page ....Recording Engineer of the Year

1978

Dave Anderson—Short Turn by Short Turn ....Best Album Graphics
Three Borodin Symphonies
—The Toronto Symphony Orchestra ....Best Classical Album of the Year
Big Band Jazz—Rob McConnell & The Boss Brass ....Best Jazz Album
Longer Fuse—Dan Hill ....Best Selling Album
Rumours—Fleetwood Mac ....Best Selling International Album
When I Need You—Leo Sayer ....Best Selling International Single
Sugar Daddy—Patsy Gallant ....Best Selling Single
Dan Hill (Co-composer) ....Composer of the Year
Carroll Baker ....Country Female Vocalist of the Year
The Good Brothers ....Country Group or Duo of the Year
Ronnie Prophet ....Country Male Vocalist of the Year
Patsy Gallant ....Female Vocalist of the Year
Gordon Lightfoot ....Folksinger of the Year
Rush ....Group of the Year
Andre Gagnon ....Instrumental Artist(s) of the Year
Dan Hill ....Male Vocalist of the Year
Lisa Dal Bello ....Most Promising Female Vocalist of the Year
Hometown Band .... Most Promising Group of the Year
David Bradstreet .... Most Promising Male Vocalist of the Year
McCauley/Mollin—Longer Fuse by Dan Hill ....Producer of the Year—Album
McCauley/Mollin—Sometimes When We Touch by Dan Hill . Producer of the Year—Single
David Greene ....Recording Engineer of the Year
Terry Brown ....Recording Engineer of the Year
Guy Lombardo ....Canadian Music Hall of Fame
Oscar Peterson ....Canadian Music Hall of Fame

1979

Alan Gee/Greg Lawson—Madcats ....Best Album Graphics
There's A Hippo in my Tub—Anne Murray .... Special Award: Children's
Hindemith, Das Marienleben
—Glenn Gould & Roxolana Roslak .... Best Classical Album of the Year

Jazz Canada Montreux
—Tommy Banks Big Band with Guest "Big" Miller ....Best Jazz Album
Dream of a Child—Burton Cummings ....Best Selling Album
Night Fever—Bee Gees ....International Best Selling Album
You're The One that I Want
—John Travolta/Olivia Newton-John ....International Best Selling Album
Hot Child in the City—Nick Gilder ....Best Selling Single
The Air Farce ....Special Award: Comedy
Dan Hill ....Composer of the Year
Carroll Baker ....Country Female Vocalist of the Year
The Good Brothers ....Country Group of the Year
Ronnie Prophet ....Country Male Vocalist of the Year
Anne Murray ....Female Vocalist of the Year
Murray McLauchlan ....Folk Artist of the Year
Rush ....Group of the Year
Liona Boyd ....Instrumental Artist(s) of the Year
Gino Vannelli ....Male Vocalist of the Year
Claudja Barry ....Most Promising Female Vocalist
Doucette .... Most Promising Group of the Year
Nick Gilder ....Most Promising Male Vocalist
Gino/Joe/Ross Vannelli ....Producer of the Year
Ken Friesen ....Recording Engineer of the Year
Hank Snow ....Canadian Music Hall of Fame

1980

New Kind of Feeling—Anne Murray ....Album of the Year
Rodney Bowes—Cigarettes The Wives ....Best Album Graphics
Smorgasbord—Sharon, Lois & Bram ....Children's Album of the Year
The Crown of Ariadne—Judy Loman ....Best Classical Recording
Sackville 4005—Ed Bickert/Don Thompson ....Best Jazz Recording
Breakfast In America—Supertramp ....International Album of the Year
Heart of Glass—Blondie ....International Single of the Year
A Christmas Carol—Rich Little ....Comedy Album of the Year
Frank Mills ....Composer of the Year
Anne Murray ....Country Female Vocalist of the Year
The Good Brothers ....Country Group of the Year
Murray McLauchlan ....Country Male Vocalist of the Year
Anne Murray ....Female Vocalist of the Year
Bruce Cockburn ....Folksinger of the Year
Trooper ....Group of the Year
Frank Mills ....Instrumental Artist of the Year
Burton Cummings ....Male Vocalist of the Year
France Joli ....Most Promising Female Vocalist
Streetheart ....Most Promising Group
Walter Rossi ....Most Promising Male Vocalist
Bruce Fairbairn ....Producer of the Year
David Greene ....Recording Engineer of the Year

I Just Fall In Love Again—Anne Murray ....Single of the Year
Paul Anka ....Canadian Music Hall of Fame

1981

Greatest Hits—Anne Murray .... Album of the Year
Jeanette Hanna—We Deliver by Downchild Blues Band .... Album Graphics
Singing 'n Swinging—Sharon, Lois & Bram ....Best Children's Album
Stravinsky—Chopin Ballads—Arthur Ozolins ....Best Classical Album
Present Perfect—Rob McConnell & The Boss Brass ....Best Jazz Album
Eddie Schwartz ....Composer of the Year
Anne Murray ....Country Female Vocalist of the Year
The Good Brothers ....Country Group of the Year
Eddie Eastman ....Country Male Vocalist of the Year
Anne Murray ....Female Vocalist of the Year
Bruce Cockburn ....Folk Artist of the Year
Prism ....Group of the Year
Frank Mills ....Instrumental Artist(s) of the Year
The Wall—Pink Floyd ....International Album of the Year
Another Brick In The Wall—Pink Floyd ....International Single of the Year
Bruce Cockburn ....Male Vocalist of the Year
Carole Pope ....Most Promising Female Vocalist
Powder Blues ....Most Promising Group
Graham Shaw ....Most Promising Male Vocalist
Gene Martynec ....Producer of the Year
Mike Jones ....Recording Engineer of the Year
Could I Have This Dance—Anne Murray ....Single of the Year
Echo Beach—Martha & The Muffins ....Single of the Year
Joni Mitchell ....Canadian Music Hall of Fame

1982

Loverboy ....Album of the Year
Hugh Syme/Deborah Samuel—Moving Pictures ....Best Album Graphics
Inch by Inch—Sandra Beech ....Best Children's Album
Ravel: Daphnis Et Chloe (Complete Ballet)
—Orchestre symphonique de Montreal,
Charles Dutoit—(conductor) ....Best Classical Album
The Brass Connection—The Brass Connection ....Best Jazz Album
The Great White North—Bob & Doug McKenzie ....Comedy Album of the Year
Mike Reno & Paul Dean ....Composer of the Year
Anne Murray ....Country Female Vocalist of the Year
The Good Brothers ....Country Group of the Year
Ronnie Hawkins ....Country Male Vocalist of the Year
Anne Murray ....Female Vocalist of the Year
Bruce Cockburn ....Folk Artist(s) of the Year
Loverboy ....Group of the Year
Liona Boyd ....Instrumental Artist(s) of the Year
Double Fantasy—John Lennon ....International Album of the Year

Bette Davis Eyes—Kim Carnes ....International Single of the Year
Bruce Cockburn ....Male Vocalist of the Year
Shari Ulrich ....Most Promising Female Vocalist
Saga ....Most Promising Group
Eddie Schwartz ....Most Promising Male Vocalist
Paul Dean/Bruce Fairbairn ....Producer of the Year
Gary Gray ....Recording Engineer of the Year
Keith Stein/Bob Rock ....Recording Engineer of the Year
Turn Me Loose—Loverboy ....Single of the Year
Neil Young ....Canadian Music Hall of Fame

1983

Get Lucky—Loverboy ....Album of the Year
Dean Motter—Metal on Metal by Anvil ....Best Album Graphics
When You Dream A Dream—Bob Schneider ....Best Children's Album
Bach: The Goldberg Variations—Glenn Gould ....Best Classical Album
I Didn't Know About You—Fraser MacPherson, Oliver Gannon ....Best Jazz Album
Bob Rock/Paul Hyde ....Composer of the Year
Anne Murray ....Country Female Vocalist of the Year
The Good Brothers ....Country Group of the Year
Eddie Eastman ....Country Male Vocalist of the Year
Carole Pope ....Female Vocalist of the Year
Loverboy ....Group of the Year
Liona Boyd ....Instrumental Artist(s) of the Year
Business As Usual—Men At Work ....International Album of the Year
Eye Of The Tiger—Survivor ....International Single of the Year
Bryan Adams ....Male Vocalist of the Year
Lydia Taylor ....Most Promising Female Vocalist of the Year
Payola$ ....Most Promising Group of the Year
Kim Mitchell ....Most Promising Male Vocalist of the Year
Bill Henderson/Brian MacLeod ....Producer of the Year
Bob Rock ....Recording Engineer of the Year
Eyes Of A Stranger—Payola$ ....Single of the Year
Glenn Gould ....Canadian Music Hall of Fame

1984

Cuts Like A Knife—Bryan Adams ....Album of the Year
Dean Motter/Jeff Jackson/Deborah Samuel
—Seamless by The Nylons ....Best Album Graphics
Rugrat Rock—The Rugrats ....Best Children's Album
Brahms: Ballades Op. 10, Rhapsodies Op. 79—Glenn Gould ....Best Classical Album
All In Good Time—Rob McConnell & The Boss Brass ....Best Jazz Album
Sunglasses at Night—Corey Hart, Rob Quartly ....Best Video
Strange Brew—Bob & Doug McKenzie ....Comedy Album of the Year
Bryan Adams/Jim Vallance ....Composer of the Year
Anne Murray ....Country Female Vocalist of the Year
The Good Brothers ....Country Group of the Year

Murray McLauchlan ....Country Male Vocalist of the Year
Carole Pope ....Female Vocalist of the Year
Loverboy ....Group of the Year
Liona Boyd ....Instrumental Artist(s) of the Year
Synchronicity—The Police ....International Album of the Year
Billie Jean—Michael Jackson ....International Single of the Year
Bryan Adams ....Male Vocalist of the Year
Sherry Kean ....Most Promising Female Vocalist of the Year
The Parachute Club .... Most Promising Group of the Year
Zappacosta .... Most Promising Male Vocalist of the Year
Bryan Adams ....Producer of the Year
John Naslen ....Recording Engineer of the Year
Rise Up—The Parachute Club ....Single of the Year
The Crewcuts ....Canadian Music Hall of Fame
The Diamonds ....Canadian Music Hall of Fame
The Four Lads ....Canadian Music Hall of Fame
J. Lyman Potts...Walt Grealis Special Achievement Award

1985

Reckless—Bryan Adams .... Album of the Year
Rob MacIntyre/Dimo Safari—Strange Animal by Gowan ....Best Album Graphics
Murmel Murmel Munsch—Robert Munsch ....Best Children's Album
Ravel: Ma Mere L'oye/Pavane pour un infante debunte/
Tombeau de Couperin and Valses nobles et sentimentales—
Orchestre symphonique de Montreal,
Charles Dutoit—(conductor).....................Best Classical Album (Large Ensemble)
W.A. Mozart—String Quartets
—The Orford String Quartet.................Best Classical Album (Solo or Chamber Ensemble)
A Beautiful Friendship—Don Thompson ....Best Jazz Album
Lost Somewhere Inside Your Love—Liberty Silver.................... Best R&B/Soul Recording
Heaven Must Have Sent You
—Liberty Silver & Otis Gayle..........................Best Reggae/Calypso Recording
You're A Strange Animal—Gowan, Rob Quartly...................................Best Video
Bryan Adams/Jim Vallance..Composer of the Year
Anne Murray...Country Female Vocalist of the Year
Family Brown...Country Group of the Year
Murray McLauchlan ....Country Male Vocalist of the Year
Luba..Female Vocalist of the Year
The Parachute Club ....Group of the Year
Canadian Brass ....Instrumental Artist(s) of the Year
Born In The USA—Bruce Springsteen..............................International Album of the Year
I Want To Know What Love Is—Foreigner ....International Single of the Year
Bryan Adams...Male Vocalist of the Year
k.d. lang ....Most Promising Female Vocalist of the Year
Idle Eyes... Most Promising Group of the Year
Paul Janz..................................... Most Promising Male Vocalist of the Year

David Foster ....Producer of the Year
Hayward Parrott...Recording Engineer of the Year
Never Surrender—Corey Hart..Single of the Year
Wilf Carter ....Canadian Music Hall of Fame
A. Hugh Joseph ....Walt Grealis Special Achievement Award

1986

Don't Forget Me (When I'm Gone)—Glass Tiger .... Album of the Year
Hugh Syme/Dimo Safari—Power Windows by Rush ....Best Album Graphics
10 Carrot Diamond—Charlotte Diamond....................................Best Children's Album
Holst: The Planets—Toronto Symphony,
Andrew Davis—(conductor) ....Best Classical Album:
Large Ensemble or Soloist(s) With Large Ensemble Accompaniment
Stolen Gems—James Campbell (Clarinet)
and Eric Robertson (Keyboard)...........Best Classical Album: Solo or Chamber Ensemble
Lights of Burgundy—Oliver Jones ....Best Jazz Album
Love Is A Contact Sport—Billy Newton-Davis............................Best R&B/Soul Recording
Tea Party—Lillian Allen ....Best Reggae/Calypso Recording
How Many (Rivers To Cross)—Luba, Greg Masuak ....Best Video
Jim Vallance ....Composer of the Year
Anne Murray ....Country Female Vocalist of the Year
Prairie Oyster ....Country Group or Duo of the Year
Murray McLauchlan ....Country Male Vocalist of the Year
Luba ....Female Vocalist of the Year
Honeymoon Suite ....Group of the Year
David Foster ....Instrumental Artist(s) of the Year
Brothers In Arms—Dire Straights ....Best Selling International Album
Live is Life—Opus ....Best Selling International Single
Bryan Adams..Male Vocalist of the Year
Kim Richardson ....Most Promising Female Vocalist of the Year
Glass Tiger .... Most Promising Group of the Year
Billy Newton-Davis .... Most Promising Male Vocalist of the Year
David Foster ....Producer of the Year
Joe/Gino Vannelli ....Recording Engineer of the Year
Don't Forget Me (When I'm Gone)—Glass Tiger ....Single of the Year
Gordon Lightfoot ....Canadian Music Hall of Fame
Jack Richardson ....Walt Grealis Special Achievement Award

1987

Shakin' Like A Human Being—Kim Mitchell .... Album of the Year
Jamie Bennett/Shari Spier
—Small Victories by The Parachute Club..............................Best Album Graphics
Drums!—Bill Usher...Best Children's Album
Holst, The Planets—Orchestre symphonique de Montreal,
Charles Dutoit—(conductor)..Best Classical Album:
Large Ensemble or Soloist(s) With Large Ensemble Accompaniment

Schubert, Quintet in C—The Orford String Quartet,
Ofra Harnoy (cello) ....Best Classical Album: Solo or Chamber Ensemble
Pages of Solitary Delights—Donald Steven, (composer)........Best Classical Composition
Atayoskewin—Malcolm Forsyth, (composer) ....Best Classical Composition
If You Could See Me Now—The Oscar Peterson Four ....Best Jazz Album
Peek-A-Boo—Kim Richardson... Best R&B/Soul Recording
Mean While—Leroy Sibbles...........................Best Reggae/Calypso Recording
Love Is Fire—The Parachute Club, Ron Berti.......................................Best Video
Bryan Adams...Canadian Entertainer of the Year
Jim Vallance...Composer of the Year
k.d. lang...Country Female Vocalist of the Year
Prairie Oyster.......................................Country Group or Duo of the Year
Ian Tyson...Country Male Vocalist of the Year
Luba...Female Vocalist of the Year
Tom Cochrane & Red Rider ....Group of the Year
David Foster ....Instrumental Artist(s) of the Year
True Blue—Madonna..............................International Album of the Year
Venus—Bananarama.................................International Single of the Year
Bryan Adams...Male Vocalist of the Year
Rita MacNeil.......................Most Promising Female Vocalist of the Year
Frozen Ghost .... Most Promising Group of the Year
Tim Feehan............................. Most Promising Male Vocalist of the Year
Daniel Lanois..Producer of the Year
Gino Vannelli/Joe Vannelli..............................Recording Engineer of the Year
Someday—Glass Tiger...Single of the Year
The Guess Who ....Canadian Music Hall of Fame
Bruce Allen ....Walt Grealis Special Achievement Award

1989

Robbie Robertson—Robbie Robertson..............................Album of the Year
Hugh Syme—Levity by Ian Thomas ....Best Album Design of the Year
Lullaby Berceuse—Connie Kaldor/Carmen Campagne.....................Best Children's Album
Fred Penner's Place—Fred Penner...Best Children's Album
Bartok: concerto for Orchestra; Music for Strings,
Percussion and Celesta—Montreal Symphony Orchestra,
Charles Dutoit—(conductor).....................................Best Classical Album:
Large Ensemble or Soloist(s) With Large Ensemble Accompaniment
Schubert: Arpeggione Sonata—Ofra Harnoy ....Best Classical Album:
Solo or Chamber Ensemble
Songs of Paradise—Alexina Louie ....Best Classical Composition
Looking Up—The Hugh Fraser Quintet.........................Best Jazz Album
Angel—Erroll Starr .... Best R&B/Soul Recording
Conditions Critical—Lillian Allen ....Best Reggae/Calypso Recording
The Return of the Formerly Brothers
—The Amos Garrett, Doug Sahm, Gene Taylor Band ....Best Roots & Traditional Album
Try—Blue Rodeo, Michael Buckley ....Best Video of the Year

Glass Tiger ....Canadian Entertainer of the Year
Tom Cochrane ....Composer of the Year
k.d. lang ....Country Female Vocalist of the Year
Family Brown...Country Group or Duo of the Year
Murray McLauchlan ....Country Male Vocalist of the Year
k.d. lang...Female Vocalist of the Year
Blue Rodeo..Group of the Year
David Foster ....Instrumental Artist(s) of the Year
Dirty Dancing—Various ....International Album of the Year
U2 ....International Entertainer of the Year
Pump Up The Volume—M.A.R.R.S. ....International Single of the Year
Robbie Robertson ....Male Vocalist of the Year
Sass Jordan ....Most Promising Female Vocalist of the Year
Barney Bentall & The Legendary Hearts......................Most Promising Group of the Year
Colin James .... Most Promising Male Vocalist of the Year
Daniel Lanois/Robbie Robertson ....Producer of the Year
Mike Fraser ....Recording Engineer of the Year
Try—Blue Rodeo ....Single of the Year
The Band ....Canadian Music Hall of Fame
Sam Sniderman ....Walt Grealis Special Achievement Award

1990

Alannah Myles—Alannah Myles............................. Album of the Year
Hugh Syme—Presto by Rush ....Best Album Design
Beethoven Lives Upstairs—Susan Hammond/Barbara Nichol........Best Children's Album
Boccherini: Cello Concertos and Symphonies
—Tafelmusik Baroque Orchestra................................Best Classical Album:
Large Ensemble or Soloist(s) With Large Ensemble Accompaniment
20th Century Original Piano Transcriptions
—Louis Lortie ....Best Classical Album: Solo or Chamber Ensemble
Concerto For Harp and Chamber Orchestra
—Oskar Morawetz...Best Classical Composition
I Beg Your Pardon (I Never Promised You A Rose Garden)
—Kon Kan .... Best Dance Recording
Skydance—Jon Ballantyne Trio Featuring Joe Henderson.....................Best Jazz Album
Spellbound—Billy Newton-Davis .... Best R&B/Soul Recording
Too Late To Turn Back Now—Sattalites............................Best Reggae/Calypso Recording
Je Voudrais Changer D'Chapeau
—La Bottine Souriante............................Best Roots & Traditional Album
Boomtown—Andrew Cash, Cosimo Cavallaro..Best Video
The Jeff Healey Band ....Canadian Entertainer of the Year
David Tyson/Christopher Ward..Composer of the Year
k.d. lang...Country Female Vocalist of the Year
Family Brown...Country Group or Duo of the Year
George Fox ....Country Male Vocalist of the Year
Rita MacNeil ....Female Vocalist of the Year

Blue Rodeo..Group of the Year
Manteca ....Instrumental Artist(s) of the Year
Girl You Know It's True—Milli Vanilli.....................International Album of the Year
Melissa Etheridge...............................International Entertainer of the Year
Swing The Mood—Jive Bunny & The Master Mixers........International Single of the Year
Kim Mitchell...Male Vocalist of the Year
Alannah Myles..Most Promising Female Vocalist
The Tragically Hip.......................................Most Promising Group of the Year
Daniel Lanois...Most Promising Male Vocalist
Bruce Fairbairn ....Producer of the Year
Kevin Doyle ....Recording Engineer of the Year
Black Velvet—Alannah Myles...Single of the Year
Maureen Forrester...Hall of Fame
Raffi .... Walt Grealis Special Achievement

1991

Unison—Céline Dion...Album of the Year
Robert leBeuf—Sue Medley by Sue Medley ....Best Album Design
Mozart's Magic Fantasy—Susan Hammond...........................Best Children's Album
Debussy: Images, Nocturnes—Orchestre symphonique de Montreal,
Charles Dutoit—(conductor)...Best Classical Album:
Large Ensemble or Soloist(s) with Large Ensemble Accompaniment
Schafer: Five Strings Quartets
—The Orford String Quartet...................Best Classical Album: Solo or Chamber Ensemble
String Quartet No. 5 'Rosalind'—R. Murray Schafer ....Best Classical Composition
Don't Wanna Fall In Love (Knife Feel Good Mix)—Jane Child .... Best Dance Recording
Presto—Rush .... Best Hard Rock/Metal Album
Two Sides—Mike Murley ....Best Jazz Album
Dance To The Music (Work Your Body)
—Simply Majestic featuring B Kool .... Best R&B/Soul Recording
Soldiers We Are All—Jayson & Friends ....Best Reggae/Calypso Recording
Dance & Celebrate—Bill Bourne & Alan MacLeod ....Best Roots & Traditional Album
Drop The Needle—Maestro Fresh Wes, Joel Goldberg ....Best Video
The Tragically Hip.................................Canadian Entertainer of the Year
Rita MacNeil ....Country Female Vocalist of the Year
Prairie Oyster ....Country Group or Duo of the Year
George Fox...Country Male Vocalist of the Year
Céline Dion...Female Vocalist of the Year
Blue Rodeo..Group of the Year
Ofra Harnoy ....Instrumental Artist(s) of the Year
Please Hammer Don't Hurt 'Em—MC Hammer ....Best Selling International Album
The Rolling Stones ....International Entertainer of the Year
Vogue—Madonna .... Best Selling International Single
Colin James ....Male Vocalist of the Year
Sue Medley........................Most Promising Female Vocalist of the Year
The Leslie Spit Treeo....................... Most Promising Group of the Year

Andy Curran....................................Most Promising Male Vocalist of the Year
David Tyson...Producer of the Year
Symphony In Effect—Maestro Fresh-Wes...............Rap Recording of the Year
Gino Vannelli/Joe Vannelli......................Recording Engineer of the Year
Just Came Back—Colin James ....Single of the Year
David Tyson..Songwriter of the Year
Leonard Cohen ....Hall of Fame
Mel Shaw ....Walt Grealis Special Achievement Award

1992

Mad Mad World—Tom Cochrane..Album of the Year
Hugh Syme—Roll The Bones by Rush....................................Best Album Design
Vivaldi's Ring of Mystery
—Classical Kids/Susan Hammond, Producer............................Best Children's Album
Debussy: Pelleas de Melisande—Orchestre symphonique de Montreal,
Charles Dutoit—(conductor)..Best Classical Album:
Large Ensemble or Soloist(s) With Large Ensemble Accompaniment
Liszt: Annees de Pelerinage—Louis Lortie (piano)..........................Best Classical Album:
Solo or Chamber Ensemble
Concerto for Piano and Chamber Orchestra
—Michael Conway Baker ....Best Classical Composition
Everyone's A Winner (Chocolate Movement Mix)—Bootsauce...... Best Dance Recording
In Transition—Brian Dickerson ....Best Jazz Album
For The Moment—Renee Rosnes ....Best Jazz Album
The Brass is Back—Rob McConnell & The Boss Brass......................Best Jazz Album
Call My Name—Love & Sas................................... Best R&B/Soul Recording
The Visit—Loreena McKennitt.......................Best Roots & Traditional Album
Saturday Night Blues—Various Artists..................Best Roots & Traditional Album
To The Extreme—Vanilla Ice ....Best Selling Album by a Foreign Artist
Sauvez Mon Ame—Luc De Larochellière.......................Best Selling Francophone Album
More Than Words—Extreme..................Best Selling Single by a Foreign Artist
Into the Fire—Sarah McLachlan, Phil Kates...Best Video
The Gathering—Various Artists...........................Best World Beat Recording
Bryan Adams..Canadian Entertainer of the Year
Cassandra Vasik....................................Country Female Vocalist of the Year
Prairie Oyster ....Country Group or Duo of the Year
George Fox...Country Male Vocalist of the Year
Céline Dion...Female Vocalist of the Year
Garth Brooks......................................Foreign Entertainer of the Year
Crash Test Dummies..Group of the Year
Roll The Bones—Rush .... Hard Rock Album of the Year
Shadowy Men On A Shadowy Planet............................Instrumental Artist(s) of the Year
Bryan Adams ....International Achievement Award
Tom Cochrane..Male Vocalist of the Year
Alanis ....Most Promising Female Vocalist of the Year
Infidels.................................. Most Promising Group of the Year

Keven Jordan..Most Promising Male Vocalist of the Year
Bryan Adams (co-producer John "Mutt" Lange)............................Producer of the Year
My Definition of a Bombastic Jazz Style—Dream Warriors....Rap Recording of the Year
Mike Fraser..Recording Engineer of the Year
Life Is A Highway—Tom Cochrane.......................................Single of the Year
Tom Cochrane...Songwriter of the Year
Ian & Sylvia...Hall of Fame
William Harold Moon ....Walt Grealis Special Achievement Award

1993

Ingenue—k.d. lang..Album of the Year
Rebecca Baird/Kenny Baird—Lost Together by Blue Rodeo................Best Album Design
Waves of Wonder—Jack Grunsky ....Best Children's Album
Handel: Excerpts from Floridante—Tafelmusik, with Alan Curtis,
Catherine Robbins, Linda Maguire, Nancy Argenta, Ingrid Attrot,
Mel Braun, Jeanne Lamon—(leader).....................................Best Classical Album:
            Large Ensemble or Soloist(s) with Large Ensemble Accompaniment
Beethoven: Piano Sonatas—Louis Lortie.................................Best Classical Album:
                                              Solo or Chamber Ensemble
Concerto for Flute and Orchestra—R. Murray Schafer..........Best Classical Composition
Love Can Move Mountains (Club Mix)—Céline Dion.................. Best Dance Recording
My Ideal—P.J. Perry...Best Jazz Album
Once In A Lifetime—Love & Sas................................. Best R&B/Soul Recording
Keep It Slammin'—Devon...Best Rap Recording
Jusqu'aux P'tites Heures—La Bottine Souriante ....Best Roots & Traditional Album
Waking Up The Neighbours—Bryan Adams ......Best Selling Album (Foreign or Domestic)
Dion Chante Plamondon—Céline Dion.................Best Selling Francophone Album
Achy Breaky Heart—Billy Ray Cyrus ....Best Selling Single (Foreign or Domestic)
Closing Time—Leonard Cohen, Curtis Wehrfritz..............................Best Video
Spirits of Havana—Jane Bunnett ....Best World Beat Recording
The Tragically Hip..Canadian Entertainer of the Year
Michelle Wright ....Country Female Vocalist of the Year
Tracey Prescott & Lonesome Daddy ....Country Group or Duo of the Year
Gary Fjellgaard..Country Male Vocalist of the Year
Céline Dion...Female Vocalist of the Year
Barenaked Ladies..Group of the Year
Doin' The Nasty—Slik Toxik ....Hard Rock Album of the Year
Ofra Harnoy ....Instrumental Artist(s) of the Year
U2..International Entertainer of the Year
Leonard Cohen...Male Vocalist of the Year
Julie Masse..Most Promising Female Vocalist of the Year
Skydiggers .... Most Promising Group of the Year
John Bottomley .... Most Promising Male Vocalist of the Year
k.d. lang/Ben Mink (co-producer Greg Penny)........................Producer of the Year
Jeff Wolpert/John Whynot............................ Recording Engineer of the Year
Beauty and the Beast—Céline Dion/Peabo Bryson..........................Single of the Year

k.d. lang/Ben Mink...Songwriter of the Year
Anne Murray...Hall of Fame
Brian Robertson ....Walt Grealis Special Achievement Award

1994

Harvest Moon—Neil Young..Album of the Year
Marty Dolan—Faithlift by Spirit of the West.............................Best Album Design
South at Eight/North at Nine—Colin Linden..................... Best Blues/Gospel Album
Tchaikovsky Discovers America
—Susan Hammond/Classical Kids..................................Best Children's Album
Gluck: Ballet Pantomime—Tafelmusik:
Jeanne Lamon, Director; Bruno Weil, (conductor) ....Best Classical Album:
            Large Ensemble or Soloist(s) with Large Ensemble Accompaniment
Debussy Songs—Claudette Leblanc,
Soprano & Valeria Tryon, Piano .....Best Classical Album: Vocal and Choral Performance
Beethoven: Piano Sonatas, Opus 10, No. 1-3
—Louis Lortie ....Best Classical Album: Solo or Chamber Ensemble
Among Friends—Chan Ka Nin ....Best Classical Composition
Don't Smoke in Bed—Holly Cole Trio .... Best Contemporary Jazz Album
Thankful—Red Light...Best Dance Recording
El Camino Real—Ancient Cultures ....Best Global Recording
Dig—I, Mother Earth ....Best Hard Rock Album
Fables and Dreams—Dave Young/Phil Dwyer Quartet........Best Mainstream Jazz Album
Wapistan—Lawrence Martin .... Best Music of Aboriginal Canada Recording
The Waltons ....Best New Group
Jann Arden..Best New Solo Artist
The Time Is Right—Rupert Gayle .... Best R&B/Soul Recording
One Track Mind—TBTBT...Best Rap Recording
Informer—Snow...Best Reggae Recording
My Skies—James Keelaghan......................Best Roots & Traditional Album
The Bodyguard—Whitney Huston........................Best Selling Album (Foreign or Domestic)
Album du Peuple Tome 2—Francoise Perusse ....Best Selling Francophone Album
I would Die For You—Jann Arden, Jeth Weinrich...........................Best Video
The Rankin Family ....Canadian Entertainer of the Year
Cassandra Vasik....................................Country Female Vocalist of the Year
The Rankin Family..................................Country Group or Duo of the Year
Charlie Major...Country Male Vocalist of the Year
Céline Dion..Female Vocalist of the Year
The Rankin Family ....Group of the Year
Ofra Harnoy ....Instrumental Artist(s) of the Year
Roch Voisine..Male Vocalist of the Year
Steven MacKinnon/Marc Jordan...Producer of the Year
Kevin Doyle ....Recording Engineer of the Year
Fare Thee Well Love—The Rankin Family...............................Single of the Year
Leonard Cohen ....SOCAN JUNO For Songwriter of the Year
Rush..Hall of Fame

John Mills, OC, QC ....Walt Grealis Special Achievement Award

1995

Colour of My Love—Céline Dion ....Album of the Year
Andrew MacNaughtan—Naveed by Our Lady Peace...........................Best Album Design
Shiver—Rose Chronicles ....Best Alternative Album
Joy to the World Jubilation V
—Montreal Jubilation Gospel Choir ....Best Blues/Gospel Album
Bananaphone—Raffi ....Best Children's Album
Bach: Brandenburg Concertos Nos. 1-6—Tafelmusik/
Jeanne Lamon, Musical Director ....Best Classical Album:
  Large Ensemble or Soloist(s) with Large Ensemble Accompaniment
Janácek: Glagolitic Mass & Sinfonietta—Choeur et Orchestre symphonique de
Montreal, Charles Dutoit—(conductor) ....Best Classical Album:
  Vocal and Choral Performance
Erica Goodman Plays Canadian Music Harp
—Erica Goodman, Harp......................Best Classical Album: Solo or Chamber Ensemble
Sketches from Natal—Malcolm Forsyth.......................Best Classical Composition
The Merlin Factor—Jim Hillman & The Merlin Factor ..... Best Contemporary Jazz Album
In the Night Club Mix—Capital Sound.......................Best Dance Recording
Africa +—Eval Manigat ....Best Global Recording
Suffersystem—Monster Voodoo Machine ....Best Hard Rock Album
Free Trade—Free Trade ....Best Mainstream Jazz Album
Arctic Rose—Susan Aglukark .... Best Music of Aboriginal Canada
Moist...Best New Group
Susan Aglukark...Best New Solo Artist
First Impression for the Bottom Jigglers—Base is Base .... Best R&B/Soul Recording
Certified—Ghetto Concept ....Best Rap Recording
Class and Credential—Carla Marshall ....Best Reggae Recording
The Mask and Mirror—Loreena McKennitt.................Best Roots & Traditional Album
Colour of My Love—Céline Dion ....Best Selling Album (Foreign or Domestic)
Coup de tête—Roch Voisine...........................Best Selling Francophone Album
Tunnel of Tree—Gogh Van Go, Lyne Charlebois..........................Best Video
Michelle Wright ....Country Female Vocalist of the Year
Prairie Oyster ....Country Group or Duo of the Year
Charlie Major..............................Country Male Vocalist of the Year
The Tragically Hip ....Entertainer of the Year
Jann Arden...Female Vocalist of the Year
The Tragically Hip...Group of the Year
André Gagnon ....Instrumental Artist(s) of the Year
Neil Young ....Male Vocalist of the Year
Robbie Robertson ....Producer of the Year
Lenny DeRose .... Recording Engineer of the Year
Could I Be Your Girl—Jann Arden...............................Single of the Year
Jann Arden..Songwriter of the Year
Buffy Sainte—Marie..Hall of Fame

Louis Applebaum ....Walt Grealis Special Achievement Award

1996

Jagged Little Pill—Alanis Morissette ....Album of the Year
Tom Wilson/Alex Wittholz—Birthday Boy by Junkhouse ....Best Album Design
What Fresh Hell Is This?—Art Bergmann.......................Best Alternative Album
That River—Jim Byrnes .... Best Blues/Gospel Album
Celery stalks At Midnight—Al Simmons ....Best Children's Album
Debussy: Children's Corner—Orchestre symphonique de Montreal,
Charles Dutoit—(conductor) ....Best Classical Album:
  Large Ensemble or Soloist(s) with Large Ensemble Accompaniment
Ben Heppner sings Richard Strauss—Ben Heppner—Tenor,
The Toronto Symphony Orchestra, Andrew Davis—(conductor).....Best Classical Album:
  Vocal and Choral Performance
Alkan: Grande Sonate/Le festin d'Esope
—Mar-André Hamelin, piano ....Best Classical Album: Solo or Chamber Ensemble
Concerto For Violin and Orchestra—Andrew P. MacDonald...Best Classical Composition
Nojo—Neufeld-Occhipinti Jazz Orchestra........................ Best Contemporary Jazz Album
A Deeper Shade of Love Extended Mix—Camille...........................Best Dance Recording
Music From Africa—Takadja ....Best Global Album
Vernal Fields—Ingrid Jensen ....Best Mainstream Jazz Album
ETSI Shon "Grandfather Song"
—Jerry Alfred & The Medicine Beat.............. Best Music of Aboriginal Canada Recording
The Philosopher Kings ....Best New Group
Ashley MacIsaac ....Best New Solo Artist
Deborah Cox—Deborah Cox .... Best R&B/Soul Recording
E-Z on Tha Motion—Ghetto Concept ....Best Rap Recording
Now And Forever—Sattalites ....Best Reggae Recording
Jagged Little Pill—Alanis Morissette .... Best Rock Album
Gypsies & Lovers—The Irish Descendants............ Best Roots & Traditional Album—Group
Hi How Are You Today?—Ashley MacIsaac.................Best Roots & Traditional Album—Solo
No Need to Argue—The Cranberries...................Best Selling Album (Foreign or Domestic)
D'eux—Céline Dion ....Best Selling Francophone Album
Good Mother—Jann Arden, Jeth Weinrich.................................Best Video
Shania Twain...Country Female Vocalist of the Year
Prairie Oyster ....Country Group or Duo of the Year
Charlie Major..............................Country Male Vocalist of the Year
Alanis Morissette ....Female Vocalist of the Year
Blue Rodeo...Group of the Year
Liona Boyd ....Instrumental Artist(s) of the Year
Shania Twain ....Levi's Entertainer of the Year
Colin James ....Male Vocalist of the Year
Michael Phillip Wojewoda ....Producer of the Year
Chad Irschick .... Recording Engineer of the Year
You Oughta Know—Alanis Morissette ....Single of the Year
Alanis Morissette ....Songwriter of the Year

David Clayton–Thomas ....Hall of Fame
Denny Doherty ....Hall of Fame
John Kay ....Hall of Fame
Domenic Troiano ....Hall of Fame
Zal Yanovsky ....Hall of Fame
Ronnie Hawkins.................................Walt Grealis Special Achievement Award

1997

Trouble at the Henhouse–The Tragically Hip .... Album of the Year
John Rummen/Crystal Heald
–Rarities, B-Sides & Other Stuff by Sarah McLachlan ....Best Album Design
One Chord to Another–Sloan......................................Best Alternative Album
Right to Sing the Blues–Long John Baldry .... Best Blues/Gospel Album
Songs From The Tree House–Martha Johnson ....Best Children's Album
Ginastera/Villa-Lobos/Evangelista–I Musici de Montréal ....Best Classical Album:
Large Ensemble or Soloist(s) with Large Ensemble Accompaniment
Berlioz: La Damnation de Faust–Choeur et orchestre symphonique de Montréal,
Charles Dutoit–(conductor)...........Best Classical Album: Vocal and Choral Performance
Scriabin: The Complete Piano Sonatas
–Marc-André Hamelin ....Best Classical Album: Solo or Chamber Ensemble
Picasso Suite–Harry Somers...Best Classical Composition
Africville Suite–Joe Sealy .... Best Contemporary Jazz Album
Astroplane–City of Love Mix–BKS .... Best Dance Recording
Africa Do Brasil–Paulo Ramos Group..............................Best Global Album
Ancestors–Renee Rosnes ....Best Mainstream Jazz Album
Up Where We Belong–Buffy Sainte-Marie... Best Music of Aboriginal Canada Recording
The Killjoys... Best New Group
Terri Clark ....Best New Solo Artist
Carlos Morgan–Feelin' Alright–Carlos Morgan......................... Best R&B/Soul Recording
What It Takes–Choclair ....Best Rap Recording
Nana McLean–Nana McLean ....Best Reggae Recording
Matapedia–Kate & Anna McGarrigle.................... Best Roots & Traditional Album–Group
Drive-in Movie–Fred Eaglesmith...................Best Roots & Traditional Album–Solo
Falling Into You–Céline Dion.......................... Best Selling Album (Foreign or Domestic)
Live á Paris–Céline Dion ....Best Selling Francophone Album
Burned Out Car–Junkhouse, Jeth Weinrich................................. Best Video
Shania Twain..Country Female Vocalist of the Year
The Rankin Family ....Country Group or Duo of the Year
Paul Brandt...Country Male Vocalist of the Year
Céline Dion...Female Vocalist of the Year
The Tragically Hip..Group of the Year
Ashley MacIsaac ....Instrumental Artist(s) of the Year
Alanis Morissette ....International Achievement Award
Céline Dion..International Achievement Award
Shania Twain...International Achievement Award
Bryan Adams...Male Vocalist of the Year

The Tragically Hip.................................North Star Rock Album of the Year
Garth Richardson ....Producer of the Year
Paul Northfield ....Recording Engineer of the Year
Ironic–Alanis Morissette...Single of the Year
Alanis Morissette (Glen Ballard, co-songwriter) ....Songwriter of the Year
Lenny Breau ....Hall of Fame
Gil Evans...Hall of Fame
Maynard Ferguson ....Hall of Fame
Moe Koffman ....Hall of Fame
Rob McConnell..Hall of Fame
Dan Gibson.................................Walt Grealis Special Achievement Award

1998

Surfacing–Sarah McLachlan...Album of the Year
Surfacing–Sarah McLachlan, John Rummen, Crystal Heald,
Stephen Chung, Andrew MacNaughtan, Justin Zivojinovich..............Best Album Design
Glee–Bran Van 3000 ....Best Alternative Album
National Steel–Colin James...Best Blues Album
Livin' in a Shoe–Judy & David ....Best Children's Album
Mozart Horn Concertos–James Sommerville, CBC Vancouver Orchestra,
Mario Bernardi ....Best Classical Album:
Large Ensemble or Soloist(s) with Large Ensemble Accompaniment
Soirée française–Michael Schade, tenor; Russel Braun, baritone;
Canadian Opera Company Orchestra; Richard Bradshaw................Best Classical Album:
Vocal and Choral Performance
Marc-André Hamelin Plays Franz Liszt
–Marc-André Hamelin ....Best Classical Album: Solo or Chamber Ensemble
Electra Rising–Malcolm Forsyth ....Best Classical Composition
Metalwood-Metalwood....................................... Best Contemporary Jazz Album
Euphoria (Rabbit in the Moon Mix)–Delerium..................... Best Dance Recording
La Llorona–Lhasa .... Best Global Album
Romantics & Mystics–Steve Bell ....Best Gospel Album
In The Mean Time–The Hugh Fraser Quintet ....Best Mainstream Jazz Album
The Spirit Within–Mishi Donovan ....Best Music of Aboriginal Canada Recording
Leahy..Best New Group
Holly McNarland...Best New Solo Artist
Things Just Ain't The Same–Deborah Cox .... Best R&B/Soul Recording
Cash Crop–Rascalz...Best Rap Recording
Catch De Vibe–Messenjah ....Best Reggae Recording
Molinos–The Paperboys .... Best Roots & Traditional Album–Group
Other Songs–Ron Sexsmith ....Best Roots & Traditional Album–Solo
Spice–Spice Girls ....Best Selling Album (Foreign or Domestic)
Marie Michèle Desrosiers chante les classiques de Noël
–Marie Michèle Desrosier ....Best Selling Francophone Album
Gasoline–Moist, Javier Aguilera ....Best Video
Clumsy–Our Lady Peace ....Blockbuster Rock Album of the Year

Shania Twain..Country Female Vocalist of the Year
Farmer's Daughter......................................Country Group or Duo of the Year
Paul Brandt...Country Male Vocalist of the Year
Sarah McLachlan...Female Vocalist of the Year
Our Lady Peace...Group of the Year
Leahy...Instrumental Artist(s) of the Year
Paul Brandt...Male Vocalist of the Year
Pierre Marchand...Producer of the Year
Michael Phillip Wojewoda.....................................Recording Engineer of the Year
Building a Mystery–Sarah McLachlan..Single of the Year
Sarah McLachlan/Pierre Marchand...............................Songwriter of the Year
David Foster..Hall of Fame
Sam Feldman..................................Walt Grealis Special Achievement Award

1999

Let's Talk About Love–Céline Dion..Best Album
Andrew McLachlan, Rob Baker, Brock Ostrom, Bernard Clark, David Ajax
–Phantom Power–The Tragically Hip...............................Best Album Design
Rufus Wainwright–Rufus Wainwright....................................Best Alternative Album
Blues Weather–Fathead..Best Blues Album
Mozart's Magnificent Voyage
–Susan Hammond's Classical Kids.........................Best Children's Album
Handel: Music For The Royal Fireworks–Tafelmusik,
Jeanne Lamon–musical director..........................Best Classical Album:
    Large Ensemble or Soloist(s) with Large Ensemble Accompaniment
Songs of Travel–Gerald Finley (baritone),
Stephen Ralls (piano)................Best Classical Album: Vocal and Choral Performance
Bach: Well-Tempered Clavier–Book 1–Angela Hewitt...............Best Classical Album:
    Solo or Chamber Ensemble
Concerto for Wind Orchestra–Colin McPhee.....................Best Classical Composition
Metalwood 2–metalwood ....Best Contemporary Jazz Album
Shania Twain...Best Country Female Vocalist
Leahy .... Best Country Group or Duo
Paul Brandt..Best Country Male Vocalist
Broken Bones–Love Inc..Best Dance Recording
Céline Dion...Best Female Vocalist
The Message–Alpha Yaya Diallo .... Best Global Album
Life Is–Sharon Riley & Faith Chorale ....Best Gospel Album
Barenaked Ladies .... Best Group
My Roots are Showing–Natalie MacMaster .... Best Instrumental Album
The Atlantic Sessions–Kirk MacDonald ....Best Mainstream Jazz Album
Jim Cuddy .... Best Male Vocalist
Contact From the Underworld of Redboy
–Robbie Robertson.........................Best Music of Aboriginal Canada Recording
Johnny Favourite Swing Orchestra ....Best New Group

Melanie Doane...Best New Solo Artist
Stunt–Barenaked Ladies...Best Pop Album
Colin James (co-producer Joe Hardy)........................Best Producer
One Wish–Deborah Cox .... Best R&B/Soul Recording
Northern Touch–Rascalz featuring Choclair, Kardinal Offishall,
Thrust and Checkmate..Best Rap Recording
Kevin Doyle..Best Recording Engineer
Vision–Frankie Wilmot..Best Reggae Recording
Phantom Power–The Tragically Hip............................... Best Rock Album
The McGarrigle Hour
–Kate & Anna McGarrigle...............Best Roots & Traditional Album–Group
Heartstrings–Willie P. Bennett.....................Best Roots & Traditional Album–Solo
Let's Talk About Love–Céline Dion...................Best Selling Album (Foreign or Domestic)
S'il Suffisait D'Aimer–Céline Dion..................Best Selling Francophone Album
One Week–Barenaked Ladies... Best Single
Bryan Adams (Phil Thornalley and Eliot Kennedy, co-songwriters)..........Best Songwriter
Forestfire–David Usher, Javier Aguilera ....Best Video
Céline Dion..............................International Achievement Award
Luc Plamondon...Hall of Fame
Allan Waters ....Walt Grealis Special Achievement Award

2000

Supposed Former Infatuation Junkie–Alanis Morissette...........................Best Album
Michael Wrycraft–Radio Fusebox by Andy Stochansky ....Best Album Design
Julie Doiron and the Wooden Stars
–Julie Doiron and the Wooden Stars .... Best Alternative Album
Gust of Wind–Ray Bonneville .... Best Blues Album
Skinnamarink TV–Sharon, Lois & Bram ....Best Children's Album
German Romantic Opera–Ben Heppner ....Best Classical Album:
    Vocal or Choral Performance
Respighi: La Boutique Fantasque
–Orchestre symphonique de Montreal/Kent Nagano.....................Best Classical Album:
    Large Ensemble or Soloist(s) With Large Ensemble Accompaniment
Schumann: String Quartets
–St. Lawrence String Quartet ....Best Classical Album: Solo or Chamber Ensemble
Shattered Night, Shivering Stars–Alexina Louie ....Best Classical Composition
. . . so far–D.D. Jackson.................Best Contemporary Jazz Album–Instrumental
Shania Twain.. Best Country Female Artist
The Rankins .... Best Country Group or Duo
Paul Brandt ....Best Country Male Artist
Silence–Delerium.. Best Dance Recording
Chantal Kreviazuk.. Best Female Artist
Omnisource–Madagascar Slim .... Best Global Album
Legacy of Hope–Deborah Klassen ....Best Gospel Album
Matthew Good Band .... Best Group

In My Hands–Natalie MacMaster .... Best Instrumental Album
Bryan Adams ....Best Male Artist
Falling Down–
Chester Knight and The Wind .... Best Music of Aboriginal Canada Recording
Sky .... Best New Group
Tal Bachman .... Best New Solo Artist
Colour and Moving Still–Chantal Kreviazuk ....Best Pop/Adult Album
Tal Bachman and Bob Rock .... Best Producer
Thinkin' About You–2Rude featuring Latoya & Miranda .... Best R&B/Soul Recording
Ice Cold–Choclair ....Best Rap Recording
Paul Northfield/Jagori Tanna .... Best Recording Engineer
Heart & Soul–Lazo ....Best Reggae Recording
Beautiful Midnight–Matthew Good Band .... Best Rock Album
Kings of Love–Blackie & The Rodeo Kings .... Best Roots & Traditional Album–Group
Breakfast In New Orleans Dinner In Timbuktu
–Bruce Cockburn ....Best Roots & Traditional Album–Solo
Millennium–Backstreet Boys .... Best Selling Album (Foreign or Domestic)
En Catimini–La Chicane ....Best Selling Francophone Album
Bobcaygeon–The Tragically Hip .... Best Single
Shania Twain (co-songwriter Robert John "Mutt" Lange).............Best Songwriter
Deep In A Dream–Pat LaBarbera ....Best Traditional Jazz Album–Instrumental
So Pure–Alanis Morissette .... Best Video
When I Look Into Your Eyes–Diana Krall ....Best Vocal Jazz Album
Sarah McLachlan ....International Achievement Award
Bruce Fairbairn .... Canadian Music Hall of Fame Award
Emile Berliner .... Walt Grealis Special Achievement Award

2001

Maroon–Barenaked Ladies ....Best Album
Stuart Chatwood (creative director), Antoine Moonen (graphic artist),
James St Laurent/Margaret Malandruccolo/Nick Sarros (photographers)
–Tangents by The Tea Party ....Best Album Design
Mass Romantic–The New Pornographers ....Best Alternative Album
Love Comin' Down–Sue Foley .... Best Blues Album
Sing & Dance–Jack Grunsky ....Best Children's Album
G.F. Handel: Apollo e Dafne Silete Venti–Karina Gauvin; Russell Braun;
Les Violons du Roy ....Best Classical Album: Vocal or Choral Performance
Sibelius: Lemminkainen Suite–Night Ride and Sunrise–Toronto Symphony Orchestra,
Jukka-Pekka Saraste–(conductor) ....Best Classical Album:
                  Large Ensemble or Soloist(s) with Large Ensemble Accompaniment
Bach: The six Sonatas & Partitas For Solo Violin
–James Ehnes ....Best Classical Album: Solo or Chamber Ensemble
From The Diary of Anne Frank–Oskar Morawetz ....Best Classical Composition
Compassion–Francois Carrier Trio + 1 .....Best Contemporary Jazz Album–Instrumental
Terri Clark .... Best Country Female Artist

The Wilkinsons .... Best Country Group or Duo
Paul Brandt ....Best Country Male Artist
Into The Night–Love Inc. .... Best Dance Recording
Jann Arden ....Best Female Artist
Ritmo + Soul–Jane Bunnett and the Spirits of Havana .... Best Global Album
Simple Songs–Steve Bell ....Best Gospel Album
Barenaked Ladies .... Best Group
Free Fall–Jesse Cook .... Best Instrumental Album
Neil Young ....Best Male Artist
Nipaiamianan–Florent Vollant .... Best Music of Aboriginal Canada Recording
Nickelback .... Best New Group
Nelly Furtado .... Best New Solo Artist
Maroon–Barenaked Ladies .... Best Pop Album
Gerald Eaton/Brian West/Nelly Furtado .... Best Producer
Sleepless–jacksoul .... Best R&B/Soul Recording
Balance–Swollen Members .... Best Rap Recording
Jeff Wolpert .... Best Recording Engineer
Lenn Hammond–Lenn Hammond ....Best Reggae Recording
Music @ Work–The Tragically Hip .... Best Rock Album
Tri-Continental–Tri-Continental: Bill Bourne,
Lester Quitzau, Madagascar Slim .... Best Roots & Traditional Album–Group
Jenny Whiteley–Jenny Whiteley ....Best Roots & Traditional Album–Solo
The Marshall Mathers LP–Eminem ....Best Selling Album (Foreign or Domestic)
Un Grand Noel d'amour–Ginette Reno ....Best Selling Francophone Album
I'm Like A Bird–Nelly Furtado .... Best Single
Nelly Furtado ....Best Songwriter
Rob McConnell Tentet
–Rob McConnell Tentet ....Best Traditional Jazz Album–Instrumental
Alive–Edwin, Rob Heydon .... Best Video
Both Sides Now–Joni Mitchell ....Best Vocal Jazz Album
Bruce Cockburn .... Canadian Music Hall of Fame Award
Daniel Caudeiron .... Walt Grealis Special Achievement Award

2002

The Look of Love–Diana Krall ....Best Album
Sebastien Toupin (art director), Sebastien Toupin, Benoit St-Jean,
Michel Valois (designers), Martin Tremblay (photographer)
–Disparu by La Chicane ....Best Album Design
Poses–Rufus Wainwright ....Best Alternative Album
Diana Krall ....Best Artist
Big Mouth–Colin Linden .... Best Blues Album
A Classical Kids Christmas–Susan Hammond ....Best Children's Album
Air Francois–Ben Heppner .... Best Classical Album: Vocal or Choral Performance
Max Brunch, Concertos 1 & 3–James Ehnes (violin), Orchestre Symphonique de
Montréal, Charles Dutoit–(conductor) ....Best Classical Album:
                  Large Ensemble or Soloist(s) With Large Ensemble Accompaniment

Bach Arrangements—Angela Hewitt...Best Classical Album: Solo or Chamber Ensemble
Par-ci, par-la—Chan Ka Nin..Best Classical Composition
Live—Francois Bourassa Trio +
André Leroux ....Best Contemporary Jazz Album—Instrumental
Carolyn Dawn Johnson..Best Country Artist/Group
Space Invader—Hatiras ....Best Dance Recording
The Journey—Alpha Yaya Diallo..Best Global Album
Downhere—Downhere..Best Gospel Album
Nickelback..Best Group
Armando's Fire—Oscar Lopez......................................Best Instrumental Album
On and On—Eagle & Hawk.................Best Music of Aboriginal Canada Recording
The Ennis Sisters..Best New Country Artist/Group
Default..Best New Group
Hawksley Workman..Best New Solo Artist
Morning Orbit—David Usher..Best Pop Album
Don't You Forget It—Glenn Lewis........................Best R&B/Soul Recording
Bad Dreams—Swollen Members..................................Best Rap Recording
Randy Staub..Best Recording Engineer
Love (African Woman)—Blessed..................................Best Reggae Recording
Silver Side Up—Nickelback..Best Rock Album
Cordial—La Bottine Souriante..................Best Roots & Traditional Album—Group
Far End of Summer—David Francey.............Best Roots & Traditional Album—Solo
Hotshot—Shaggy..............................Best Selling Album (Foreign or Domestic)
Les vents ont changé—Kevin Parent.............Best Selling Francophone Album
How You Remind Me—Nickelback..Best Single
Jann Arden..Best Songwriter
Murley, Bickert & Wallace: Live at the Senator
—Mike Murley..............................Best Traditional Jazz Album—Instrumental
Jealous of Your Cigarette—Hawksley Workman, Sean Michael Turrell...........Best Video
The Look of Love—Diana Krall..Best Vocal Jazz Album
Daniel Lanois (co-producer Brian Eno)........................Jack Richardson Best Producer
Daniel Lanois..Canadian Music Hall of Fame
Michael Cohl................................Walt Grealis Special Achievement Award

2003

Lovesick Blues—Derek Miller........................Aboriginal Recording of the Year
Steve Goode (director/designer), Margaret Malandruccolo/
Nelson Garcia (illustrator/photographer)—Exit by k-os..........Album Design of the Year
Let Go—Avril Lavigne..Album of the Year
You Forgot It In People—Broken Social Scene..................Alternative Album of the Year
Shania Twain..Artist of the Year
6 String Lover—Jack de Keyzer..Blues Album of the Year
Sing With Fred—Fred Penner..................................Children's Album of the Year
Bruch Concertos: Vol II—James Ehnes/Mario Bernardi/
Orchestre symphonique de Montréal....................Classical Album of the Year:
Large Ensemble or Soloist(s) with Large Ensemble Accompaniment

Liszt: Paganini Studies & Schubert March Transcriptions—
Marc-André Hamelin..................Classical Album of the Year: Solo or Chamber Ensemble
Mozart Requiem—Les Violons Du roy..Classical Album of the Year:
Vocal or Choral Performance
Requiem for a Charred Skull—Bramwell Tovey............Classical Composition of the Year
Instrument of Praise—Toronto Mass Choir....................................Contemporary Christian/
Gospel Album of the Year

Tales From the Blues Lounge
—Richard Underhill....................................Contemporary Jazz Album of the Year
I'm Gonna Getcha Good!—Shania Twain................Country Recording of the Year
Billie Jean—The Sound Bluntz........................Dance Recording of the Year
Daniel Bélanger..Francophone Album of the Year
Sum 41..Group of the Year
Allegro—Robert Michaels........................Instrumental Album of the Year
The Eminem Show—Eminem........................International Album of the Year
Alanis Morissette........................Jack Richardson Producer of the Year
Shania Twain..Juno Fan Choice Award
Avril Lavigne..New Artist of the Year
Theory of A Deadman..New Group of the Year
Let Go—Avril Lavigne..Pop Album of the Year
The Way I Feel—Remy Shand........................R&B/Soul Recording of the Year
Monsters In The Closet—Swollen Members........................Rap Recording of the Year
Denis Tougas..Recording Engineer of the Year
You Won't See Me Cry—Sonia Collymore....................Reggae Recording of the Year
Gravity—Our Lady Peace..Rock Album of the Year
Chicken Scratch—Zubot & Dawson..............Roots & Traditional Album of the Year: Group
Unravel—Lynn Miles........................Roots & Traditional Album of the Year: Solo
Complicated—Avril Lavigne..Single of the Year
Chad Kroeger/Nickelback..Songwriter of the Year
Life on Earth—Renee Rosnes........................Traditional Jazz Album of the Year
Weapon—Matthew Good, Ante Kovac........................Video of the Year
Live In Paris—Diana Krall..Vocal Jazz Album of the Year
Balagane—Jeszcze Raz..World Music Album of the Year
Tom Cochrane..Canadian Music Hall of Fame
Terry McBride................................Walt Grealis Special Achievement Award

2004

Big Feeling—Susan Aglukark........................Aboriginal Recording of the Year
Garnet Armstrong/Susan Michalek (director/designer); Andrew MacNaughtan
(photographer)—Love Is The Only Soldier by Jann Arden........Album Design of the Year
We Were Born In a Flame—Sam Roberts..Album of the Year
Talkin' Honky Blues—Buck 65........................Alternative Album of the Year
Sam Roberts..Artist of the Year
Painkiller—Morgan Davis..Blues Album of the Year
A Duck In New York City—Connie Kaldor....................Children's Album of the Year

CONCERTOS: Music of Jacques Hétu—Andre Laplante (piano),
Christopher Millard (bassoon), Robert Cram (flute),
Joaquin Valdepenas (clarinet), CBC Radio Orchestra,
Mario Bernardi—(conductor)..Classical Album of the Year:
           Large Ensemble or Soloist(s) with Large Ensemble Accompaniment
Murphy, Chan, Hatzis, Kulescha: Canadian Premiers
—Gryphon Trio.....................Classical Album of the Year: Solo or Chamber Ensemble
Azulão—Isabel Bayrakdarian, James Parker,
Cello Ensemble.......................Classical Album of the Year: Vocal or Choral Performance
String Quartet No. 8—R. Murray Schafer.....................Classical Composition of the Year
Jill Paquette—Jill Paquette................Contemporary Christian/Gospel Album of the Year
bLOW tHE hOUSE dOWN
—Great Uncles of the Revolution.....................Contemporary Jazz Album of the Year
Up!—Shania Twain..Country Recording of the Year
Something About You—The Sound Bluntz......................Dance Recording of the Year
Wilfred Le Bouthillier—Wilfred Le Bouthillier...................Francophone Album of the Year
Nickelback...Group of the Year
Italian Love Songs—I Sorenti.......................................Instrumental Album of the Year
Get Rich or Die Tryin'—50 Cent...................................International Album of the Year
Gavin Brown...Jack Richardson Producer of the Year
Nickelback...Juno Fan Choice Award
Rush, Andrew MacNaughtan/Dan Catullo (directors), Allan Weinrib/Pegi Cecconi/
Ray Danniels (producers)—Rush In Rio.................................Music DVD of the Year
Michael Bublé...New Artist of the Year
Billy Talent..New Group of the Year
Afterglow—Sarah McLachlan..Pop Album of the Year
The Master Plan—In Essence.......................................R&B/Soul Recording of the Year
Flagrant—Choclair...Rap Recording of the Year
Mike Haas/Dylan Heming/Jeff Wolpert....................Recording Engineer of the Year
Rent A Tile—Leroy Brown....................................Reggae Recording of the Year
We Were Born In A Flame—Sam Roberts.........................Rock Album of the Year
Maudite Moisson—Le Vent du Nord............Roots & Traditional Album of the Year: Group
Skating Rink—David Francey...........................Roots & Traditional Album of the Year: Solo
Powerless (Say What You Want)—Nelly Furtado...........................Single of the Year
Sarah McLachlan...Songwriter of the Year
Lost in the Stars—Guido Basso.........................Traditional Jazz Album of the Year
Fighter—Christina Aguilera, Floria Sigismondi.............................Video of the Year
Shade—Holly Cole...Vocal Jazz Album of the Year
Beyond Boundaries—Kiran Ahluwalia....................World Music Album of the Year
Bob Ezrin..Canadian Music Hall of Fame
Walt Grealis...Walt Grealis Special Achievement Award

2005
Taima—Taima..Aboriginal Recording of the Year
All Of Our Names—Sarah Harmer...................Adult Alternative Album of the Year

Billy Talent—Billy Talent...Album of the Year
Let It Die—Feist..Alternative Album of the Year
Avril Lavigne...Artist of the Year
I'm Just A Man—Garrett Mason...Blues Album of the Year
Vincent Marcone—It Dreams by Jakalope.................CD/DVD Artwork Design of the Year
A Poodle In Paris—Connie Kaldor.................................Children's Album of the Year
Dardanus/Le temple de la gloire: Music of Jean-Philippe Rameau
—Jeanne Lamon, Tafelmusik Baroque Orchestra....................Classical Album of the Year:
           Large Ensemble or Soloist(s) with Large Ensemble Accompaniment
Bach: The English Suites
—Angela Hewitt............................Classical Album of the Year: Solo or Chamber Ensemble
Cleopatra—Isabel Bayrakdarian,
Tafelmusik Baroque Orchestra...Classical Album of the Year:
           Vocal or Choral Performance
The Tents of Abraham—Istvan Anhalt.....................Classical Composition of the Year
Here To Stay—Greg Sczebel...............Contemporary Christian/Gospel Album of the Year
New Danzon—Hilario Durán Trio..........................Contemporary Jazz Album of the Year
One Good Friend—George Canyon.............................Country Recording of the Year
All Things (Just Keep Getting Better)
—Widelife with Simone Denny..Dance Recording of the Year
Marie-Elaine Thibert—Marie-Elaine Thibert.....................Francophone Album of the Year
Billy Talent..Group of the Year
Mi Destino/My Destiny—Oscar Lopez....................Instrumental Album of the Year
American Idiot—Green Day..................................International Album of the Year
Bob Rock...Jack Richardson Producer of the Year
Avril Lavigne...Juno Fan Choice Award
Ron Mann/Blue Rodeo—In Stereovision—Blue Rodeo....................Music DVD of the Year
Feist..New Artist of the Year
Alexisonfire..New Group of the Year
Under My Skin—Avril Lavigne...Pop Album of the Year
Keshia Chanté—Keshia Chanté.........................R&B/Soul Recording of the Year
Joyful Rebellion—k-os..Rap Recording of the Year
L. Stu Young..Recording Engineer of the Year
WYSIWYG—Sonia Collymore..............................Reggae Recording of the Year
Chuck—Sum 41...Rock Album of the Year
40 Days—The Wailin' Jennys........................Roots & Traditional Album of the Year: Group
Hopetown—Jenny Whiteley.........................Roots & Traditional Album of the Year: Solo
Crabbuckit—k-os...Single of the Year
Ron Sexsmith...Songwriter of the Year
Vivid: The David Braid Sextet Live—David Braid.......Traditional Jazz Album of the Year
B-Boy Stance—k-os,
The Love Movement feat. k-os & Micah Meisner......................................Video of the Year
The Girl In The Other Room—Diana Krall.............................Vocal Jazz Album of the Year
African Guitar Summit—Mighty Popo, Madagascar Slim, Donné Roberts,
Alpha Ya Ya Diallo, Adam Solomon, Pa Joe....................World Music Album of the Year

The Tragically Hip...Canadian Music Hall of Fame
Allan Slaight ....Walt Grealis Special Achievement Award

2006

Hometown—Burnt Project 1 .... Aboriginal Recording of the Year
Prairie Wind—Neil Young ....Adult Alternative Album of the Year
It's Time—Michael Bublé... Album of the Year
Broken Social Scene—Broken Social Scene.............. Alternative Album of the Year
Michael Bublé.. Artist of the Year
Let It Loose—Kenny 'Blues Boss' Wayne .... Blues Album of the Year
Rob Baker (director/illustrator); Garnet Armstrong (director/designer);
Susan Michalek (designer); Will Ruocco (illustrator)
—Hipeponymous by The Tragically Hip.......................CD/DVD Artwork Design of the Year
Baroque Adventure: The Quest For Arundo Donax
—Tafelmusik Baroque Orchestra.....................Children's Album of the Year
Beethoven: Symphonies nos. 5 et 6
—Tafelmusik Baroque Orchestra, Bruno Weil.......................Classical Album of the Year:
Large Ensemble or Soloist(s) with Large Ensemble Accompaniment
Albéniz: Iberia—Marc-André Hamelin ....Classical Album of the Year:
Solo or Chamber Ensemble
Viardot-Garcia: Lieder Chansons Canzoni Mazurkas
—Isabel Bayrakdarian, Serouj Kradjian........................Classical Album of the Year:
Vocal or Choral Performance
String Quartet No. 1 (The Awakening)
—Christos Hatzis...Classical Composition of the Year
Amanda Falk Amanda Falk .... Contemporary Christian/Gospel Album of the Year
Radio Guantánamo (Guantánamo Blues Project Vol. 1)
—Jane Bunnett...Contemporary Jazz Album of the Year
The Road Hammers—The Road Hammers....................Country Recording of the Year
Spanish Fly—Hatiras & Macca feat. Shawna B.....................Dance Recording of the Year
Pages blanches—Jim Corcoran .... Francophone Album of the Year
Nickelback..Group of the Year
Belladonna—Daniel Lanois.................................Instrumental Album of the Year
Monkey Business—The Black Eyed Peas ....International Album of the Year
X&Y—Coldplay ....International Album of the Year
Neil Young .... Jack Richardson Producer of the Year
Simple Plan ....Juno Fan Choice Award
Pierre Lamoureux/Christopher Mills, Gord Downie/Allan Reid/
Shawn Marino—Hipeponymous by The Tragically Hip ....Music DVD of the Year
Daniel Powter ....New Artist of the Year
Bedouin Soundclash ....New Group of the Year
It's Time—Michael Bublé...Pop Album of the Year
Back For More—Shawn Desman....................R&B/Soul Recording of the Year
The Dusty Foot Philosopher—K'naan .... Rap Recording of the Year
Vic Florencia ....Recording Engineer of the Year
Reggae Time—Blessed..Reggae Recording of the Year

All The Right Reasons—Nickelback.............................Rock Album of the Year
The Duhks—The Duhks .... Roots & Traditional Album of the Year: Group
Hair In My Eyes Like A Highland Steer
—Corb Lund..............................Roots & Traditional Album of the Year: Solo
Home—Michael Bublé...Single of the Year
Arcade Fire ....Songwriter of the Year
Ask Me Later—Don Thompson Quartet ....Traditional Jazz Album of the Year
Devil's Eyes—Buck 65, Micah Meisner .... Video of the Year
Christmas Songs—Diana Krall .... Vocal Jazz Album of the Year
Humo De Tabaco—Alex Cuba Band ....World Music Album of the Year
Bryan Adams ....Canadian Music Hall of Fame
Bernie Finkelstein ....Walt Grealis Special Achievement Award
Bruce Cockburn ....Allan Waters Humanitarian Award

2007

Sedzé—Leela Gilday................................... Aboriginal Recording of the Year
The Light That Guides You Home—Jim Cuddy ....Adult Alternative Album of the Year
Loose—Nelly Furtado .... Album of the Year
Sometimes—City and Colour .... Alternative Album of the Year
Nelly Furtado .... Artist of the Year
House of Refuge—Jim Byrnes.. Blues Album of the Year
Chloe Lum & Yannick Desranleau for Seripop (director/designer/illustrator/
photographer)—The Looks by MSTRKRFT ....CD/DVD Artwork Design of the Year
My Beautiful World—Jack Grunsky ....Children's Album of the Year
Mozart: Violin Concerti—James Ehnes/
Mozart Anniversary Orchestra ....Classical Album of the Year:
Large Ensemble or Soloist(s) with Large Ensemble Accompaniment
Piazzolla—Les Violons du Roy, Jean-Marie Zeitouni.............Classical Album of the Year:
Solo or Chamber Ensemble
Mozart: Arie e Duetti—Isabel Bayrakdarian, Michael Schade,
Russell Braun, Canadian Opera Company Orchestra/
Richard Bradshaw..Classical Album of the Year:
Vocal or Choral Performance
Clere Vénus Á L'AVENTURE!—Denis Gougeon................Classical Composition of the Year
Wide Eyed and Mystified—Downhere .... Contemporary Christian/
Gospel Album of the Year
From The Heart
—Hilario Durán and His Latin Jazz Big Band........Contemporary Jazz Album of the Year
Somebody Wrote Love—George Canyon............................Country Recording of the Year
Sexor—Tiga ....Dance Recording of the Year
Il était une fois dans l'est—Antoine Gratton.................... Francophone Album of the Year
Billy Talent...Group of the Year
Run Neil Run—Sisters Euclid..............................Instrumental Album of the Year
Taking The Long Way—Dixie Chicks ....International Album of the Year
Brian Howes .... Jack Richardson Producer of the Year
Nelly Furtado ....Juno Fan Choice Award

Andy Keen, Sarah Harmer, Patrick Sambrook, Bryan Bean
—Escarpment Blues—Sarah Harmer ....Music DVD of the Year
Tomi Swick ....New Artist of the Year
Mobile ....New Group of the Year
Loose—Nelly Furtado ....Pop Album of the Year
mySOUL—jacksoul ....R&B/Soul Recording of the Year
Black Magic—Swollen Members ....Rap Recording of the Year
John "Beetle" Bailey ....Recording Engineer of the Year
Xrated—Korexion ....Reggae Recording of the Year
II—Billy Talent ....Rock Album of the Year
Bloom—The McDades ....Roots & Traditional Album of the Year: Group
Yellowjacket—Stephen Fearing ....Roots & Traditional Album of the Year: Solo
Promiscuous ft. Timbaland—Nelly Furtado ....Single of the Year
Gordie Sampson ....Songwriter of the Year
Avenue Standard—Jon Ballantyne ....Traditional Jazz Album of the Year
Bridge To Nowhere—Duplex (aka Dave Pawsey and Jonathan Legris),
Sam Roberts ....Video of the Year
From This Moment On—Diana Krall ....Vocal Jazz Album of the Year
Kaba Horo—Lubo Alexandrov ....World Music Album of the Year
Bob Rock ....Canadian Music Hall of Fame
Donald K. Tarlton ....Walt Grealis Special Achievement Award
Tom Jackson ....Allan Waters Humanitarian Award

2008

The Dirty Looks—Derek Miller ....Aboriginal Recording of the Year
Small Miracles—Blue Rodeo ....Adult Alternative Album of the Year
The Reminder—Feist ....Album of the Year
Neon Bible—Arcade Fire ....Alternative Album of the Year
Feist ....Artist of the Year
Building Full of Blues—FATHEAD ....Blues Album of the Year
Tracy Maurice (director/designer); Francois Miron (photographer)
—Neon Bible by Arcade Fire ....CD/DVD Artwork Design of the Year
Music Soup—Jen Gould ....Children's Album of the Year
Korngold, Barber & Walton Violin Concertos—James Ehnes, Bramwell Tovey,
Vancouver Symphony Orchestra ....Classical Album of the Year:
          Large Ensemble or Soloist(s) with Large Ensemble Accompaniment
Alkan Concerto for Solo Piano—Marc-André Hamelin ....Classical Album of the Year:
          Solo or Chamber Ensemble
Surprise—Measha Brueggergosman ....Classical Album of the Year:
          Vocal or Choral Performance
Constantinople—Christos Hatzis ....Classical Composition of the Year
Holy God—Brian Doerksen ....Contemporary Christian/Gospel Album of the Year
Almost Certainly Dreaming
—The Chris Tarry Group ....Contemporary Jazz Album of the Year
Risk—Paul Brandt ....Country Recording of the Year
All U Ever Want—Billy Newton-Davis vs. Deadmau5 ....Dance Recording of the Year

L'échec du matériel—Daniel Bélanger ....Francophone Album of the Year
Blue Rodeo ....Group of the Year
The Upmost—Jayme Stone ....Instrumental Album of the Year
Good Girl Gone Bad—Rihanna ....International Album of the Year
Joni Mitchell ....Jack Richardson Producer of the Year
Michael Bublé ....Juno Fan Choice Award
Pierre & Francois Lamoureux, Billy Talent, Pierre Tremblay,
Steve Blair—666 Live—Billy Talent ....Music DVD of the Year
Serena Ryder ....New Artist of the Year
Wintersleep ....New Group of the Year
The Reminder—Feist ....Pop Album of the Year
Revival—Jully Black ....R&B/Soul Recording of the Year
The Revolution—Belly ....Rap Recording of the Year
Kevin Churko ....Recording Engineer of the Year
Don't Go Pretending—Mikey Dangerous ....Reggae Recording of the Year
Them Vs. You Vs. Me—Finger Eleven ....Rock Album of the Year
Key Principles—Nathan ....Roots & Traditional Album of the Year: Group
Right of Passage—David Francey ....Roots & Traditional Album of the Year: Solo
1 2 3 4—Feist ....Single of the Year
Feist ....Songwriter of the Year
Debut—Brandi Disterheft ....Traditional Jazz Album of the Year
C'Mon—Blue Rodeo, Christopher Mills ....Video of the Year
Make Someone Happy—Sophie Milman ....Vocal Jazz Album of the Year
Agua Del Pozo—Alex Cuba ....World Music Album of the Year
Triumph ....Canadian Music Hall of Fame
Moses Znaimer ....Walt Grealis Special Achievement Award
Paul Brandt ....Allan Waters Humanitarian Award

2009

Running For The Drum—Buffy Sainte-Marie ....Aboriginal Recording of the Year
Is it o.k.—Serena Ryder ....Adult Alternative Album of the Year
Dark Horse—Nickelback ....Album of the Year
Oceans Will Rise—The Stills ....Alternative Album of the Year
Sam Roberts ....Artist of the Year
Ramblin' Son—Julian Fauth ....Blues Album of the Year
Anouk Pennel; Stéphane Poirier—En concert dans la forêt des mal-aimés
avec l'Orchestre Métropolitain du Grand Montréal
by Pierre Lapointe ....CD/DVD Artwork Design of the Year
Snacktime!—Barenaked Ladies ....Children's Album of the Year
Beethoven: Ideals Of The French Revolution
—Orchestre symphonique de Montreal/Kent Nagano ....Classical Album of the Year:
          Large Ensemble or Soloist(s) with Large Ensemble Accompaniment
Homage—James Ehnes ....Classical Album of the Year: Solo or Chamber Ensemble
Gloria! Vivaldi's Angels—Ensemble Caprice ....Classical Album of the Year:
          Vocal or Choral Performance
Flanders Fields Reflections—John Burge ....Classical Composition of the Year

Ending Is Beginning—Downhere .... Contemporary Christian/Gospel Album of the Year
Embracing Voices—Jane Bunnett .... Contemporary Jazz Album of the Year
Beautiful Life—Doc Walker .... Country Recording of the Year
Random Album Title—Deadmau5 .... Dance Recording of the Year
Tous les sens—Ariane Moffatt .... Francophone Album of the Year
Nickelback .... Group of the Year
Nostomania
—DJ Brace and The Electric Nosehair Orchestra .... Instrumental Album of the Year
Viva La Vida—Coldplay .... International Album of the Year
Daniel Lanois .... Jack Richardson Producer of the Year
Nickelback .... Juno Fan Choice Award
Blue Road—Blue Rodeo, Christopher Mills, Geoff McLean .... Music DVD of the Year
LIGHTS .... New Artist of the Year
The Stills .... New Group of the Year
Flavors of Entanglement—Alanis Morissette .... Pop Album of the Year
The Love Chronicles—Divine Brown .... R&B/Soul Recording of the Year
Not 4 Sale—Kardinal Offishall .... Rap Recording of the Year
Kevin Churko .... Recording Engineer of the Year
Everything—Humble .... Reggae Recording of the Year
Love At The End Of The World—Sam Roberts .... Rock Album of the Year
Chic Gamine—Chic Gamine .... Roots & Traditional Album of the Year: Group
Proof of Love—Old Man Leudecke .... Roots & Traditional Album of the Year: Solo
Dangerous—Kardinal Offishall .... Single of the Year
Dallas Green .... Songwriter of the Year
Second Time Around—Oliver Jones .... Traditional Jazz Album of the Year
Honey Honey—Feist, Anthony Seck .... Video of the Year
Lucky—Molly Johnson .... Vocal Jazz Album of the Year
Africa to Appalachia—Jayme Stone & Mansa Sissoko ...... World Music Album of the Year
Loverboy .... Canadian Music Hall of Fame
Fred Sherratt .... Walt Grealis Special Achievement Award
Sarah McLachlan .... Allan Waters Humanitarian Award

2010

We Are—Digging Roots .... Aboriginal Album of the Year
Three—Joel Plaskett .... Adult Alternative Album of the Year
Crazy Love—Michael Bublé .... Album of the Year
Fantasies—Metric .... Alternative Album of the Year
K'naan .... Artist of the Year
The Corktown Sessions—Jack de Keyzer .... Blues Album of the Year
Love My New Shirt—Norman Foote .... Children's Album of the Year
Mathieu, Shostakovich, Mendelssohn: Concertino & Concertos
—Alain Lefèvre & London Mozart Players .... Classical Album of the Year:
                Large Ensemble or Soloist(s) with Large Ensemble Accompaniment
Joel Quarrington: Garden Scene—Joel Quarrington .... Classical Album of the Year:
                Solo or Chamber Ensemble
Adrianne Pieczonka Sings Puccini—Adrianne Pieczonka ..... Classical Album of the Year:
                Vocal or Choral Performance

Lament In The Trampled Garden—Marjan Mozetich .... Classical Composition of the Year
Where's Our Revolution—Matt Brouwer .... Contemporary Christian/
                Gospel Album of the Year
The Happiness Project—Charles Spearin .... Contemporary Jazz Album of the Year
Dance With Me—Johnny Reid .... Country Album of the Year
For Lack of a Better Name—Deadmau5 .... Dance Recording of the Year
Les sentinelles dorment—Andrea Lindsay .... Francophone Album of the Year
Metric .... Group of the Year
As Seen Through The Windows—Bell Orchestre .... Instrumental Album of the Year
Only By The Night—Kings Of Leon .... International Album of the Year
Bob Rock .... Jack Richardson Producer of the Year
Michael Bublé .... Juno Fan Choice Award
Sam Dunn, Scott McFadyen Rod Smallwood,
Stefan Demetriou, Andy Taylor—Iron Maiden Flight 666 .... Music DVD of the Year
Drake .... New Artist of the Year
Arkells .... New Group of the Year
Crazy Love—Michael Bublé .... Pop Album of the Year
Lonesome Highway—jacksoul .... R&B/Soul Recording of the Year
So Far Gone—Drake .... Rap Recording of the Year
Dan Brodbeck .... Recording Engineer of the Year
Martin Bernard; Stephane Cocke;
Thomas Csano for Beats on Canvas .... Recording Package of the Year
Gonna Be Alright—Dubmatix ft. Prince Blanco .... Reggae Recording of the Year
III—Billy Talent .... Rock Album of the Year
Good Lovelies—Good Lovelies .... Roots & Traditional Album of the Year: Group
Hunter, Hunter—Amelia Curran .... Roots & Traditional Album of the Year: Solo
Haven't Met You Yet—Michael Bublé .... Single of the Year
K'naan .... Songwriter of the Year
It's About Time—Terry Clarke .... Traditional Jazz Album of the Year
Little Bit of Red—Serena Ryder, Marc Ricciardelli .... Video of the Year
Ranee Lee Lives Upstairs—Ranee Lee .... Vocal Jazz Album of the Year
Comfortably Mine—Dominic Mancuso .... World Music Album of the Year
April Wine .... Canadian Music Hall of Fame
Ross Reynolds .... Walt Grealis Special Achievement Award
Bryan Adams .... Allan Waters Humanitarian Award

CARAS BOARD OF DIRECTORS
PRESENT–1975

2009/10

Ed Robinson	Chair
Melanie Berry	President
Steve Kane	1st Vice-President
Randy Lennox	2nd Vice-President
Humphrey Kadaner	Secretary-Treasurer
Bruce Allen	Director
Vivian Barclay	Director
Deane Cameron	Director
Shane Carter	Director
Vinny Cinquemani	Director
Rob Farina	Director
Paul Haagenson	Director
Ralph James	Director
Aideen O'Brien	Director
Julien Paquin	Director
Ed Robertson	Director
Patti-Anne Tarlton	Director
Chris Taylor	Director
Louis Thomas	Director

2008/09

Stephen Stohn	Chair
Melanie Berry	President
Deane Cameron	1st Vice-President
Steve Kane	2nd Vice-President
Darren Throop	Secretary-Treasurer
Bruce Allen	Director
Vivian Barclay	Director
Shane Carter	Director
Vinny Cinquemani	Director
Kim Cooke	Director
Jim Cuddy	Director
Rob Farina	Director
Paul Haagenson	Director
Ralph James	Director
Humphrey Kadaner	Director
Randy Lennox	Director
Aideen O'Brien	Director
Julien Paquin	Director
Patti-Anne Tarlton	Director
Chris Taylor	Director
Louis Thomas	Director

2007/08

Stephen Stohn	Chair
Melanie Berry	President
Deane Cameron	1st Vice-President
Steve Kane	2nd Vice-President
Darren Throop	Secretary-Treasurer
Jully Black	Director
Kim Cooke	Director
Vinny Cinquemani	Director
Jim Cuddy	Director
Denise Donlon	Director
Rob Farina	Director
Paul Haagenson	Director
Ralph James	Director
Randy Lennox	Director
Pierre Marchand	Director
Aideen O'Brien	Director
Samantha Pickard	Director
Chris Taylor	Director
Louis Thomas	Director
Pierre Tremblay	Director

2006/07

Stephen Stohn	Chair
Melanie Berry	President & Executive Producer
Deane Cameron	1st Vice-President
Steve Kane	2nd Vice-President
Darren Throop	Secretary-Treasurer
Jully Black	Director
Vinny Cinquemani	Director
Kim Cooke	Director
Jim Cuddy	Director
Denise Donlon	Director
Rob Farina	Director
Paul Haagenson	Director
Ralph James	Director
J.J. Johnston	Director
Randy Lennox	Director
Pierre Marchand	Director
Aideen O'Brien	Director
Samantha Pickard	Director
Chris Taylor	Director
Louis Thomas	Director
Pierre Tremblay	Director

2005/06

Ross Reynolds	Chair
Melanie Berry	President
Deane Cameron	1st Vice-President
Jim West	2nd Vice-President
Darren Throop	Secretary-Treasurer
Jully Black	Director
Elaine Bomberry	Director
Kim Cooke	Director
Jim Cuddy	Director
Denise Donlon	Director
Rob Farina	Director
Gary Furniss	Director

2004/05

Ross Reynolds	Chair
Melanie Berry	President
Deane Cameron	1st Vice-President
Jim West	2nd Vice-President
Steve Herman	Secretary-Treasurer
Jully Black	Director
Elaine Bomberry	Director
Kim Cooke	Director
Jim Cuddy	Director
Denise Donlon	Director
Sam Feldman	Director
Gary Furniss	Director
J.J. Johnston	Director
Randy Lennox	Director
Samantha Pickard	Director
Gary Slaight	Director
Louis Thomas	Director
Darren Throop	Director
Pierre Tremblay	Director
Matt Zimbel	Director

2003/04

Ross Reynolds	Chair
Melanie Berry	President
Deane Cameron	1st Vice-President
Jim West	2nd Vice-President
Steve Herman	Secretary-Treasurer
Kim Cooke	Director
Jim Cuddy	Director
Denise Donlon	Director
Gary Furniss	Director
J.J. Johnston	Director
Tim Potocic	Director
Gary Slaight	Director
Chris Smith	Director
Donald Tarlton	Director
Darren Throop	Director (Replacing Roger Whiteman)
Pierre Tremblay	Director
Randy Lennox	Director
Sheri Jones	Director
Matt Zimbel	Director

Also appearing (column 3, top):

J.J. Johnston	Director
Ralph James	Director
Samantha Pickard	Director
Steve Kane	Director
Stephen Stohn	Director
Louis Thomas	Director
Chris Taylor	Director
Pierre Tremblay	Director

2002/03

Ross Reynolds..Chairman
Melanie Berry..President
Sheri Jones..1st Vice-President
Randy Lennox..2nd Vice-President
Steve Herman..Secretary-Treasurer
Laura Bartlett..Director
Deane Cameron..Director
Gary Furniss..Director
Cliff Jones..Director
Garry Newman..Director
Tim Potocic..Director
Gary Slaight..Director
Donald Tarlton..Director
Jim West..Director
Roger Whiteman..Director
Matt Zimbel..Director

2001/02

Stan Kulin..Chairman
Daisy Falle..President
Lisa Zbitnew..1st Vice-President
Sheri Jones..2nd Vice-President
Jason Sniderman..Secretary-Treasurer
Laura Bartlett..Director
Pat Campbell..Director
Steve Herman..Director
Cliff Jones..Director
Randy Lennox..Director
Garry Newman..Director
Tim Potocic..Director
Gary Slaight..Director
Jim West..Director
Matt Zimbel..Director
Mark Lazare..Director

2000/01

Stan Kulin..Chairman
Daisy Falle..President
Chip Sutherland..1st Vice-President
Gilles Paquin..2nd Vice-President
Lisa Zbitnew..Secretary-Treasurer
Ric Arboit..Director
Pat Campbell..Director
Steve Herman..Director
Cliff Jones..Director
Mark Lazare..Director
Randy Lennox..Director
Garry Newman..Director
Jane Bunnett..Director
Gary Slaight..Director
Sheri Jones..Director
Jason Sniderman..Director

1999/2000

Stan Kulin..Chairman
Daisy Falle..President
Ross Davies..1st Vice-President

Chip Sutherland..2nd Vice-President
Ross Reynolds..Secretary-Treasurer
Jane Bunnett..Director
Daniel Caudeiron..Director
Cliff Jones..Director
Mario Lefebvre..Director
Garry Newman..Director
Gilles Paquin..Director
Holger Petersen..Director
Jason Sniderman..Director
Lisa Zbitnew..Director

1998/99

Lee Silversides..President
Ross Davies..1st Vice-President
Chip Sutherland..2nd Vice-President
Ross Reynolds..Secretary-Treasurer
Jane Bunnett..Director
Rick Camilleri..Director
Daniel Caudeiron..Director
Cliff Jones..Director
Mario Lefebvre..Director
Gilles Paquin..Director
Holer Petersen..Director
John Reid..Director
Jason Sniderman..Director
Daisy Falle..Executive Director

1997/98

Lee Silversides..President
Stan Kulin..1st Vice-President
Ross Davies..2nd Vice-President
Chip Sutherland..Secretary-Treasurer
Jane Bunnett..Director
Daniel Caudeiron..Director
Ross Reynolds..Director
Mario Lefebvre..Director
Gilles Paquin..Director
Holger Petersen..Director
Jason Sniderman..Director
Rick Camilleri..Director
Shari Ulrich..Director
Daisy Falle..Executive Director

1996/97

Lee Silversides..President
Stephen Stohn..1st Vice-President
Doug Chappell..2nd Vice-President
Stan Kulin..Secretary-Treasurer
Paul Alofs..Director
Daniel Caudeiron..Director
Ross Davies..Director
Mario Lefebvre..Director
Gilles Paquin..Director
Holger Petersen..Director
Ross Reynolds..Director
Lesley Soldat..Director
Chip Sutherland..Director

Sylvia Tyson..Director
Shari Ulrich..Director
Rick Camilleri..Director
Daisy Falle..Executive Director

1995/96

Lee Silversides..President
Doug Chappell..1st Vice-President (part only)
Stephen Stohn..2nd Vice-President (later 1st Vice-President)
Earl Rosen..Secretary-Treasurer
Paul Alofs..Director
Deane Cameron..Director
Daniel Caudeiron..Director
Ross Davies..Director
Bob Jamieson..Director
Stan Kulin..Director
Mario Lefebvre..Director
Eddie Schwartz..Director
Lesley Soldat..Director
Ted Southam..Director
Chip Sutherland..Director
Tony Tobias..Director
Sylvia Tyson..Director
Shari Ulrich..Director
Daisy Falle..Executive Director

1994/95

Dave Charles..President (Resigned)
Lee Silversides..President (after Mr. Charles' reisgnation)
Duff Roman..1st Vice-President
Doug Chappell..2nd Vice-President
Earl Rosen..Secretary-Treasurer
Deane Cameron..Director
Terry Flood..Director
Allan Gregg..Director
Tim Rooney..Director
Eddie Schwartz..Director
Lesley Soldat..Director
Ted Southam..Director
Stephen Stohn..Director
Tony Tobias..Director
Sylvia Tyson..Director
Shari Ulrich..Director
Bob Roper..Director
Daisy Falle..Executive Director
Bob Jamieson..Director
Stan Kulin..Director
Steve Thomson..Director

1993/94

Dave Charles..President
Duff Roman..1st Vice-President
Doug Chappell..2nd Vice-President
Earl Rosen..Secretary-Treasurer
Deane Cameron..Director
Terry Flood..Director
Allan Gregg..Director
Bob Jamieson..Director

Michael Godin...Director
Tim Rooney..Director
Bob Roper..Director
Eddie Schwartz...Director
Lesley Soldat..Director
Ted Southam..Director
Stephen Stohn...Director
Steve Thomson..Director
Sylvia Tyson...Director
Daisy Falle..............................Executive Director
Tony Tobias..Director

1992/93
Peter Steinmetz..............................President
Bill Henderson.............................1st Vice-President
Donald Tarlton.............................2nd Vice-President
Duff Roman......................Secretary-Treasurer
Paul Burger..Director
Deane Cameron...Director
Doug Chappell...Director
Dave Charles..Director
Terry Flood..Director
Michael Godin...Director
Earl Rosen..Director
Eddie Schwartz...Director
Lee Silversides...Director
Ted Southam..Director
Tony Tobias..Director
Daisy Falle..............................Executive Director
Lee Aaron..Director
Allan Gregg..Director
Steve Thomson..Director

1991/92
Peter Steinmetz..............................President
Gil Moore......................................1st Vice-President
Don Tarlton....................................2nd Vice-President
Duff Roman......................Secretary-Treasurer
Lee Aaron..Director
Paul Burger..Director
Deane Cameron...Director
Bill Henderson...Director
Dave Charles..Director
Terry Flood..Director
Michael Godin...Director
Allan Gregg..Director
Earl Rosen..Director
Eddie Schwartz...Director
Lee Silversides...Director
Ted Southam..Director
Steve Thomson..Director
Tony Tobias..Director
Bob Muckle..Director
Leonard Rambeau...Director
Daisy Falle..............................Executive Director

1990/91
Peter Steinmetz..............................President

Gil Moore......................................1st Vice-President
Frank Davies.................................2nd Vice-President
Don Kollar........................Secretary-Treasurer
Andre Menard..Director
Bill Henderson...Director
Bob Muckle..Director
Daisy Falle..............................Executive Director
Peter Parrish...Director
Don Tarlton...Director
Duff Roman..Director
Earl Rosen..Director
Eddie Schwartz...Director
Gerry Lacoursiere...Director
Lee Silversides...Director
Leonard Rambeau...Director
Michael Godin...Director
Muriel Sherrin...Director
Neill Dixon...Director
Steve Thomson..Director
Terry Flood..Director

1989/90
Peter Steinmetz..............................President
Gil Moore......................................1st Vice-President
Frank Davies.................................2nd Vice-President
Don Kollar........................Secretary-Treasurer
Wayne Baguley...Director
Neill Dixon...Director
Terry Flood..Director
Bill Henderson...Director
Gerry Lacoursiere...Director
Peter Parrish...Director
Duff Roman..Director
Muriel Sherrin...Director
Don Tarlton...Director
Steve Thomson..Director
Daisy Falle..............................Executive Director
Michael Godin...Director
Andre DiCesare...Director
Bernie DiMatteo...Director
Ian Thomas..Director
Lee Silversides...Director
Leonard Rambeau...Director

1988/89
Peter Steinmetz..............................President
Gil Moore......................................1st Vice-President
Frank Davies.................................2nd Vice-President
Don Kollar........................Secretary-Treasurer
Wayne Baguley...Director
Neill Dixon...Director
Terry Flood..Director
Michael Godin...Director
Gerry Lacoursiere...Director
Peter Parrish...Director
Leonard Rambeau...Director
Duff Roman..Director
Muriel Sherrin...Director

Don Tarlton...Director
Steve Thomson..Director
Daisy Falle..............................Executive Director

1987/88
Peter Steinmetz..............................President
Gil Moore......................................1st Vice-President
Frank Davies.................................2nd Vice-President
Jim Sward........................Secretary-Treasurer
Neill Dixon...Director
Brian Ferriman...Director
Don Kollar...Director
Muriel Sherrin...Director
Donald Tarlton...Director
Ian Thomas..Director
Daisy Falle..............................Executive Director
Bill Henderson...Director
Gerry Lacoursiere...Director
Wayne Baguley...Director
Michael Godin...Director
Peter Parrish...Director
Leonard Rambeau...Director

1986/87
Peter Steinmetz..............................President
Andrew Hermant..........................1st Vice-President
Frank Davies.................................2nd Vice-President
Jim Sward........................Secretary-Treasurer
Brian Ferriman...Director
Don Kollar...Director
Gil Moore...Director
Lynne Partridge...Director
Muriel Sherrin...Director
Ian Thomas..Director
Bill Henderson...Director
Gerry Lacoursiere...Director
Donald Tarlton...Director
Daisy Falle..............................Executive Director
Neill Dixon...Director
Jane Bell...Director
Bernie Finkelstein...Director

1985/86
Peter Steinmetz..............................President
Andrew Hermant..........................1st Vice-President
Frank Davies.................................2nd Vice-President
Jim Sward........................Secretary-Treasurer
Jane Bell...Director
Neill Dixon...Director
Brian Ferriman...Director
Bernie Finkelstein...Director
Stan Kulin..Director
Gil Moore...Director
Lynne Partridge...Director
Joe Summers...Director
Norman Perry...Director
Muriel Sherrin...Director
Ian Thomas..Director

Don Tarlton...Director
Steve Thomson..Director
Daisy Falle..............................Executive Director

John Watt .... Director
Daisy Falle .... Executive Director

1984/85
Peter Steinmetz .... President
Les Weinstein .... 1st Vice-President
Sam Sniderman .... 2nd Vice-President
Andrew Hermant .... Secretary-Treasurer
Frank Davies .... Director
Neill Dixon .... Director (Part)
Arnold Gosewich .... Director
Stan Kulin .... Director
Gil Moore .... Direcor
Norman Perry .... Director
Joe Summers .... Director
Jim Sward .... Director
John Watt .... Director
Vic Wilson .... Director
Ross Reynolds .... Director
Muriel Sherrin .... Director
Daisy Falle .... Executive Director

1983/84
Peter Steinmetz .... President
Les Weinstein .... 1st Vice-President
Sam Sniderman .... 2nd Vice-President
Andrew Hermant .... Secretary-Treasurer
Neill Dixon .... Director
Arnold Gosewich .... Director
Stan Kulin .... Director
Norman Perry .... Director
Ross Reynolds .... Director
Muriel Sherrin .... Director
Joe Summers .... Director
Jim Sward .... Director
John Watt .... Director
Vic Wilson .... Director
Daisy Falle .... Executive Director

1982/83
Brian Robertson .... President
Les Weinstein .... 1st Vice-President
Sam Sniderman .... 2nd Vice-President
Peter Steinmetz .... Secretary
Andrew Hermant .... Treasurer
Daisy Falle .... National Co-ordinator
Bruce Allen .... Director
Deane Cameron .... (January 1983) Director
Ray Danniels .... Director
Arnold Gosewich .... Director
Norman Perry .... Director
Ross Reynolds .... Director
Jim Sward .... Director
John Watt .... Director
Vic Wilson .... Director

1981/82
Brian Robertson .... President

Les Weinstein .... 1st Vice-President
Sam Sniderman .... 2nd Vice-President
Peter Steinmetz .... Secretary
Tom Williams .... Treasurer
Deane Cameran .... Director
Ray Danniels .... Director
Arnold Gosewich .... Director
Andrew Hermant .... Director
Ross Reynolds .... Director
Jim Sward .... Director
John Watt .... Director
Norman Perry .... Director

1980/81
Brian Robertson .... President
Les Weinstein .... 1st Vice-President
Sam Sniderman .... 2nd Vice-President
Peter Steinmetz .... Secretary/Legal Counsel
Tom Williams .... Treasurer
Ray Danniels .... Director
Ross Reynolds .... Director
John Watt .... Director
Michael Cohl .... Director
Daisy Falle .... National Co-ordinator

1979/80
Brian Robertson .... President
Joe Summers .... 1st Vice-President
Les Weinstein .... 2nd Vice-President
Tom Williams .... Secretary-Treasurer
Mike Cohl .... Director
Ray Danniels .... Director
Ross Reynolds .... Director
Sam Sniderman .... Director
Daisy Falle .... National Co-ordinator
Peter Steinmetz .... (October 1979–Not appointed)

1978/79
Brian Robertson .... President
Joe Summers .... 1st Vice-President
Les Weinstein .... 2nd Vice-President
Tom Williams .... Secretary-Treasurer
Ray Danniels .... Director
Ross Reynolds .... Director
Bob Morten .... Director
Sam Sniderman .... Director
Mike Cohl .... Director
Daisy Falle .... (February 1978) National Co-ordinator

1977/78
Leonard Rambeau .... President (Resigned)
Brian Robertson .... Secretary-Treasurer, President
                                  (After Rambeau Resignation)
Joe Summers .... 1st Vice-President
Tom Williams .... 2nd Vice-President/Secretary-Treasurer
George Struth .... Director
Ray Danniels .... Director
Terry Brown .... Director

Bob Morten .... (replaced Terry Brown) Director
Les Weinstein .... Director

1976/77
Mel Shaw .... President
Leonard Rambeau .... 1st Vice-President
Tom Williams .... 2nd Vice-President
Brian Robertson .... Secretary-Treasurer
Ray Danniels .... Director
George Struth .... Director
Ross Reynolds .... Director

1975/76
Mel Shaw .... President
Leonard Rambeau .... 1st Vice-President
Martin Onrot .... 2nd Vice-President
Brian Robertson .... Secretary-Treasurer
Greg Hambleton .... Director
George Struth .... Director
Ross Reynolds .... Director

MusiCounts Advisory Committee 2010 – 2011
Melanie Berry .... President & CEO
Steve Cranwell .... Executive Director
Ed Robinson .... Chairman

Deane Cameron	Jim Cuddy	Ross Davies
Denise Donlon	Bob Ezrin	Michael Hurley
David Kines	Randy Lennox	Margaret McGuffin
Aideen O'Brien	Johnny Reid	Ross Reynolds
Stephen Stohn		

Previous Members
Christine Amendola .... 2008 - 2009
Jully Black .... 2004 - 2009
Sarah Crawford .... 2004 - 2009
Leisa Peacock .... 2003 - 2007
Gary Slaight .... 2004 - 2007
Srinka Wallia, Executive Director .... 2003 - 2009

CARAS Staff 2010/2011
Melanie Berry, Laura Bryan, Jackie Dean, Jade Goulet, Kathryn
Hamilton, Alex Heming, Brenna Knought, Jaime MacGillivray,
Meghan McCabe, Josh McIntyre, Jacqueline O'Brien, Jill Primeau,
Denise Rayner, Carolyn Richardson, Chris Topping.
Our gratitude to: Daisy Falle (1980-2002)

MusiCounts Staff 2010/2011
Steve Cranwell, Mike Hurley, Noreen Malazo
Special thanks to: Srinka Wallia (2004-2009)

INDEX